On Pilgrimage

On Pilgrimage

Sacred Journeys around the World

Jennifer Westwood

First published as *Sacred Journeys* by Henry Holt and Company in 1997.

Library of Congress Cataloging-in-Publication Data

Westwood, Jennifer.
    On pilgrimage : sacred journeys around the world / by Jennifer Westwood.
      p. cm.
    Rev. ed. of: Sacred journeys. 1997.
    Includes bibliographical references and index.
    ISBN 1-58768-015-7
    1. Pilgrims and pilgrimages. 2. Shrines. 3. Sacred space. I. Westwood,
Jennifer. Sacred journeys. II. Title.
    BL619.P5 W37 2002
    291.3'5—dc21

                                      2002007626

Published by
HiddenSpring
an imprint of Paulist Press
997 Macarthur Boulevard
Mahwah, New Jersey 07430

www.hiddenspringbooks.com

Printed and bound in the
United States of America

Contents

Introduction. ix

Part I *The Pilgrim's Path* 1

CHAPTER 1
Longing. 3
Mecca 8
Canterbury. 14
Benares 24

CHAPTER 2
Getting Ready 29
Glastonbury 34
Camargue 40

CHAPTER 3
Setting Out. 45
Kateri Tekakwitha. 50
Mount Athos 62

CHAPTER 4
Sacred Way. 65
Santiago de Compostela. 68
Mount Kailash 80
Shikoku 86

CHAPTER 5
Adventures and Difficulties. 91
Croagh Patrick 94
An American Desert Retreat. 106

CHAPTER 6
Midway: Going on or Turning Back. 111
Sainte-Baume. 122

CHAPTER 7
Doubt and Hope 129
Chaco Canyon. 134
St. Catherine's Monastery. 140

CHAPTER 8
Drawing Near: Anticipation 145
Sodo. 148
Our Lady of Guadalupe 154

CHAPTER 9
Arrival: Excitement and Preparation. 161
Sainte Anne de Beaupré. 166
Assisi. 170

CHAPTER 10
Climax: Encounter with the Unknown . . 177
The Western Wall. 190
Home Dance of the Hopi. 194

CHAPTER 11
Reflection and Redirection 201
War Graves of the Somme 204
Arunachala 208

CHAPTER 12
Coming Home 217
Saint Winifred's Well 220

Part II *Guide to Sacred Places* 229

Journeys to Sacred Landscapes 231
Journeys to Sacred Temples 248
Journeys to Sacred Shrines 273

Bibliography 292

Index 296

Acknowledgments 305

Contributors 306

Picture Credits 310

Introduction

When I was first asked to write Part I of this book, I hesitated. Accustomed to writing about ancient places from the point of view of the myths and legends attached to them, rather than any sacred use today, I thought I had nothing to say about pilgrimage. The one thing in my favor seemed to be that I had spent a lot of time on the business of getting to sacred places—temples, shrines, churches, stone circles, standing stones, and tombs.

"Every man and woman has two journeys to make through life. There is the outer journey, with its various incidents, and the milestones of youth, marriage, middle age, and senility. There is also an inner journey, a spiritual Odyssey, with a secret history of its own."

W. R. Inge, *More Lay Thoughts of a Dean* (1931)

Also, because of the nature of pilgrimage, there was not much possibility of following the normal procedure in writing about folklore: Stand back from the material, and keep your commentary on what you see as free of subjective interpretation as possible. Writing any other way seemed exposing. But as some of the other contributors found, a pilgrimage only becomes a truly revelatory experience once you start looking from inside out and not from outside in.

Eventually, I decided that I would treat the entire writing process as a pilgrimage. Although the research began much earlier, I started writing in May during a pilgrimage to Les Saintes-Maries-de-la-Mer in the Camargue, France, and finished within days of returning there for the October Grand Pélérinage des Saintes Maries Jacobé et Salomé.

There were other pilgrimages in between, including a magical one to the cave at Sainte-Baume in Provence, France, located in a silent, primeval forest, where Mary Magdalene is said to have lived for thirty years as a hermit clothed only in her hair. For me, participating in pilgrimage, and watching and reading about other people's participation, stirred up many issues. Much of the documentation made painful reading from the humanitarian point of view, and there was necessarily some rummaging around in my own belief system. I am not a practicing member of any faith and was surprised at how upset I was at uncovering some of my own beliefs.

Jewish legend says that the Rock of Jerusalem (now under the Dome of the Rock) is the foundation stone of the world. King David came upon it when building the Temple, and the rock warned him not to move it. It said that the world had once started slipping through the hole that lay beneath it into the waters under the earth—the chaos of preexistence. Only the rock's action in plugging the hole prevented the whole world from sliding into this chaos.

This legend has manifold meanings: At one level it seems to be speaking of religion itself, at another of Judaism, and at another of the operations of the human mind. Certainly, the turbulence that uncovering hidden beliefs creates is like chaos welling up when the rock has been lifted. My pilgrim road has not been smooth, and I don't expect yours to be: I see this as a major benefit.

Aims and methods

Pilgrimage exists in a multitude of variations. For all the work religious historians, anthropologists, sociologists, and geographers have devoted to in recent decades, there seems as yet no clear, overall picture of its nature.

Part I discusses issues raised by pilgrimage generally. The material is drawn from anthropologists and others writing over the past forty years, mainly from the world religions, within most of which there is a long tradition of individual pilgrims testifying to their experiences. Not all the pilgrimage places I mention are necessarily open to those who do not share the religion practiced at the shrine. Having said that, I have used examples mainly from world religions that have some pilgrimage shrines open to those of other faiths, rather than from tribal and ecstatic religions, whose rites are normally closed.

If you wish to observe or join in a pilgrimage outside your own locality, remember that pilgrimages to local shrines are often private community events. For example, a Portuguese *romaria* may involve only a single village in celebrating its patron saint, who symbolizes the community and is the focus of its sense of identity. To put it bluntly, local people may not want you there.

On a more general note, visitors *en masse* physically damage sites. Minor ancient monuments and small-scale landscape features, such as holy wells and wayside crosses and tombs, often cannot sustain the annual descent of even moderate numbers of people. However, I do not subscribe to the elitist view that the "public" should be denied access. We must compromise, so I ask you to treat every sacred landscape (however humdrum) with the reverence that the Japanese poet Issa (1763–1827) accorded Mount Kamji, the Shinto holy hill in the inner precincts of the Ise Shrine:

> "Kamji Yama.
> My head bent
> Of itself."

Because it is the very nature of pilgrimage to stand slightly to one side of organized religion, some of the practices I describe in Part I and the quotations I have chosen to illustrate its themes may displease orthodox practitioners. Nothing is intended to offend.

Attitudes and discoveries

In 1994, the body of a fifteenth-century pilgrim, with rough robe and staff, was found buried in Worcester Cathedral, England. To me, the discovery of his remains is more touching than are some real-life pilgrims, in the same way that souvenirs of medieval Christian pilgrimages—amulets, holy water flasks, and pilgrim badges—seem more attractive than most modern pilgrim souvenirs. This is partly because I am conditioned by my British background, which places emphasis on traditional and conservative values, to see them in an approving way.

It is easy to patronize pilgrimage. Holy places the world over are often artistically more mediocre and gaudier than

Western aesthetics can accommodate. Bernadette Soubirous, on seeing the statue of the Blessed Virgin made for the grotto at Lourdes, exclaimed, "My God, how you deface her!" But, really, what is "taste" in this context? The Lourdes statue may not be great art, but how could human hands represent the transcendental beauty of Bernadette's vision? The creators of the greatest religious art in the world cannot give us more than the faintest foreshadowing of divinity—not even the cave painters of Lascaux in France and Altamira in Spain nor the carvers of the Cycladic deities of ancient Greece with their "archaic smiles." As an aid to focusing the mind on God, for the right person the most sentimental statue of the Sacred Heart may be as effective as a Michelangelo sculpture.

When we see the souvenir shops that line the streets leading to the shrine at Lourdes, we need to see the rosaries, medals, T-shirts, statues, and pictures in the light of the function they will serve: as gifts of love and as badges of religious devotion and affiliation. Often the objects pilgrims buy become the focus of shrines in the family home, reminders of the sacred journey and in some cases (as with water from the spring at Lourdes) representing the transfer into the home of the power of the holy place visited.

We have to learn to accommodate the fact that the sanctity of pilgrimage shrines is often underpinned by a chain of reasoning that we would not accept in any other context. Images depicting the Virgin of Loreto have been carried on historic flights, including Lindbergh's crossing of the Atlantic in the *Spirit of St. Louis* in 1927 and in the 1969 *Apollo 9* space mission. This is because in 1920, Pope Benedict XIV proclaimed the Virgin of Loreto the patron saint of air travelers. The connection between the Virgin of Loreto and aviators arises from the original reason for Loreto's existence as a pilgrimage place: the Sancta Casa (Holy House), now encased in marble within the basilica. According to tradition, the Sancta Casa was the Virgin Mary's house at Nazareth, which on May 10, 1291, was carried by angels first to Tersatto near Fiume (Rijeka, in the former Yugoslavia), and finally, on December 2, 1295, to the Italian town of Loreto. Miracles took place there, and in 1507, Pope Julius II approved the Holy House as an object of pilgrimages.

This story of the Holy House's coming to Loreto, first recorded in Italian around 1472, received the caveat from Pope Julius *ut pie creditur et fama*—"as is piously and traditionally believed." In other words, he left it an open question as to whether or not the story was pious fiction. It does not alter the fact that the association of the Virgin of Loreto with aviation rests on the story of the flying angels and on the magical principle that "like produces like." We no longer think like this, so should we say (as many do) that the Holy House is just a symbol, that it is the Virgin who is potent and not the Holy House? But then why come to Loreto? Why don't aviators carry holy medals from Guadalupe or Lourdes?

Pilgrimage shrines worldwide raise similar questions; and we have, each of us, to accommodate the meanings attached to pilgrimage sites to our own belief systems.

Signs on the horizons

I usually say "pilgrimage" rather than "sacred journey." To me, they mean the same thing, and I see no reason to use two words where one would do. On the same grounds, I say "God" rather than using some circumlocution such as "the divine principle." These are the words for sacred journey and deity in my culture: Brought up in a Christian country, I naturally use the vocabulary of Christianity to describe religion. This implies nothing about my personal beliefs, and you should substitute words with which you are comfortable. (Anyone worried that the word *God* necessarily implies a male figure should read Mother Julian of Norwich's *Revelations of Divine Love* [c. 1393], in which this medieval mystic uses the word *mother* in addressing Jesus.)

If I hold any belief with conviction, it is roughly this: Muslim writers have seen one category of seekers after God as *salik*, or wayfarers, whom God guides on the active way through asceticism and prayer. Their journey begins with learning to read the "signs on the horizon"—developing an awareness of the effects of God's actions in the world. "O God," wrote the ninth-century Egyptian mystic Dhu 'l-Nun, "I never hearken to the voices of the beasts or the rustle of the trees, the splashing of waters or the song of birds, the whistling of the wind or the rumble of thunder, but I sense in them a testimony to Thy unity... O God I acknowledge thee in the proof of thy handiwork and the evidence of thy acts...."

I once experienced a literal "sign on the horizon." It was in the Finger Lakes district of New York State, and I was heading north. Suddenly, I noticed a great black scribble that began as a black dot and gradually sprawled across the sky as if someone were writing his signature: God's handwriting. It was like being at Belshazzar's Feast (Dan 5), and I was very apprehensive. Of course, it was only wild geese flying south for the winter. I'd never before witnessed their migration. But now that I have seen and pondered it, I know what Dhu 'l-Nun meant by "evidence of thy acts."

There is rather more to this than the simple thought that "Nature" is a wonderful thing, and someone must have made it. While theologians through the ages have been troubled by the question of whether God is immanent (implicit in the universe) or transcendent (totally separated), the folk experience of divinity is not far removed from that of the solitary Hindu mystic who experiences oneness by reaching into the inner core, the *atman*, that he believes exists identically in all creation.

In myth and folklore, there is a running theme of Universal Sympathy—that all things resonate together, and a pang that is experienced in one part of the universe will be experienced in the rest. It often takes the form of universal lamentation at the death of a god—the Greek Pan, the Norse Balder, even Christ. The orthodox Christian tradition that at the Crucifixion "the sun was darkened, and the veil of the temple was rent" (Luke 23:45) was matched in folk tradition with the belief that the whole world wept. And to balance the tears, the sun dances on Easter Morning with joy at the Resurrection; and at midnight on Christmas Eve, cattle kneel reverentially in their stalls, the bees hum in their hives, and the Holy Thorn blooms at Glastonbury, England.

What these traditions are saying is affect the part and you affect the whole. All things are one. It is almost a commonplace today that physicists have arrived at much the same conclusion: All creation is interconnected. I stand with them.

"I am not of this world nor the next...
I have seen that the two worlds are one:
One I seek, One I know, One I see, One I call...
If once in this world I win a moment with thee,
I will trample on both worlds,
I will dance in triumph forever."

Jala al-din Rumi (d. 1273),
Divani Shamsi Tabiz, R. A. Nicholson, trans.

Part I

The Pilgrim's Path

CHAPTER 1

Longing

*T*he greatest regular assemblies of human beings on Earth are those of pilgrims. They arrive in their tens of thousands for Holy Week in Rome and Passover in Jerusalem; and at Mecca, there gathers annually more than a million of the faithful from every part of the Islamic world. The Kumbha Mela, celebrated every twelve years at the river confluence at Allahabad in India, draws more than ten million people.

Why do they come in such numbers? What is it that they seek? Why in all ages and all over the world have people felt this same desire to set out, to launch themselves as it were by a springboard out of their normal lives and familiar places, on a journey into the unknown? The answer seems to be that, to whatever faith they belong, wherever their footsteps are directed, and whichever immediate reasons they give for going, at bottom, all pilgrimages spring from an inborn yearning for an encounter with the divine. This yearning is compounded of the desire to revere deity in its own special place and the hope of persuading it to pay heed to individual prayer. Pilgrimage to a special place, where the divine pierces through the mundane, holds out the promise of help and comfort in this world and of a living encounter with deity.

The place

First, the place. For Hindu mystics and for Sufis, this sacred place is within themselves: Their pilgrimage is a journey with no physical movement, but a personal seeking within mind and body. For others, the sacred place may have a physical existence, but the journey there be symbolic, as when medieval Christian pilgrims trod the foot mazes known as the Path to Jerusalem on the floors of cathedrals.

Not even all real journeys had a geographic goal. The word *pilgrim* comes from the Latin *peregrinus*, meaning, "a wanderer or stranger," and early Christians saw a pilgrimage as the search for a place of exile. On his landing in Cornwall, England, in the sixth century, the hermit St. Meriasek exclaimed, "Jesus be thanked, to a foreign country here have I come...." Detaching themselves from their roots, they chose to live as in every place a stranger, trading the fleeting companionship of this world in exchange for the everlasting company of the blessed in Heaven.

The idea of pilgrimage as a journey with no fixed goal is illustrated in the ninth-century *Voyage of St. Bréanainn* (St. Brendan). This fantastical account describes a sea voyage by the sixth-century Irish saint who, with fourteen of his monks, embarked in a boat covered with oxhides and sailed westward, entrusting their fate to God. After seven years, they finally arrived at a marvellous island called the Land of Promise, after which they sailed home. Not all of Bréanainn's monks survived the adventure: His *Voyage* is partly based on mythic voyages to the Otherworld by Irish heroes such as Maol Dúin (Maeldun), and the journey to the Land of Promise is a metaphor for death.

Though Bréanainn's voyage is mainly fantasy, it also echoes the real-life practice of Irish monks such as the three — Dubslane, Machbethu, and Maelinmun — who in 891 landed in Cornwall and went to the court of King Alfred the Great, having cast themselves off from Ireland in a coracle without any oars "because they wished for the love of God to be in foreign lands, they cared not where." Similarly, some European pilgrims of the Middle Ages roamed from place to place, and the Japanese beggar pilgrims of Edo wander from shrine to shrine on a pilgrimage that lasts the whole of their lives. *Pilgrimage* has become a metaphor for life itself, the journey we set out on the moment we are born, the road to the Otherworld, the Celestial City.

But most pilgrims make real, purposeful journeys, temporarily abandoning their normal lives to travel, often in great hardship, to a particular place. Although these places may have acquired their reputations for sanctity for different reasons, all seem to pilgrims to offer the possibility of closer contact with the divine. Often this springs from the deep-seated belief that a deity or saint is eternally accessible at the point where he or she lived or visited or appeared. Although the faithful can pray to the Blessed Virgin for help in any church, they believe that she is most likely to answer their prayers where she has manifested herself on Earth, in places such as Fátima, Lourdes, La Salette, and Guadalupe.

Particularly holy in pilgrims' eyes are places that prophets and saints knew in their lifetimes. The earliest Christian pilgrims sought out the Holy Land and the scenes of Christ's life and Passion. In the same way, Hindu pilgrims are drawn to places where human saints or *avataras* (deities who have descended to Earth) have dwelt, and the four most sacred Buddhist pilgrimage sites in India are places that have direct associations with the life of the Buddha.

Especially potent is the place where the saint or deity trod and left a permanent footprint. At the church in Rome that medieval pilgrims knew as the Palmalle, they could see the mark of Christ's foot, which was believed to have been impressed on the marble when he appeared to Peter before his execution. Another sacred footprint has made Sri Pada in Sri Lanka an even more universal pilgrimage center than Jerusalem. The footprint on the peak is said by Buddhists to be that of Buddha; by Hindus to be that of Shiva; by Christians, St. Thomas, Apostle of the Indians; and by Muslims, Adam, the first man.

Pilgrims also eagerly seek the shrines of dead holy people and saints. The Jewish *Lives of the Prophets* from around 50 C.E. gives the location of numerous tombs of Jewish saints. The Pilgrim of Bordeaux, whose *Itinerary*, written in 333 C.E., is the earliest description of a pilgrimage to the Holy Land to have come down to us, visited more sites connected with the Old Testament than with the New. Probably Christian pilgrimages grew out of the Jewish practice of visiting the tombs of prophets and saints. The Jewish followers of Jesus, who regarded him as "a prophet mighty in deed and word," would have found it natural to preserve his tomb as a site to which they could come as pilgrims. Islam also preserves the shrine tombs of its saints, at which miracles are asked of them.

To medieval Christian pilgrims, and to some Christians today, the tombs of saints and the relics they contained were so nearly identical with the saints' living presence that spiritual benefit might be passed to the pilgrim by contact with them. The practice of sleeping near the shrine (known as incubation), especially at healing shrines, presumed that the remains of the saint emitted a kind of radiation that was more effective the longer the exposure to it. Relics are also treasured in other faiths. Although Buddha himself did not advocate pilgrimage, after his death his relics were distributed and placed in monuments known as *stupas*, which became a goal for pilgrims. Outside India the best known is the Temple of the Tooth in Kandy, Sri Lanka, where in an inner chamber one of Buddha's teeth is preserved on a golden lotus flower inside nine golden caskets.

"Alone in my little hut without a human being in my company, dear has been the pilgrimage before going to meet death."
Irish hermit, eighth or ninth century

The goal of a pilgrimage is often described as a geographical location that attracts pilgrims because they deem it worthy of reverence

"...behold, I saw a man cloathed with rags, standing in a certain place, with his face from his own house...and a great burden upon his back. I...saw him...burst out...crying, What shall I do to be saved? I saw also that he looked this way and that way, as if he would run, yet he stood still, because...he could not tell which way to go. I looked then, and saw a man named Evangelist coming to him, and asked....Do you see yonder shining light? He said, I think I do. Then said Evangelist, Keep that light in your eye....So I saw in my dream that the man began to run."
John Bunyan, *The Pilgrim's Progress,* Part I (1678)

7

MECCA

MIN

Uniting in a single belief

I had read a lot about the *hajj*, its rituals, obligations, and prohibitions. But because of the lack of information about the very few people who had journeyed to Mecca from Communist Russia, I had some misconceptions. One of these was that it was forbidden for women. I never dreamed that I would be able to perform it twice: first, the *hajj* proper, with my father in 1993, and then the *Umrah* (little pilgrimage) with my mother in 1995.

This second pilgrimage was both the more interesting journey and the more meritorious from the Muslim point of view. We performed it during Ramadan, the season of fasting, and were told by our Imam that *Umrah* during Ramadan is equivalent to the pilgrimage made with the prophet Muhammad. We traveled from Kazan by bus, a journey of more than nine days of nonstop driving and fasting. We crossed Western Russia, Ukraine, Romania, Bulgaria, Turkey, Syria, Jordan, and part of Saudi Arabia without the comforts of long stops, hotels, or hot meals.

The first group of pilgrims (men only) from Tartarstan had journeyed to Mecca in 1992. The following year, my father and I joined a group of 170 pilgrims from Tartarstan and several other republics of the former USSR. Everything was new to us! We had been raised under the banner of state atheism and lived in a secular society in which no distinctions existed in any sphere of life between men and women. We were accustomed to having independence and the freedom to make our own decisions.

Thus, for most of us, the *hajj* came as a culture shock. It was our first experience of the fully fledged Muslim way of life, and many of us were unprepared. To start with, although views differ on this question, most modern Islamic scholars insist that women participating in the *hajj* must be accompanied by either their husbands

Rituals of the hajj

Before they arrive in Mecca, pilgrims wash and dress in white to enter the state of *ihram* (purity). In Mecca, they first visit the sacred Mosque, washing again before entering. There, they circle the Ka'ba seven times counterclockwise and kiss the black stone. Then, at the well of Zamzam they drink water before walking seven times between the hills of Safa and Marwa. At Arafat, where Muhammad preached his last sermon, they pray until sunset. The following day, an animal sacrifice at Mina celebrates Eid-ul-Adha, and pilgrims throw stones at pillars in a symbolic rejection of evil. Finally, they return to Mecca to circle the Ka'ba again.

A sacred privilege

The Qur'an says that it is the duty of all Muslims to go to Mecca, provided that they can afford to do so. Pilgrims on the *hajj* regard themselves as privileged, and pray for their less fortunate friends and relatives who have not been able to accompany them.

JZDALIFAH

ARAFAT

or a close male relative—father, brother, or son. For Russian women, this rule proved very difficult: Many are single, and as the journey is expensive, few families can afford to send more than one member on the pilgrimage.

This rule is not without good reason: The *hajj* is very strenuous physically. For instance, women are permitted to approach and kiss the black stone of the Ka'ba, but in the overcrowded mosque, it is often physically impossible for a woman to do so. Moreover, some rituals can only be performed by men. For example, the *Talbiya* (sacred formula) has to be spoken aloud, but women are not permitted to speak in the presence of strange men.

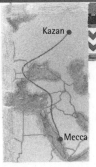

When we started our journey, given our preconceptions, we were surprised to find that nearly half of our group were women. We were even more surprised to discover that women constitute half of all pilgrims on the *hajj*. We were amazed, too, to see how many young pilgrims there were, since the *hajj* is traditionally performed by older people.

The *hajj* begins with entering the state of *ihram* (ritual purity), which has both a spiritual and material aspect. For women, *ihram* means wearing a long white dress and a veil covering the head. Nothing must emphasize the woman's figure: In fact, she must hide her age, beauty, and physical merits. Any man in the street is entitled to upbraid her if she infringes this rule.

Despite the difficulties and the patience needed to complete the rituals, the *hajj* gave us a unique religious experience. Nothing in the world can compare with the atmosphere in Mecca, with its sea of people dressed in white, with tears in their eyes, all directing their thoughts toward a common goal. Coming from a society in which religion is synonymous with backwardness and ignorance, being part of the three million pilgrims in Mecca, seeing faces filled with passion, ecstasy, and exultation, and meeting people from all over the world united in one belief, was a truly extraordinary experience.

Gÿlnar R. Baltanova

as the scene of a divine manifestation or association with some holy person. In other words, human beings put the value of holiness on it. But, is it possible that some places are holy per se, regardless of their meaning for human beings? Some cultures have thought so. Places of pilgrimage are often places of great natural grandeur, possibly less in acknowledgment of a masterwork of the Creator than of a human propensity for investing certain kinds of geographical feature with symbolism. Certain places, particularly mountains, caves, rivers, and springs, have from ancient times been thought of as the dwelling places of the gods or places where the world of the gods and the human world intersect. The place itself was (and often still is) regarded as holy, regardless of what human history has been enacted there.

This belief is sometimes formalized in mythology. According to ancient Hindu tradition, in the Himalayas lies Devabhumi, the country of the gods. The very mountain names proclaim this: *Nanda Devi*, "the Goddess Nanda," *Chomo Lhari*, "Goddess of the Holy Mountain," *Chomo Lungma*, "Mother Goddess of the Land" (the Tibetan name for Mount Everest). In both Hindu and Buddhist mythology, at the center of Earth stands a mountain around which sun, moon, and stars revolve. This mountain is Mount Meru, which Hindus believe is Mount Kailash in Tibet. Here is Svarga, Indra's Heaven, a paradise of the blessed who wait until the time of their next rebirth on Earth.

The belief in the holiness inherent in certain places caused Roman farmers to invoke the spirits of the countryside before extending their cultivated land and encroaching on the wild. Other Romans dedicated certain sites to the *genius loci*, or nameless spirit of the place, notifying passersby of the fact in an inscription. In the Viking era, Icelanders similarly venerated the *landvættir*, the spirits of the land, who were guarding and cherishing the land before the first settlers ever arrived from Norway. Even today, it is hard not to believe that some places (particularly deserts) are of themselves filled with *numen*, a kind of overflowing of the divine that enfolds us when we visit.

11

Because of the worldwide belief in inherently sacred locations, some places remain a lodestone for pilgrims through changes of religion. At Mecca, which has the longest unbroken tradition of pilgrimage in the world, pilgrims were seeking that mysterious black stone enshrined in the Ka'ba well before Muhammad made pilgrimage to Mecca one of the Five Pillars of Islam.

The prayer

Sharing the common lot of people the world over and throughout recorded history—conflict, suffering, and death—all spiritual seekers ask and all religions try to answer the same fundamental, impossible question: Why? We are all, from the moment we are born until the moment that we die, engaged in this search for meaning. Children in perplexity and trouble run to their parents; adults for the most part run to "god." Not for nothing does mythology use the language of parenthood: *Alföðr* (All-Father) and *Jaganmata* (Mother of the World). We know that life is a hard road and uncertain, that we stumble, but that "he" or "she" is up ahead. A pilgrimage dramatizes the journey through life. In conventional pilgrimages, a physical shrine or other holy place—having acquired a reputation for sanctity—exerts a spiritual magnetism that draws pilgrims to some fixed geographical location in the quest for the divine.

What we beg of our god may be something specific that is ardently desired—children, practical advantage, social status, even worldly gain. People yearn for personal miracles—what Shi'a Muslims in Iran call *kiramat*—modest miracles that solve

12

a problem. At Iranian *imamzadeh,* shrine tombs of the descendants of the Imams, one girl may ask specifically for her moustache to disappear, another more generally for a husband, a new wife will pray for a son, a pregnant woman for an easy delivery. Hindus in Bengal seek divine aid in curing baldness, passing an exam, or saving a declining business. Haitian pilgrims to Sodo may want a particular job or to win promotion. King Henry VII of England went to the shrine at Walsingham in 1487 to pray for preservation from the machinations of his enemies. In India, a Jain businessman may pay all the expenses of a communal pilgrimage to win both moral status (by eschewing the sin of satisfaction in possessions) and a sound financial reputation (by demonstrating that he has the ability to spend).

Chaucer's mixed bag of saints and sinners on the road to Canterbury is a lesson to all of us not to be too precious in our notions of who makes a sacred journey and why. There is seemingly no limit to the range of desires of the human heart laid bare before deity. In Culiacán, Mexico, the *narcotraficantes,* or drug traffickers, seek the shrine of a dead bandit named Jesús Malverde, who was hanged from a tree in 1909. Although unrecognized by the Church, he has his feast day, May 3, when crowds gather at the shrine illuminated by dozens of candles. The *narcotraficantes* are devoutly religious, practicing the Catholicism of rural Mexico, with its folk saints and visions and miracles. They wear Malverde scapulars and are said to ask him for a bountiful harvest for the cocaine and marijuana farmers in the Sierra Madre and to bless their drugs for the journey to the United States. Their hit men reputedly ask him to bless their bullets. Ordinary people are thankful not only for the employment

A walk on the Pilgrim's Way

It is an Indian tradition that when you are fifty you should go on a pilgrimage. You have given enough attention to your family and your career; now is the time to pay attention to your soul, your spirit, your imagination, your divinity, and your creativity. From now on, whatever you do should be in the service of the spirit. So a few years ago, I embarked on a journey to the holy places of Britain. I would walk from my home in Devon to Glastonbury, Canterbury, Walsingham, Lindisfarne, and Iona; I would take in many sacred places along the way and return home down the west side of the country.

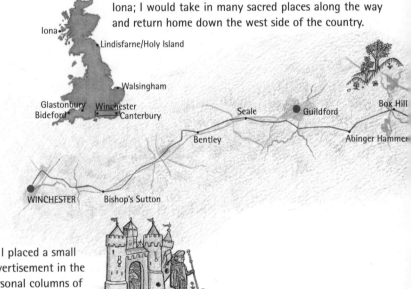

I placed a small advertisement in the personal columns of *Resurgence*: Could readers offer me a bed for the night along the way? The response was tremendous. When I set out, I had an offer of hospitality in most of the places I was to visit. Each day I would try to walk 20 miles, starting at 9:00 A.M. and arriving at my host's house between 4:00 and 6:00 P.M. I started out with a small backpack, one change of clothes, and the pair of Polish shoes I was wearing. I took no book, no diary, no camera, and no money.

On the twelfth day, starting from Salisbury Cathedral and following the old Roman road, I came to Winchester. As I walked the Pilgrim's Way to Canterbury, I was on the same path that many thousands of pilgrims had walked before. I had a sense that I was in the company of those people who had preceded me. As I stepped in their footprints, I felt I was in touch with their dedication, their purity, their sense of divinity.

The Pilgrim's Way

Pilgrims have followed this prehistoric route across southern England to the holy relics in Canterbury since the cathedral was founded in the sixth century.

Practicalities

Traditional dates to make the pilgrimage to the tomb of Thomas à Becket are the anniversary of his martyrdom (December 29) and the Feast of the Translation (July 7). Pilgrims enter the walled city by the medieval West Gate and walk through the narrow streets to the cathedral.

The very beauty of the Pilgrim's Way is refreshing. In most parts, it follows the ridge of the North Downs. Even though Surrey and Kent are riddled with highways, cities, and built-up areas, I was able to escape the secular world in the woods of the North Downs. Now and then, I had to cross the highways and divided roads full of rushing trucks and speeding cars; I was amazed to see the madness of it all. The speed of my two legs and the speed of highway traffic are worlds apart. Happily, I realized that for a pilgrim, slow is always beautiful.

In spite of our society's obsession with speed, I was impressed with the way this ancient pilgrim's path, more than one hundred miles in length, is maintained. The Pilgrim's Way is not the same as it was in the Middle Ages, as in some places industrial growth has swallowed it; but fortunately, a new footpath—the North Downs Way—that goes all the way to Canterbury has been created. It is clearly marked and well defined, and I met a number of people walking it.

After thirty days of walking purification, I entered the holy city of Canterbury. The first glimpse of the magnificent cathedral filled me with joy and delight. I felt the spirit of Canterbury enter into me. I rejoiced among the Christians without being a "Christian." On my arrival at the cathedral I went to an area designated for silent prayer and meditation where pilgrims light a candle. In this dark corner of the cathedral, lit only by the many candles, I too lit a candle and said the Prayer for Peace. After giving his blessings, Canon Brett led me to the chapel of Thomas à Becket. A sword hanging above the altar spoke the language of power and pain. The story Canon Brett told me of Becket's martyrdom caused my doubts and hesitations to vanish and my preoccupations with home and worldly responsibility to diminish.

Satish Kumar

of growing and transporting the crop, but also for the benefits of hospitals, orphanages, and schools endowed by the drug barons—not to mention the Jesús Malverde Funeral Service that is provided free for the Culiacán poor. They, too, come to thank Malverde, who they say—like Robin Hood—robbed the rich to give to the poor. Who can say whose prayers God answers?

It is, of course, easier to empathize with the desperate longing for health that draws pilgrims to many shrines, in the hope that their health will improve by exposure to holiness whether this holiness resides in the general sanctity of a place, or in the specific virtues of healing waters, or in the *mana*, or life force, radiating from the relics of departed saints. Hindus resort to Baba Taraknath, the local deity of Tarakeshwar in West Bengal, in the belief that he can and does cure, among other illnesses, coughs, dysentery, gonorrhoea, tuberculosis, and leprosy. The most active Christian shrines today are places that have reputations for miraculous cures: Pilgrims arrive, with a hope bolstered by the shrine's tradition of miracles, to Lourdes in the Pyrenees, where in 1858 the Blessed Virgin reputedly appeared to the French peasant girl, Bernadette Soubirous. The characteristics of Lourdes—a manifestation of the divine, associated with a sacred spring at which miracles of healing subsequently take place—are repeated at other Christian pilgrimage places, including the important New World shrine of Sainte Anne de Beaupré in Quebec.

Among the poor and in poorer countries, this quest for well-being is perhaps a pilgrim's most urgent motive and one that transcends the barriers of formal religion. In India, a land of many faiths, the desire for miracles of healing leads to shrines of one religion attracting supplicants from others, notably the shrines of the Hindu mother goddesses, of the *pirs* (Sufi elders) and the saints of Islam, places associated with the lives of Sikh gurus, and Roman Catholic shrines of the Blessed Virgin Mary. Hindus, Muslims, and Sikhs all ask for mental health in Badaun, at the shrine of two Muslim saints, Sayyed Hasan (Bare Sarkar) and Shah Vilayat (Chhote Sarkar). Ajmer, in Rajasthan, the Medina of Asia, is visited also by Hindus. Many seek cures for the incurable, regardless of their religion, at the Roman Catholic shrine to Our Lady of Health at Velankanni in Tamil Nadu.

Like Christian in John Bunyan's *The Pilgrim's Progress*, some pilgrims are more concerned for their souls. Medieval Christians carried with them on the road the fear of Hell and a desperate hope that the pil-

> "The lovers of Brahman ask: What is the source of this universe? ...From where do we come? By what power do we live? Where do we find rest?"
>
> The Upanishads

grimage, because the way was hard and long, would serve as an expiation of their sins. The medieval doctrine of Purgatory—as a staging post to Heaven where sins could be atoned for, and the belief that a person's time there could be reduced by his or her own or his or her relatives' merit—led to the Church's practice of offering indulgences (essentially promises of time off in Purgatory) as a reward to pilgrims. A fourteenth-century pilgrim's guide to the Holy City, *The Stacions of Rome*, details the number of years' remission of suffering in Purgatory acquired at each "stacion," or shrine: at St Thomas of India's, 14,000 years; at St. Lawrence's, 7,000 years; at the Church of Holy Rood, 250 years, pardon every Sunday and Wednesday and 100 every other day. The Crusaders, essentially fighting pilgrims, were promised instant salvation if they were killed while liberating the sacred places of the Holy Land from the "infidel."

Hindu pilgrims, too, regard the mortification and disciplining of the body as a way of acquiring merit. One of the hardest of all sacred journeys is the Ganges pilgrimage between the pilgrimage centers of Gangotri, Kedarnath, and Badrinath, at the confluences of the Bhagirathi, the Mandakini, and the Alaknanda Rivers with the sacred Ganges. The pilgrimage, performed in May, June, and July each year, covers 600 miles, much of it on foot and in harsh conditions. Buddhist pilgrims, like their Hindu counterparts, believe that the merit gained on a pilgrimage leads to higher status in the next life and eventually, if enough is accumulated, to freedom from the cycle of existence.

> "The pilgrimage is like an ever flowing river... at the banks of which Muslims may always wash from their faces the dusts of hardship and suffering, pollution and malaise..."
>
> Ayatollah al-Udhma Khamenei
> on the occasion of *hajj* 1416/1996

Sometimes the will to go on a pilgrimage is a desire to fulfill an obligation. Islam enjoins all Muslims who are able to do so to visit Mecca once in their lifetime. Obligatory in a different way were the pilgrimages imposed by Church or State in medieval Europe as punishments or penance. Convicted criminals were sent on penitential journeys to Santiago de Compostela in northern Spain. Others were condemned to wander from shrine to shrine until their iron fetters were worn through by dragging along the road. Also involving obligation are pilgrimages undertaken in the fulfillment of a vow. In the late Middle Ages, the Englishman Roger of Wansford left directions in his will for his executors to send someone on a pilgrimage to fulfill a vow he had made in peril of his life, "almost suffocated by the waves of the sea between Ireland and Norway."

For some, the sacred journey begins in the desire to participate in a ritual cycle concerned with the round of passing seasons, like the pilgrim festivals of Old Testament times — Weeks, Tabernacles, and Passover — when all Hebrew men would come to the temple at Jerusalem. Or it may have to do with the human life cycle, as among Hindus, for whom a pilgrimage often serves as an initiation into a new stage of life. Children are fed

The Pulley

When God at first made man,
Having a glass of blessings standing by,
"Let us," said he, "pour on him all we can:
Let the world's riches which dispersèd lie,
Contract into a span."

So strength first made a way;
Then beauty flowed, then wisdom, honour, pleasure:
When almost all was out, God made a stay,
Perceiving that, alone of all his treasure,
Rest in the bottom lay.

"For if I should," said he,
"Bestow this jewel also on my creature,
He would adore my gifts instead of me,
And rest in Nature, not the God of Nature:
So both should losers be.

"Yet let him keep the rest,
But keep them with repining restlessness:
Let him be rich and weary, that at least,
If goodness lead him not, yet weariness
May toss him to my breast.

George Herbert (1593–1633)

19

their first solid food at pilgrimage shrines or have their hair cut for the first time. The first act of newlyweds is often to make a pilgrimage. The elderly and the sick congregate at shrines in the belief that death at a pilgrimage center will free them from the cycle of rebirth. It is not unknown for the aged to commit ritual suicide at places such as Puri and Allahabad. The sacred space, filled with the immanence of the divine, is the blessed and the safe place for new beginnings.

This motive overlaps with the initiatory: the sacred journey undertaken from the desire to work some kind of transformation on the self. The Muslim who goes to Mecca returns home with both a new moral authority and a new social rank, and is henceforth distinguished by the title *hajji*. The reshaping or awakening of the self to the divine is perhaps the main motive for New Age pilgrimage.

The world-famous musician Yehudi Menuhin delivered this sad epitaph on the twentieth century: "I would say that it raised the greatest hopes ever conceived by humanity, and destroyed all illusions and ideals." Many would agree. Probably the most violent and destructive century on record, it also saw in the Western world a weakening of organized religion, a growing cynicism concerning human responsibility and accountability, and the loosening of social and family bonds. Our

> "...what he is who is in truth Maker, Keeper, and Lover I cannot tell, for until I am essentially united with him I can never have full rest....He is true rest. It is his will that we should know him, and his pleasure that we should rest in him. Nothing less will satisfy us."
>
> Mother Julian of Norwich (1342–c. 1416), *Revelations of Divine Love*

traditional support systems are either weakened or gone. Perhaps at no time in history has the individual felt so truly alone.

We are also recoiling from the true cost of the technological explosion to the planet and our co-heirs in it (the rest of life). Where our ancestors perceived the inherent nobility in humankind and placed them at the center of creation, we have become ashamed of our species ("only man is vile").

However, this modern Western malaise of alienation from ourselves, from each other, and from the rest of creation, is producing its own cure. Spiritual warriors are arising, learning from our past traditional strategies for dealing with despair and self-loathing (medieval monks suffered from it, too), and out of them are evolving new ones. One of these old-new strategies is the sacred journey.

The journey

Many seekers see their attempt to find an ideal to live by in terms of a journey. Some join the pilgrimages of the world religions to experience *communitas*, a kind of spiritual solidarity. This solidarity is what brings tens of thousands of young adults of all Christian denominations and other faiths from all over the world on a "pilgrimage of trust" to Taizé in eastern France, to share in the worship of a Christian monastic community.

Others devise their own sacred journeys. A journey to a place that has mainly a personal meaning is as much a pilgrimage as a journey to a recognized sacred site if the desire to go there is strong and the experience spiritually uplifting. A journey of remembrance, such as a longed-for visit to a distant place

21

where someone we love is buried or their ashes are interred, whether in a churchyard or garden of rest in our own country or a war cemetery in some "foreign field," is a pilgrimage. All of these journeys represent the search for an ideal, something that the individual pilgrim values.

We are the heirs of a long and complex tradition in which the sacred is entwined with the profane. Not the least impulse at the heart of many pilgrims has always been wanderlust, the desire for travel for its own sake. This desire was a strong motive in Europe in the Middle Ages when a pilgrimage was the only opportunity for many to leave their towns and villages and see the wonders of the world, in the security of the company of other travelers, on a well-known route, and with some prospect of accommodation in established pilgrim inns. Organized pilgrimages to Santiago de Compostela or to Thomas à Becket's tomb at Canterbury offered all the mental if not physical comforts of a packaged tour.

For women in particular, this was the great escape, for they could travel on escorted pilgrimages without their menfolk, as did the religious ecstatic Margery Kempe, born in 1364, wife of a burgess of Lynn (now King's Lynn), in Norfolk, England, and mother of fourteen children. Her pilgrimages to Jerusalem and Germany allowed her to set aside her role as wife and mother and globetrot a little while pursuing her own private journey into the divine. These pilgrimages are recorded with all their trials and tribulations in her spiritual biography, *The Book of Margery Kempe*—the first autobiography ever to be written in English.

We may find it difficult to perceive any inwardness in modern mass tourism and deplore the commercialization of holy places and of sacred journeying itself. But few world traditions of pilgrimage are free from an element of tourism: Medieval Christian pilgrims went to Rome to see the "sights"; not just the tombs of the apostles and the churches, but Roman antiquities, the traces of a great and vanished empire. They were drawn to Jerusalem not only because it acted as a spiritual powerhouse, as a place important in the sacred history of Jews and Christians (they ignored its importance to Muslims), but also because the journey to Outremer, the "land across the sea," was the ultimate journey of travel and adventure.

In the Holy Land, pilgrims could engage directly with their sacred history by walking in the footsteps of biblical characters. When the German pilgrim Theoderich made a pilgrimage between 1171 and 1173, he was shown, among other things, a grotto under the Church of Our Lady in Nazareth said to be the scene of the Annunciation by the Angel Gabriel, and in the same church, the burial place of St. Joseph and the very spot where Our Lady came forth from her mother's womb. In Nazareth, too, he saw a fountain spouting from the mouth of a marble

"A man once wished to go to Jerusalem, and since he did not know the way, he called on another man...and asked him for information. 'The way is long,' he said, 'and there is great danger....Furthermore, there are many different roads which seem to lead towards it, but every day men are killed and robbed, and never reach their goal....' The pilgrim replied: 'I do not mind how much hardship I have to undergo on the road, so long as...I reach my destination....' The other answered, 'I will set you on the right road....keep your mind constantly on Jerusalem. If you will keep to this road...you will arrive at the place for which you long.'"

Walter Hilton (d. 1395),
The Ladder of Perfection

BENARES

City of Light

City of Light, City of the Dead, the Forest of Bliss, the Never-Forsaken, the City of Shiva—call it what you will (and it is known by all these names), Benares has to be one of the maddest, holiest, most entrancing cities on Earth. Every trick in the book is used by the hawkers, the rickshaw wallahs, the boatmen, the hangers-on, to part another fool from his or her money. The assault is continuous and only ceases when one flees to the Ganges in a boat of one's own.

Floating down the Ganges through the City of the Gods: Then the light falls on the temples, the palaces, the water, in a shimmering haze. The whole riverfront takes on a dreamlike air—buffalo lounge in the water, a man meditates by the shore, a sadhu walks by with staff and water pot, and children play chase among the funeral pyres. The ghats, colossal stone steps leading down to the water's edge, glow pink and gold in the afternoon sun. The washermen make use of them to dry their day's work—yards of sari, blue and bright yellow, stretch down to the water. Just by the washing a huddle of people, all dressed in white, gaze on as the body of one of their relatives crackles and dissolves in the flames of a great fire.

Badrinath

Dwarka

Puri

Rameshwaram

Kanpur

Allahabad

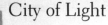

BENARES

Varana

Adi Keshava

Panchaganga

Manikarnika

Dashashwamedha

Ganges

Asi Ghat

Somewhere bells are ringing, firecrackers are being set off. Overhead, two vultures are circling.

Hindus from all over the world come to Benares to die. It is their Holy of Holies, where the soul is guaranteed a speedy return to the celestial fields. Benares is "older than history," said Mark Twain after his visit there; "older than tradition, older even than legend." For more than three thousand years, this city has been at the heart of an unbroken spiritual tradition. I, a Christian by culture, went there not to die, as it turned out, but to reflect upon my own mortality. I have never forgotten the principle that the mystic philosopher G. I. Gurdjieff always emphasized to his pupils that the awareness of our own inevitable end is the most powerful spiritual lesson that we can learn. Benares brings this home more than most places.

Half a dozen fires are burning day and night by the water, and a row of corpses, trussed in yellow and gold cloth on bamboo stretchers, await their turn nearby. The family members sit on the ghats up above, watching the proceedings in silence. I sit with them, in an almost casual atmosphere. No one is shedding a tear because mourning is considered bad luck for the dead, and everyone knows that the Hereafter is an easier place to be than the life we all share on Earth.

One day, I passed a procession of pipers and drummers leading a flower-covered bier down to the water. Just before the fire they stopped, and two young men leaped out in front of the body, which was still on the shoulders of the bearers, and threw themselves into a wild sexual dance—one with a stick

Dhaka

Calcutta

in his trousers that seemed to give him a massive erection, the other gyrating his pelvis like a woman, with his arms and forefingers prodding the air. Round and round each other they turned, the musicians drumming them into an ecstatic frenzy. By now everyone was clapping and laughing, and the dancers motioned to me to come and join them. I had never been to a funeral like this before, and I backed away, embarrassed. Later, too late, I wished I had danced that cremation dance.

Roger Housden

> ### Practicalities
> The best time to make a pilgrimage to Benares is from October to November for the Ramlila Festival and the Durga Goddess Festival. Bathing in the Ganges is particularly auspicious at this time. Be prepared to negotiate firmly if you want to rent a boat to catch the dawn. Pilgrims seeking the undiluted magic of Benares are recommended to rent accommodations in small lodges among the lanes of Vishwanatha near the ghats.

lion's head, "from which the child Jesus often used to draw water and take it to his mother." Such sites, some of them no doubt bogus, nevertheless, through the exercise of the historical imagination, added color and immediacy to the visit and served to reinforce faith (proving the Bible "true").

They also allowed the pilgrim to "fold" time, notably to share in Christ's passion by walking the Via Dolorosa, his journey to the Cross. Although raised to a higher power, such places functioned rather like well-managed sites of Civil War battles, such as Bull Run, Virginia; or light and sound performances in Europe and the Middle East—Karnak in Egypt, for example; or the reenacting of ancient dramas in the open-air amphitheatres for which they were designed, such as Epídhavros in Greece. By focusing the attention and manipulating the emotions through sight and sound, they create an acute awareness that allows the spectator or participant to "be there." While saints and mystics might be able to empathize with the sufferings of Christ to the extent that they receive the stigmata, others less spiritually disciplined may need sensory aids. (It is for this reason that the Via Dolorosa is still recreated symbolically at many Christian pilgrimage sites.)

Nowadays tourism is often marketed as pilgrimage. No longer a simple journey to visit the sights (and sites), the sightseeing tour has become a "pilgrimage" to the famous places of antiquity, a "pilgrimage" to great works of nature, or a "pilgrimage" to the home of some famous writer or poet or painter or musician. Here the tour promoters have the truth of it: Anthropologist Alan Morinis has written that the term *pilgrimage* can be put to use "wherever journeying and some embodiment of the ideal intersect." Often there is very little distance between sacred journeys to recognized holy places and shrines and secular pilgrimages to pay homage to some historical hero or modern icon, such as visits to Mount Vernon, the home of George Washington, or to Graceland, virtually the shrine of Elvis Presley.

The diverse strands of pilgrimage give us something with which to work when seeking the focus and intent of our own sacred journey. We do not need to be alone on our spiritual quest: We can engage in a historical process. Treading in the steps of revered ancestors is an act that unites and reconciles modern tourism, pilgrimage within living faiths and orally transmitted sacred journeying, such as native Australian "travel" along the Songlines, where the journey is not a memorialization of times past but a mythic act.

According to this ancient way of thinking, one does not reenact the myths of how things came to be but participates in the very act of Creation. Participating in making a brave new spiritual world is perhaps in the end why, at a time when we are told that formal religion is losing ground, the impulse to undertake a pilgrimage seems to be gathering strength. In 1993, when the feast of St. James fell on a Sunday and it was declared Compostellan Holy Year, 99,436 pilgrims walked the whole length of the 500-mile-long Camino de Santiago (Way of St. James), the 1,000-year-old pilgrim trail to Santiago de Compostela in Spain. Roughly another 4.5 million arrived by coach or bus. Yet this pilgrimage had been all but abandoned by the late-nineteenth century, the markers along the way and the pilgrim shelters vanished. It was only in the 1960s that the Camino was restored.

Essentially all pilgrims are seeking to access, by way of a significant site, a spiritual reservoir charged in the past and constantly refilled. For the pilgrim not only takes but gives, drawing spiritual sustenance, and at the same time by an act of faith in the place of pilgrimage, replenishing the never-failing spring. To be a pilgrim is not to perform an individual act of devotion, but to engage in humankind's dialogue with the divine: not in time, but eternity.

CHAPTER 2

Getting Ready

"*T*he gods seemed to have possessed my soul and turned it inside out, and roadside images seemed to invite me from every corner, so that it was impossible for me to stay idle at home. Even while I was getting ready, mending my torn trousers, tying a new strap to my hat, and applying *moxa* to my legs to strengthen them, I was already dreaming of the full moon rising over the islands of Matsushima." So in the seventeenth century wrote the Japanese poet and pilgrim Matsuo Basho. Your pilgrimage, too, has begun. The place you want to be is in sight. You have embraced it in your mind: Let your feet follow.

The practical preparations that you make for your sacred journey are as much a part of your pilgrimage as the traveling itself. Once you have decided on your goal, it is time to research the practical aspects of your journey: when to make the journey, whether to go alone or with others, how long the journey will take, and how much it will cost. You may also wish to make spiritual preparation, perhaps as required by your religious faith or as a personal preparation for your sacred journey. In this planning and preparation stage, there are many questions to consider.

When?

When will you set out? There are traditional seasons of pilgrimage, governed by the weather. Chaucer's pilgrims rode on the road from London to Canterbury in April; Basho likewise felt the quickening of spring. Hindus still arrive at Badrinath, high in the Himalayas and snowbound for half the year, between May and October. Other considerations apart, like an ordinary vacationer you will probably choose to let good weather guide you.

However, if you belong to one of the world's great faiths, you may want to attend some important festival in the religious calendar, when your community of belief gathers together not only in sacred space but in sacred time. For Sikhs, that space is the Golden Temple at Amritsar, and the time is *Baisakhi* (the Punjabi New Year's Day, April 13). For Hindus with devotion to Vithoba, it is Pandharpur on Vithoba's special day, the *sukla ekadasi*, or "bright eleventh." This is the eleventh lunar day of the waxing part of the month of Asadha. (As usual with festivals regulated according to the lunar calendar, the equivalent date in the Roman calendar varies.) Suppose you are Christian, wishing to make a pilgrimage to Walsingham, England. A Protestant may want to join the Anglican National Pilgrimage on May 27; but a Catholic may choose September 8, the feast of the Nativity of Mary, and the Catholic pilgrimage, which begins with a mass at the former Slipper Chapel.

Those of other faiths, or none, will probably also prefer to time their visits to a sacred place to coincide either with a festival or in accordance with some other traditional association. For example, local people and those who are historically minded may visit Walsingham in late January or early February when snowdrops carpet the woods, mindful that these "Mary's Tapers" were traditionally used to decorate English churches on the feast of the Purification of the Blessed Virgin Mary, celebrated on February 3.

The "when" of your sacred journey depends on more than flight availabilities.

How?

Then there's the "how." Down the centuries, pilgrims of all faiths have elected to go on an organized tour in company with others: a kind of spiritual Cook's Tour. When the Englishman Sir Richard Torkington set out for Jerusalem on March 20, 1517, he made his way to Venice, Italy, where he found a "patron," a courier who specialized in transporting pilgrims by sea to Palestine. Although the ship did not stick to the scheduled route, they eventually docked in Jaffa, from where the Warden of the Mount Sion Convent conducted them to Jerusalem. They were shown the sights—rather more than are shown today: "We went to the house where the sins of Mary Magdalen were forgiven"— and on the last day of July, apparently all present and correct, set sail again for the return journey from Jaffa. This style of escorted tour was necessitated by the Muslims controlling Jerusalem at that time. Even today some journeys will lead a pilgrim to parts of the world where it is unwise to travel alone.

As with ordinary travel abroad, there are sights and experiences you may miss without guidance. There are also religious observances you may fumble. This worries even pilgrims in their native country: In India, on arrival at their destination, Hindus often put themselves in the hands of *pandas* or *purohits*, guides who provide not only food and lodging but also ritual instruction.

A guided tour may not be your idea of a sacred journey. But the meaning of what you do is in how you see it. Think of yourself as participating in an age-old tradition of companionship in spiritual adventure. You will be sharing good times and bad — excitement and boredom, ease and discomfort, revelation and doubt. Not the least of your sharing will be the act of eating together, which even in everyday life has a symbolic dimension and which in many religions is ritualized as the communal sacrificial feast. Seen in this light, the greasiest café becomes the Grail Castle.

"Whan that Aprill with his shoures soote
The droghte of March hath perced to the
roote,...Thanne longen folk to goon on
pilgrimages."

Geoffrey Chaucer, *The Canterbury Tales*,
fourteenth century

The determined lone wolf's first step will be to consult a guidebook. Here, too, you are identifying yourself with a hallowed tradition: A pilgrim from Bordeaux, France, produced an itinerary of the road to Jerusalem for other travelers in 333 C.E. *Information for Pilgrims unto the Holy Land* (c. 1498) gives alternative routes and rates of exchange, hints on choosing a pilgrim ship out of Venice, and what herbs and spices, crockery, and utensils to take. It advises the pilgrim on how to hire a mule in Jaffa and what fresh foodstuffs to buy for a trip to Jericho. It also gives vocabularies in Greek and Turkish. No wonder it ran to more than one edition, exactly like its modern equivalents, volumes in classic guidebook series such as the *Fodor's* or *Frommer's* Guides.

If you are traveling in a culture whose religion you do not share, look for a guidebook that gives precise information about visiting holy places. "When in Rome, do as the Romans do" may not get you by. You need to know how you as a foreigner are expected to behave. You may on arrival find locally published guidebooks that better answer your questions. Otherwise, you may need a human guide. Again, this is not only a problem for nonbelievers. A British Hindu woman who wished to fulfill a vow to go to Varanasi (Benares) in India enlisted her father's help in making the arrangements for her journey. "He wrote to relatives in India, who contacted a priest attached to one of the Varanasi temples. My son and daughter accompanied me and when we arrived, it was this priest who met us at the railway station and took us to our lodgings. He also acted as our guide around the city and made sure that the religious actions I carried out were correct so that my pilgrimage would be successful."

> "Don't wait to be ready. Everything you need for this journey is available to you right now."
>
> K. Bradford Brown, *Point Counter Point* (1988)

Organizing your trip

So, you have decided how you will travel. If you are joining a party, most of the logistics will be handled for you. If you are traveling independently, you will have more to think about— not least, your own personality. Are you an anxious traveler (you may call it "organized"), making "to do" lists, practicing packing,

GLASTONBURY

A spiritual magnet

"Glastonbury—Ancient Isle of Avalon" reads the town sign, capturing the juxta-position of location and legend, fact and faith, present and past, which pervades the place. As one woman told me, "There's a new myth created every day around Glastonbury." Described as a spiritual magnet, it is a "multiple-choice" pilgrimage site, for a number of different Glastonburys coexist in time and space. People have been drawn here for centuries, bringing a variety of traditions and worldviews that currently interact. It is for individuals to discover which Glastonbury is "real" for them.

Christian Glastonbury is shaped by the traditions that have earned the town the title "cradle of English Christianity." According to legend, Joseph of Arimathea, provider of the tomb for Jesus and thought by some to be Jesus' uncle, landed at Glastonbury (2,000 years ago it was beside the sea) where he built a simple church dedicated to the Virgin Mary. Some claim that Joseph, a tin merchant, had already visited the area and might have brought his nephew on such a trip. This idea con-tinues to capture the imagination, expressed most eloquently by William Blake in his poem *Jerusalem:*

"And did those feet in ancient time
Walk upon England's mountains green?
And was the holy Lamb of God
On England's pleasant pastures seen?"

Joseph's staff, thrust into the ground on his arrival, flourished to become the famous Glastonbury Thorn, which flowers both in spring and at Christmas. He also reputedly carried with him another, more precious relic—the Grail. As the cult of Joseph developed and Arthurian romances proliferated, the Grail was variously described as the dish in which Joseph had collected Jesus' blood after the crucifix-ion, two cruets filled with the blood and sweat of Jesus, and the chalice used at the Last Supper.

Inextricably linked with the Grail are tales of King Arthur and his Knights of the Round Table. According to legend, after his last battle, Arthur was taken for healing to Avalon, where some believe he remained, the once and future king, to return at some hour of great need. The twelfth-century "discovery" of the bodies of King

Arthur and his queen in the Abbey grounds seemed to confirm the identification of Glastonbury with Avalon and Arthur in popular tradition.

The Abbey was built over the site of St. Joseph's Church, regarded in the words of one medieval poet as the "holyest erth of england." After the Benedictine monks were forced to leave it by the Dissolution of the Monasteries in the sixteenth century, it fell into disrepair. It is now administered as a historic site. At the annual pilgrimage weekend in June, which has attracted crowds of around 14,000, some of the Abbey's original function and flavor—if not its magnificence—are recaptured.

Many contemporary pilgrims are attracted by Glastonbury's pre-Christian connections. Some claim that the Abbey lies on an ancient site of goddess worship and regard the banks around the sides of the Tor, perhaps created by prehistoric peoples, as a complex three-dimensional ritual maze. The Tor, with a fourteenth century church tower at its summit, rises dramtically out of a flat plain on the edge of the town. For others, Glastonbury's significance lies in its presumed association with ancient Druids: They maintain that it was a great center of Druidic learning—a sort of Druidic Oxford or Cambridge—attracting students from Europe and beyond.

Glastonbury is now also hailed as "the epicenter of the New Age in England," a center of converging lea lines and the "heart chakra" of planet Earth. People journey there to find themselves. Arthur is often invoked by people embarking on their own spiritual quest, symbolically rising again "to lead us into a New Age, a new cycle, a new beginning, a new phase in world evolution."

Marion Bowman

turning up at the airport too early? You might want to work on this—you will not be able to control a journey that is "sacred" so tightly. You are entering a different space and time, stepping into the unknown: This is the nature and the purpose of your journey.

Are you at the other pole, forever unforewarned and unforearmed (you may think of yourself as "spontaneous"—others might say "feckless")? On your voyage of the soul, choose to be the burden on no one's back—neither your country's nor someone else's. Doing so entails being:

legal   (passport, perhaps visas)

viable (money in foreign currency, travelers' checks, or credit cards; medical insurance)

able   (supplies of ongoing medication, up-to-date vaccinations—your doctor will have a list of which vaccinations are needed for which countries).

This is not the mundane coming between you and your sacred journey—this is your journey. You are already (especially if you are not used to organizing such things) on your road.

"I had a desire to see the places where He [our Lord] was born...and died....And while I was feeling these desires, our Lord spoke in my mind and told me to go to Rome, Jerusalem, and the shrine of St. James. This was two years before I went, because I wanted to go but could not afford it." This is the illiterate English pilgrim Margery Kempe, dictating her story to a priest in the fifteenth century. You may feel that you have been as imperatively summoned on your pilgrimage as Margery, but can you afford to go? Muslims commonly wait to make the *hajj* until they can do so without depriving their families. Pilgrims from other cultures defer their journeys to sacred places for the same reason. Journeys abroad, in particular, have a way of costing more than you think, and it is the essence of sacred journeys that they spring surprises, leading you down byways you had not expected to tread, offering challenges you had not expected to meet. Sad to be unable to respond and to take the chances offered to you because you have given no thought to your budget!

Margery again: "When the time came for me to visit the holy places...I asked the parish priest...to make an announcement from the pulpit for me: any man or woman with a claim for debt against myself or my husband was to come and have a word with me before I left and I would settle things to their satisfaction—which is what I did." Without going to the lengths of having your affairs announced from the pulpit, you might want to follow her example and settle outstanding business. This was more urgent for pilgrims of the Middle Ages, whose travels might last a year or more and whose chances of a safe return from almost anywhere were considerably less than ours. Still, you might regard this reckoning as they did, as being also a symbolic leave-taking, a letting go of worldly concerns, a marking of the division between secular and sacred time.

Packing

For the pilgrims of many faiths, this separation of sacred from secular time was, or is, marked by the putting on of ritual garments. These are signs that proclaim a people temporarily set apart, treading the same roads as other travelers but marching to a different drum. The staff and scrip (satchel) are no longer the marks of the Christian pilgrim; yet still today, to fulfill the requirement for an unstitched white cotton garment (symbolic of the equality of all Muslims) an American Muslim man going to Mecca will pack two white sheets—one to be wrapped round the lower half of his body, the other to be thrown over his shoulder. A Muslim woman will take a clean, plain, long dress and a white scarf to cover her head. At their local airport, before their flight, they will perform the ritual washing known as *wudu* and don their pilgrim's garments. They do this in case their flight passes over Mecca, because before they reach the goal of their sacred journey they must enter into the state of ritual purity known as *ihram*. (Pilgrims not already prepared are warned by the pilot so that they can wash and change on board.)

"Give me my Scallop shell of quiet,
   My staffe of Faith to walke upon,
My Scrip of Joy, Immortall diet,
   My bottle of salvation:
My Gowne of Glory, hopes true gage,
   And thus Ile take my pilgrimage."
                Sir Walter Raleigh,
                The Pilgrimage (1604)

Common sense dictates that, like any other traveler, you will pack suitable garments of the right weight for the climate in the country you are visiting, comfortable and hard-wearing footwear, enough of both but not too much. If your journey is taking you to acknowledged holy places, be mindful that your dress should be respectful of the traditions of the faith and country.

Dress makes all sorts of statements and consequently is a touchy subject all round. It is a frequently observed phenomenon that people often become unreasonably truculent if asked to amend their dress, for example, in restaurants. A pilgrim cannot afford to pack this attitude in his or her baggage. If you come from a liberal society where almost anything (or nothing) can be worn on the street, be prepared to abandon your own notions of suitability. Except for wilderness journeys, shorts won't see you through. Even on men, and especially when combined with bare chests, they are widely regarded as impolite in public.

In a number of religious faiths, including the more traditional branches of Christianity, displays of female flesh in holy places are particularly unacceptable. Women going to Islamic countries should take clothes that are extremely discreet. In Iran, in particular, *hejab* (Islamic dress) must be worn by all women in public. When visiting certain Islamic shrines, women should also prepare themselves mentally to wear the *chador* (floor-length veil). You will normally be lent one at the entrance. You do not have a choice here: "will not comply" equals "cannot go."

Don't forget the head: The significance of a covered or uncovered head differs between cultures. Some American men may need reminding that, whereas at home baseball caps (and stetsons) are often left on the head indoors in public places, in Europe it is considered uncouth, and in churches and cathedrals, irreverent. Conversely, in many Christian shrines worldwide it is still considered respectful for women to cover their heads with a scarf, as it is in many other religions.

People may warn you if you are infringing on their notions of propriety: But do you want it to come to that? Do you truly mean to give them the message that their spiritual tranquillity is less important than your search for the divine? If not, accept finding out about, buying, and wearing appropriate clothes as part of the disciplines of a pilgrimage. (Don't go to the other

The Marys of the sea

The paradox of a people always on the move going on pilgrimage brings us to Les Saintes-Maries-de-la-Mer in the Camargue, a region of lagoons and salt marsh, white horses and black bulls, flamingos and mosquitoes. The press call it the "Gypsy Pilgrimage." Certainly, gypsies arrive from all over Europe, defying expectations: Mobile homes fill the parking lots, men carry mobile phones, girls wear orange day-glo leggings, singers working restaurants offer tapes.

But gypsies are only the half of it. May 25 is the Feast of the Three Marys—Magdalene, Jacobé, and Salomé—first witnesses of the Resurrection and for whom the town is named. According to Provençal legend, these three faithful women were set adrift in a rudderless boat from Palestine in 45 C.E., together with their black servant, Sara, and several other saints. Eventually their boat was washed ashore in the Camargue. Its cargo of saints, including Mary Magdalene, with her sister Martha and their brother Lazarus, dispersed to evangelicize Provence. The elderly Marys Salomé and Jacobé, with Sara, stayed and built themselves an oratory. Here they were buried; here pilgrims came; here was built the church.

On May 24, the Eve of the Feast, we arrive in the church for the "Descente des Châsses" at 3:00 P.M. These *châsses* are painted reliquaries containing the relics of the Marys, which were discovered by "Good King René" of Provence in 1488. Soon, the church is packed. A steady trickle of gypsies flows up the aisle and down into the crypt to pay respect to a diminutive statue with a nut-brown face—Sainte Sara, their adopted patron.

Before the reliquaries descend from an upper chapel—tantamount to the coming among us of the holy women themselves—the bishop asks us not to take photographs, but flashlights pop, and TV cameras roll. The reliquaries are winched down in stages, and at each halt, bunches of florists' flowers, wrapped in cellophane, are tied to the ropes. Gypsies reach up with their candles and their hands to touch the wonder-working caskets, which will return to their aerie tomorrow at 3:00 P.M. Now, Sara is carried down to the sea.

The next day, a Missa Solemnis at 10:00 A.M. launches the Marys on the same journey. Charged with the energy of the Mass, we struggle out of the crowded church and hurry to the beach. We station ourselves beside a retired fishing boat. Presently, the bishop and parish priest climb aboard. "Will it be launched?" we ask fishermen. "Heavens no," they say. (Tourists!) Half a dozen *gardians* (herdsmen) on the famous horses of the Camargue mark the seaward limit of the procession.

D58

Etang de Vaccarès

D570

Petit Rhône

PARC REGIONAL DE CAMARGUE

LES SAINTES-MARIES-DE-LA-MER

Now, come the Marys in the little blue boat, in which they normally sit in the church, amid votive plaques that thank them for prayers answered and miracles performed. Borne shoulder high, they are grave little persons, uncommonly like Queens Mary and Anne of England. We join the rush to touch them or their gauzy cloaks. Camarguais, gypsies, and—catching the infection—tourists transfer that touch to companions and bless themselves and each other with seawater made holy by the saints' presence.

We are in the surf, beside a horse who stamps as waves wash in behind him. His *gardian* watches out for our bare feet—everyone here looks out for pilgrims. I have heard that the saints' blessings are reserved for Provençals and gypsies. Perhaps other years, surely not this: For these people catch us up in their own open generous spirituality. It is as natural as breathing to reach up our arms in church and sing with them over and over: *"O Saintes de Provence, Nous vous tendons les bras, Venez..."*

We may burst if we don't join their shouts in the church and in the streets: *"Vive les Saintes Maries, Vive Sainte Sara!"* They are why, contrary to expectation and in my go-to-church outfit, I stand here beside the horses, up to my waist in the sea.

Jennifer Westwood

Practicalities

The seaside resort of Les Saintes-Maries-de-la-Mer is at the tip of the Camargue in southern France, just over an hour's drive from Marseille.

There are two pilgrimages a year: *Le Pélérinage des Saintes Maries* on May 24/25 is followed by a civic celebration on May 26 in honor of the *gardians'* champion, the Marquis de Baroncelli. The *Grande Pélérinage des Saintes Maries Jacobé et Salomé,* on the penultimate Sunday in October, is also attended by gypsies but does not include a procession for their patron saint, Sara.

extreme, and play Lawrence of Arabia by dressing up as a local—
that is impertinent.)

Taking thought for others

Amid the excitement of getting ready, take thought for
those you leave behind. If your way lies somewhere that to them
seems remote and alien, they may harbor unfounded fears. Try
to allay these fears before you go by sharing information. Once
embarked, send regular messages home, although this may not
be easy. (We all know about the wish-you-were-here postcard that
arrives three weeks after our return.)

One way of staying in touch is to identify yourself with
another old tradition and keep a diary of your journey, like
Nikulás, abbot of the monastery of Munkatherá, Iceland, who set
out for the Holy Land in 1154 and recorded his impressions of
sights and people en route. Every so often, post a copy of your
entries home. One of your family or friends may be willing to
make photocopies and circulate them to others. That way you
preserve your memories while they are fresh, and the people you
love go with you on your journey, almost step by step.

Think, too, of all those unknown souls you may encounter.
Among the more useful things to lug around the world are "trade
goods"—small presents to express gratitude and love—and a
Polaroid camera. In cultures where these are not commonplace,
people often appreciate instant pictures of themselves with the
exotic stranger (you). You will need to do some homework as to
what gifts are likely to be acceptable (and importable) where you

are going, and whether there are any reasons of belief for personal photographs to be taboo.

Caring for yourself

You may not want to emulate Basho by putting dried leaves of *Artemisia moxa* on your legs in order to strengthen them, but if you intend to walk any distance and are unaccustomed to exercise you might want to build some stamina. If you are considering walking barefoot, like medieval pilgrims before you, remember that you may be walking on hot metalled roads, not the soft (albeit sometimes stony) dirt tracks of their time. Remember, too, that their feet were often already hardened and calloused from going barefoot or wearing ill-fitting shoes. Seek advice on foot care and appropriate footwear from long-distance walkers.

Finally, your inner self. Our religions will enjoin some of us to make spiritual preparation. This may entail ritual fasting or cleansing, abstinence from sex, learning special prayers, or studying sacred texts. We may be required to treat the world around us better than usual. Among the rules Muslims must follow to maintain *ihram* (a state of purity) throughout the *hajj* is to do nothing dishonest or unkind, neither uproot nor damage any plant, neither kill nor harm any animal or insect.

Both followers of organized religions and other spiritual adventurers may prepare by spending time in meditation. From the Christian tradition comes this definition: "Meditation is the deliberate...reflection on some truth or passage of Scripture. It has a threefold purpose: to instruct the mind, to move the will, and to warm the heart for prayer." To warm the heart for prayer—not bad preparation for any sacred journey.

"When you feel...that he is calling you to this work...lift your heart to God....A naked intention directed to God...is wholly sufficient. If you want this intention summed up in a word, to retain it more easily, take a short word...to do so. The shorter...the better....A word like 'GOD' or 'LOVE'....And fix this word fast to your heart, so that it is always there....It will be your shield and spear in peace and war alike. With this word you will hammer the cloud and the darkness above you."

Anonymous author,
The Cloud of Unknowing, fourteenth century

CHAPTER 3

Setting Out

The moment has arrived. You are physically and intellectually prepared, with bags packed, tickets booked, and guidebooks studied.

But are you *really* ready? Western preachers and poets have for generations used *pilgrimage* as a metaphor for life's journey toward death and eternity. This is why Bunyan wrote in *The Pilgrim's Progress* of Christian: "Now he had not run far from his own door, but his wife and children…began to cry after him to return; but the man put his fingers in his ears, and ran on, crying, Life! Life! Eternal life! So he looked not behind him…."

No one is suggesting that you apply this ruthless attitude to real life, or that you emulate the Roman matron Paula, who in 382 C.E. embarked for the Holy Land, ignoring her young son piteously stretching his arms out to her from the shore and her older daughter, who "by her tears silently besought her mother to stay until she was married." Pilgrimage is a journey *to*, not an escape *from*.

However, this is the point at which the pilgrim must shed his or her security blanket, the web of everyday concerns and people that makes us feel safe and competent and on familiar ground.

Pilgrimage itself is a "rite of passage." All human life involves transitions (passages) in space, time, and social condition. Some of these transitions—notably, marriage and death—are judged critical and marked by rites. This is as true of Judaism, Christianity, and Islam as of Greek and Roman paganism or as of the religions of tribal societies.

The anthropologist Arnold van Gennep divided "rites of passage" into three phases. In the first phase, people become separated from their social condition; in the second phase, they lead a marginal existence, separated from their normal lives; and in the third phase, they either rejoin their former condition or join a new one.

This is a description of pilgrimage. The Muslim on the *hajj* is separated from his or her previous life by adopting ritual dress; existing outside normal life during the *hajj*; and returning to a new condition of improved status within the community, marked by the respectful title, *hajji*.

> "Here among the shadows in a lonely land,
> With strangers we're a band of pilgrims on the move;
> Thru dangers burdened down with sorrows,
> And we're shunned on ev'ry hand,
> But we are looking for a city built above."
>
> W. Oliver Cooper (1885–1963),
> *"Looking for a City"*

Crossing the threshold

All sacred journeys, great and small, are rites of passage. The word *liminal*, used to describe the second phase of such transitions, comes from Latin *limen*, the Roman word for a threshold: the slab or bar at the main doorway that prevents water or mud from flowing into the house. It is the thing that separates outside from inside. Such a significant place was the threshold that it was sometimes taboo (forbidden). The worshipers of the Philistine god Dagon, so the Old Testament tells us, took care not to step on the threshold of his temple, a practice echoed by pilgrims in Syria in the nineteenth century, who still thought it unlucky to step on the threshold of a saint's shrine or of a mosque. According to the thirteenth-century traveler Marco Polo, visitors to the marvellous palace of Kublai Khan in Beijing were prevented from stepping on the threshold by guards stationed at every doorway for that purpose.

In ancient times, the threshold was built with ritual, sometimes with sacrifice and the burial of the sacrificial victim beneath it to provide a ghostly protector for the house. Roman thresholds were presided over by a pair of deities, male and female, one on each side, Limentius and Lima. In India, the threshold is the seat of the goddess Lakshmi. Doorways all over the world in ancient times were guarded by statues of monsters: winged bulls in Mesopotamia, sphinxes in Egypt, dragons in China. Doorways all over the world today are still hung with sacred, protective objects. British people often fix a horseshoe over the main door to the outside world. Although they say it is "for luck," it began as an evil-averting magical practice to keep out witches. Orthodox Jews still fix the *mezuzah*, a small case of religious texts, to their doorways.

These beliefs externalize a psychological truth. The threshold of a house marks not only a place of physical movement, inside to outside, but also a transition from one world of experience to another—from the familiar (from Latin *familia*, family) to the unfamiliar, from the known to the unknown, from the safe grip on the hem of the mother's skirt to the hand timidly held out to a potentially hostile stranger. We make this transition every day without noticing it: But children notice it on their first day at play group or school.

The mother who kisses her child goodbye at the door in the mornings is "noticing" it in another sense—marking it, by engaging in protective magic as old as time. The Western bride carried over the threshold of her new home by her husband is sharing the experience of Roman brides and that of brides in China today, where care is taken that her foot does not touch the threshold when she first goes to her husband's home.

When we cross the threshold on entering a temple, we are passing not

Pūsan on the Road

"Traverse the ways, Pūsan, and keep away anguish,
O child of the unharnessing. Stay with us,
O god going before us...

Lead us past our pursuers; make our paths pleasant and easy to travel. Find for us here, Pūsan,
the power of understanding.

Lead us to pastures rich in grass; let there be no
sudden fever on the journey. Find for us here, Pūsan,
the power of understanding.

Use your powers, give fully and lavishly, give eagerly and fill the belly. Find for us here, Pūsan,
the power of understanding.

We do not reproach Pūsan, but sing his praises with well-worded hymns..."

From *Pūsan on the Road*, a hymn to the solar charioteer Pūsan who presided over roads and journeys, from the Rig Veda (c.1200–900 B.C.E.)

only from known to unknown, but also from the profane (the realm of everyday) to the sacred (the realm of God). When we cross our own threshold to set out on our pilgrimage, we are making the same transition. In the words of van Gennep, "to cross the threshold is to unite oneself with a new world."

"Noticing"

The step that takes us across the threshold on to the path of pilgrimage is momentous. We do not know where it will lead. We do not know who we will become on our sacred journey.

And so that first step demands "noticing." Most organized pilgrimages within world religions begin with an opening ritual on the eve of the pilgrimage or on the day itself. This ritual formally marks the moment when we pass from secular to sacred time. A Roman Catholic pilgrimage may begin with high mass, during which pilgrims fortify themselves spiritually by taking Holy Communion. Hindus—for whom sacred journeys involve austerities and are often physically extremely arduous—will, before departing, offer worship to Ganesh, the god of beginnings and of difficulties over which to be triumphed. If your pilgrimage is short, involving not much of a journey, or no journey at all, there is all the more reason to mark its beginning.

The raw material for such "markers" lies all around. I opened my week of pilgrimage in May 1996 to Les Saintes-Maries-de-la-Mer in the Camargue, France, with a visit to Saint Walstan's Well at Bawburgh, England. Allegedly buried there in 1016 amid miraculous happenings, Walstan was once patron saint of farm laborers, and water from his well was used locally to cure

Three shrines of simplicity

North America is not well known for its pilgrimage shrines. Yet some of the most interesting and most popular pilgrimages in the world are found here. Millions travel each year to Our Lady of Guadalupe in Mexico City, to Sainte Anne de Beaupré near Quebec City, and to St. Joseph's Oratory in Montreal. There are more than a hundred pilgrimage shrines located throughout the United States, some of which attract several hundred thousand pilgrims each year. Many of these shrines are associated with ethnic devotions and particular religious orders, with only a few devoted to indigenous saints such as John Neumann, Mother Cabrini, or the North American martyrs. The three shrines associated with the life of the Blessed Kateri Tekakwitha are unique in North America because they span the border between the United States and Canada.

As I departed with a bus load of pilgrims to visit the Kateri shrines, I was hoping to experience the unfolding history of this Native American woman, a convert to the Catholic faith, who is also known as the "Lily of the Mohawks." The first shrine we visited is in Auriesville, New York, where in 1656, Blessed Kateri was born to a Mohawk father and an Algonquin mother.

When she was four years old, a smallpox epidemic killed her parents and left her scarred with pock marks and nearly blind for the rest of her life. The Auriesville shrine stands on a hill overlooking the Mohawk River. Here, several Jesuits were killed during their missionary work. Today, the shrine attracts thousands of pilgrims like us, interested in both the Jesuit martyrs and their famous convert, Blessed Kateri Tekakwitha.

We journeyed to the second site in this pilgrimage cycle—Fonda, New York. It was here, a few miles farther up the Mohawk River, that Blessed Kateri experienced her first deep encounter with Christianity. Resisting her uncle's attempts to force her into marriage, Tekakwitha (as she was then known) was baptized into the Christian Church and given the baptismal name *Kateri* (Catherine). The wooden shrine at Fonda is very much appreciated by the Mohawk people because of its unpretentious simplicity.

Pilgrims visit the Native American Museum under the church, climb the hill overlooking the Mohawk River, and view the excavations showing the outlines of the original village. There is a small stream that is believed to be where Blessed Kateri was baptized. Pilgrims may purchase holy water or take home sacred earth from this tranquil place.

The journey to Kahnawake, the Mohawk reservation near Montreal, is one of the most moving parts of this pilgrimage cycle. In 1676, the Blessed Kateri fled here to the newly established Jesuit mission, to escape persecution by non-Christian Mohawks. Her remains are enshrined at the St. Francis-Xavier Mission on the banks of the St. Lawrence River, where pilgrims have a strong feeling that they have stepped back several hundred years into the past. This shrine is all the more remarkable because it is the only major place of a pilgrimage situated in an American Indian reservation.

Blessed Kateri lived a devout and pious life for three years in Kahnawake before she died at the tender age of twenty-four. In the words of the Church, she lived an "exemplary life," engaging in severe penances, proposing to found a community of American Indian nuns, and taking a private vow of perpetual virginity. It is said that at the time of her death her face became radiant, and many miracles were reported. Today, pilgrims come in the thousands, and from all parts of the world, to pray at the site where Blessed Kateri lived during her final years.

Dr. James Preston

sick animals until well into the nineteenth century. Usually I join the annual procession to the holy well on the Sunday nearest May, 30, Walstan's pre-Reformation feast day. This year I would be in the Camargue, but it seemed right not to neglect my own humble local saint, even if (as historians suspect) he is mostly mythical.

Other markers to open my pilgrimage might have been a prayer at the shrine of the medieval anchoress Mother Julian in

Norwich, England, or at the tomb
of John Bunyan in the Non-
conformist Cemetery in
Bunhill Fields, London,
both places that for me hold
personal meaning. But neither shrines nor tombs, neither churches nor temples nor
mosques, are needed for this
moment of dedication and leave-taking. In the
quiet of your own home—or better still, in your garden as an
image of Paradise—a piece of music, a poem, a prayer, a minute
or two's silent contemplation will serve. It is the act of "noticing"
itself that opens the way.

> "God over me, God under me,
> God before me, God behind me,
> I on thy path, O God,
> Thou, O God, in my steps."
> *Carmina Gadelica*
> *(Charms of the Gaels)*
> Collected in the nineteenth century

Letting go and taking hold

Formal openings to pilgrimages also help pilgrims to notice
in the ordinary sense: They wake us, make us alert to what is happening to us, change our mind-set. The early Romans again provide illustration of this. Basically countrymen and farmers, they
saw the world as charged with *numen,* an outpouring of the
divine. (*Numen* literally means "a nod"—deities need only nod
to get things done.) This *numen* was embodied in the nature spirits who inhabited the landscape—every spring, lake, hill, valley,
rock, and tree had its caretaker—and the sometimes barely personified gods who presided over human life.

Central to early Roman life was the home, in which the
paterfamilias, father of the family, also acted as priest, conduct-
ing the rites that kept household and farm in spiritual health.

Central to the home was the hearth, for which the Latin word is *focus*. We speak of being focused, as often as not unaware that the word carries a charge of historical and psychological meaning from archaic times, when the fire was literally in the middle of the hut. Before the days of the emperors, the hearth rites were the center of Roman worship. It is no accident that the goddess of the hearth, Vesta, was one of the few old Roman deities to survive throughout the Roman period, holding her own against incomers from Greek mythology and eastern mystery cults.

The farther from his hearth a Roman traveled, the greater the psychic exposure. His progress from the hearth outward took him gradually out of the guardianship not only of Vesta, but of the Lares and Penates, the household spirits. Once past Limentius and Lima on the threshold, he was also beyond the protection of Janus, the two-faced god of the gate or door and also of the month of January, looking both in and out, behind and before. Last,

The pilgrim caravan sets out for Mecca

"It is their caravan prudence, that in the beginning of a long way, the first shall be a short journey....Of a few sticks (gathered hastily by the way), of the desert bushes, cooking fires are soon kindled....In the first evening hour there is some merrymaking of drum-beating and soft fluting, and the Arcadian sweetness of the Persians singing in the tents about us; in others they chant together some piece of their devotion. In all the pilgrims' lodgings are paper lanterns with candles burning; but the camp is weary and all soon is at rest. The hajjies lie down in their clothes the few night hours till the morrow gun-fire; then to rise suddenly for the march...not knowing how early they may hear it....At half past five o'clock was the warning shot for the second journey."

C. M. Doughty,
Passages from Arabia Deserta (1888)

he passed Terminus, the boundary god, symbolized by a great stone marking the limit of the property. Each year on February 23 (once the last or "terminal" day of the year), Roman neighbors would meet at the boundary stone between their properties. Together they would garland the stone with flowers and sprinkle it with the blood of sacrifice, recharging the *numen* that would safeguard their adjoining lands for another year and reaffirming their own concord.

Beyond Terminus, the Roman was outside his familiar support system, in "liminal" territory, in a land he perceived as crowded with alien gods looking after other people's interests. He would attempt to establish friendly relations with these local deities by building them altars, even if, not knowing their names, he had to dedicate them vaguely to the *genius loci*, the "spirit of this place," or *si deus si dea*, "whether you be god or goddess." The farther he traveled away from his hearth, the more "unfocused" he became — but the more aware that the world was full of both dangers and manifold wonders.

Waking up

Detachment from the familiar, coupled with acute awareness, is exemplified by the travels of the Japanese poet Basho, especially those recorded in an account that has become a classic of Japanese literature, *The Narrow Road to the Deep North*. In the spring of 1689, accompanied by one friend, Basho set out on foot from Fukagawa, on the outskirts of Edo (old Tokyo), along the Oshukaido, the great road north through the eastern coastal plain up into the remote province of Oshu. Turning inland, he finally reached the sanctuary of the *yamabushi*, the hermit priests of the northern mountains, and spent a week with them before walking south for two and a half months in the summer heat down the Hokurikudo, the highway leading back along the coast of western Japan to the town of Ogaki.

This was a pilgrimage in something of the Western sense, in that he had a physical goal—the hermits. But more than that, it was a journey of self-exploration. Basho separated himself from the material world before he went, selling his house as if he did not expect to return, and this was not only because of his own frailty or the physical dangers of the journey. The far North in the Japanese imagination of that time was the Other, mysterious and remote from the civilized world of Edo. For Basho, it represented the unfathomable mystery of the universe. He traveled along the Narrow Road to the Deep North as he traveled through his life on Earth—seeking a vision of eternity in the every day.

The things Basho thought worthy of contemplation on his journey included sights that any ordinary tourist might have wanted to see. In his six months on the road (he reached Ogaki in

> "[U]pon the sliding doors, or immediately above the principal entrance of nearly every house, are pasted oblong white papers bearing ideographic inscriptions....The white papers...are ofuda, or holy texts and charms...one...can nearly always discern at a glance the formula of the great Nichiren sect...all bristling with long sharp points and banneret zigzags, like an army; the famous text Namu-myo-ho-ren-ge-kyo....Any pilgrim belonging to this sect has the right to call at whatever door bears the above formula and ask for alms or food."
>
> Lafcadio Hearn,
> *Glimpses of Unfamiliar Japan* (1894)

the autumn), he visited not only temples and shrines but also places that had inspired poets in the past, historical monuments, and other local "wonders." In going out of his way to visit such famous landmarks, Basho might have seemed to be connecting himself to the Japanese past, defining his own cultural identity. But, he sought the ancient monument of Tsubo-no-Ishibumi no more fervently than he sought the species of iris known as *katsumi* in the hills of Asaka. "I went from pool to pool, asking every soul I met on the way where I could possibly find it, but strangely enough no one had ever heard of it, and the sun went down before I caught even a glimpse of it." Perhaps as a consolation prize, perhaps because he reached the city of Sendau on May 4, when it was the custom to throw fresh leaves of iris on the roof and pray for good health, the painter Kaemon whom he met there gave him two pairs of sandals with deep blue laces, of which he wrote:

> "It looks as if
> Iris flowers had bloomed
> On my feet…"

The Narrow Road to the Deep North is often said to be essential reading for pilgrims. But Basho's style of pilgrimage is different from the prevailing "great religion" models, with fixed goals and hopes of specific benefits—so many years' remission in Purgatory, or as Imam Reza is traditionally said to have promised Shi'ite pilgrims to Mashad:

"…an 'opening of one's eyes,' a revelation, can never be given directly in so many words. We see inner reality only through an 'aha!' experience, a sudden insight into our own being."

John Sanford, *The Kingdom Within* (1987)

"Whoever makes the pilgrimage to my tomb will have my presence with him at three important times: First, when the good and bad are separated to the right and left; second, at the bridge of Sirát; and third, at the weighing of merits."

We can learn from Basho, instead, to look at the world with the unfocused but all-seeing eye, making everything the matter of our pilgrimage. During his time in his little house in Fukagawa (given to him in 1680), Basho had practiced Zen meditation. He often claimed to have one foot in the Otherworld, and one in this: In other words, he had not attained enlightenment. Nevertheless, he arrived at a truth that he summed up as: "No matter what we may be doing at a given moment, we must not forget that it has a bearing upon our everlasting self which is poetry."

He sought his "everlasting self" through traveling. For other pilgrims, too, the journey may prove more insightful than the destination. Whether we are on the road to Compostela or on a tour of stone circles and standing stones, even with a fixed itinerary and a tight schedule, we can lay down the agendas that we carry like burdens on our backs and simply be aware. We can open ourselves in readiness, waiting on our moment with the divine (enlightenment, whatever), which may come to us not on top of the mountain or in the cave where it has revealed itself to others but by the way, in the grain of a stone or the petal of a daisy. We, too, can have blue laces.

Taking courage

Basho's account is not all mystical insights: "my bony shoulders were sore because of the load I had carried"; an inn "was a filthy place....A storm came upon us toward midnight, and between the noise of thunder and leaking rain and the raids of mosquitoes and fleas, I could not get a wink of sleep.

> Bitten by fleas and lice,
> I slept in a bed,
> A horse urinating all the time
> Close to my pillow."

"Who would true valor see, Let him come hither," begins Bunyan's well-known hymn "To be a pilgrim." Valor is certainly needed by anyone embarking on a physically hard journey or stepping into unfamiliar situations: loneliness for the normally gregarious, the harassment of large crowds for the normally solitary. From the early stages of the journey, some pilgrims will encounter and have to adapt to physical discomfort and psychological uncertainty.

Those who have chosen the walkers' road will soon find out just how hard it can be. Satish Kumar writes of his walk to Canterbury across southern England: "Why, oh why are a pilgrim's legs lacking in strength? In India, walking was my birthright. From the age of five I walked every day with my mother to our smallholding. From the ages of nine to eighteen I was a wandering monk of the Jain order. And then I had walked almost around the world! However, since that long walk I had become a householder and lost touch with walking."

Calling on both his own personal valiancy and his spiritual tradition, he went on: "I knew that walking was not solely a means to get somewhere; it was an end in itself, a form of meditation, a way of being. Reflecting in this way, I gathered strength and kept going."

Pilgrims who walk to the shrine of Saint Giles, in a crypt below the half-ruined hilltop abbey of Saint-Gilles in Provence, leave their pilgrim staffs behind the rails of his tomb with a justifiable sense of achievement, as thanksgiving for having completed their journey. Sights such as these inspire others when the pain begins to bite.

Those who have elected to catch a bus to a local shrine or to re-create a mythic journey from sacred site to sacred site from the comfort of a car, need valor of a different order. Even before they have crossed their own threshold, some will assuredly fall to doubting their own purposes, thinking that their journey is not "real," and that in the world of pilgrimages, they are second-class citizens. They may receive little support from others, who have fixed ideas of what constitutes spiritual endeavor.

But, although pain and hardship are historically associated with pilgrimage, the idea that a sacred journey must be one long slog—"no pain, no gain"—is a cultural value that we put on it and a part only of some religious traditions, particularly Christianity, that equate suffering with redemption. Outside these, reaching back to rites of separation and initiation from very ancient times, are philosophies that accept that physical hardships, including hunger and lack of sleep, may have to be endured but that do not ascribe to them a redemptive purpose or result. These hardships are used (as in intensive military training, for example by the French Foreign Legion) to jolt the mind out of a rut and into awareness.

So long as the pilgrim becomes and remains aware (and this takes practice), sacred journeys do not have to be all misery and mosquitoes. Basho, already infirm when he embarked on his journey, did indeed suffer, but not for any virtue in the pain (he took the chance to soak his aching bones in hot springs, and when things got too bad, he borrowed a horse). His walk up the Narrow Road was not penance but an awakening.

If self-doubt creeps in, we can take support from the good historical precedent for a symbolic pilgrimage. In China before communism, there existed "mountain societies" for making the journey to the Great Mountain, T'ai Shan. The societies were of two sorts: "traveling" and "stationary." Both collected a fixed amount of money per month from members. Soon after the New Year, members of traveling societies went to the Great Mountain, while members of the stationary societies celebrated a festival involving worship at a paper "mountain" — for all religious purposes held to be identical with the real T'ai Shan.

> "Three young clerics, of the men of Ireland, went on their pilgrimage...there was no provision taken to sea save three cakes. 'I will bring the little cat,' says one of them. Now when they reached the shoulders of the main, 'In Christ's name,' say they, 'let us cast away our oars into the sea, and throw ourselves on the mercy of our Lord!' This was done. Not long afterwards they came...to a beautiful island....The little cat goes from them. It draws to them a veritable salmon....'O God,' say they, 'our pilgrimage is no pilgrimage now!...'
>
> Thereafter they abode for six watches without food, until a message came from Christ that some was on the altar...half a cake of wheat for each man, and a piece of fish."
>
> *The Book of Lismore* (1890)
> Whitley Stokes, trans.

Although the stationary societies were sometimes referred to disparagingly as "squatting and fattening societies" because of the feasts entailed, such symbolic pilgrimages prevented people who

MOUNT ATHOS

SALONIKA

The garden of the Mother of God

Mount Athos forms the tip of a finger of land that juts into the sea east of Salonika in northern Greece. For almost two millennia the peninsula has been revered as the sacred territory of the Virgin Mary, and twenty monasteries of the various Orthodox faiths—Greek, Russian, Serbian, and Bulgarian—are spread along its shores and among its wild mountains. Some 1,500 monks live there now—women and "beardless boys" have been forbidden access to the Holy Mountain for centuries.

My papers in hand, I boarded the ferry from the tiny port on the border of Athos—the name that generally signifies the whole peninsula. We chugged for an hour or more along the Athos coast, passing monasteries with onion towers and massive stone ramparts along the way. The boat, filled with Greek pilgrims, finally anchored in Daphni. We made our way to Karies, the administrative center for the Holy Mountain, and then we were on our own.

The only transport on the peninsula is an ancient bus that rattles over the hills from Karies to Iviron monastery, on the northern coast. The best way to travel on Athos is on foot, along the pilgrim paths that thread their way from one monastery to the next. This is what I had come for, to set my body in motion in the rarefied air and the natural elements of the Holy Mountain, to join the countless pilgrims, who had traveled these paths down through the centuries and made of their walking an active communion with the world about them.

I was given permission to stay for two weeks. I would walk all day and arrive in the late afternoon at the gates of a monastery, usually to be greeted by the guest master with the traditional glass of ouzo. I often walked, or scrambled, over the cliff paths hanging precariously over steep drops of shale that plunged into the dazzling water below; through forests where the paths would peter out and leave me turn-

Trypiti
Ouranópolis
KARIES
Iviron
DAPHNI
Megistis Lavra
MOUNT ATHOS
6,700FT

ing in circles; up steep crags and rocky bluffs, where everything was sky, a vast canopy of blue; and through sheaves of white and silver light.

When I reached a monastery in the evening, I was always surprised to notice how little food I wanted. A bowl of thin soup and a slice of bread filled me until morning, when I would take another slice of bread with thin black coffee. I would never have lunch, and yet my body was humming with a living energy that I have only rarely known again since.

Suddenly, one morning on the path above the ocean, I realized what it was: I was being fed, literally filled, with the wind, the water, the hard earth, the slant of Greek light, and the vibrations of tens of thousands of monks who had lived out their lives on this land in an intensity of prayer.

Roger Housden

could not make a "real" pilgrimage from suffering spiritual deprivation. This may also have been the main purpose of the medieval pavement labyrinths in European cathedrals sometimes known as *Chemins de Jérusalem*, "Paths to Jerusalem." They provided a stage for a pilgrim to act out his or her soul's voyage.

If we are too solemn about pilgrimage, we may miss the spiritual insights that may arrive in the midst of fun. The turf mazes that were once plentiful in Britain are often claimed gloomily to have been traversed by people on their knees as a penance. But their names—Shepherd's Race, Trojaburg, Troy Town—and their frequent association with sites of fairs and gatherings, suggest that they may have been used to play a game linked to an ancient Roman sport. However they were used originally, "maze running" today can generate something of the euphoria that, as athletes know, often carries with it moments of startling clarity. Jeff Saward, the founder in 1980 of the Caerdroia Project in Essex, England, dedicated to labyrinth research, speaks of "the intense concentration required to keep from straying from the path and the momentary flash of revelation as one reaches the sudden center."

What happens to a pilgrim's feet is important: More important is what happens to the head and the heart. Pilgrimage is about willingness and trust: willingness to open ourselves however briefly to the divine in the world around us, trust that the "flash of revelation" will come. We do not know what form it will take or when it will arrive. In the movie *Mermaids*, Charlotte (Winona Ryder) says something like: "Whoever heard of anyone hearing the Voice of God doing 70 miles per hour down the freeway?" She couldn't be more wrong.

CHAPTER 4

Sacred Way

You are on your road, literally or metaphorically, your body and mind adjusting to your journey in this marvelous time and space outside normality. Hopefully, you are wide awake and aware, even if you are sitting comfortably. If you travel by air, put your consciousness into takeoff and landing, not letting yourself be distracted by the strategies employed by cabin crew and other passengers to "take your mind off" these most hazardous moments in any flight. This is your life: Live it.

Pilgrimage is about receiving what there is, all of it, as part of the liminal experience. Even on a day trip, there will be some stretching of the mind and spirit so that a new person goes back home. If you are on a journey in a strange land, you are missing something if at times you are not half drunk with seeing, smelling, hearing, tasting, feeling as well as with spiritual exaltation. It is not suffering that keeps the true pilgrim going but expectation and joy.

In the summer of 1983 for the third time in five years, a Westerner made the entire pilgrimage on foot from Alandi to Pandharpur in India. Hindu Varkaris (devotees of this pilgrimage), when asked about this, said that they were very pleased that others were experiencing the pilgrimage but were anxious that in focusing on the laboriousness of the journey, Westerners were missing its essential joy.

People have different expectations of a pilgrimage. Largely this is a matter of culture. The Latin word for *pilgrimage, peregrinatio*, comes from *per ager*, "through the fields." The idea of a journey is uppermost and because of the laboriousness of that journey in historical times, the word *pilgrimage* often implies hardship or discomfort. The Greek word for *pilgrimage*, however, *proskynesis*, means "prostration or veneration": Focusing on the goal, it relates to what you do when you arrive at your pilgrimage destination, rather than how you get there. It contains no implication of suffering.

Both words contain the idea of movement: movement toward deity, or in its presence. As we shall see in a later chapter, on closer approach to the sacred destination, walking may be replaced by dancing, crawling on the knees, or prostrations. This movement creates a kind of sacred choreography. All pilgrimages have shapes, which may be functional but which also assume a symbolic dimension. The contemplation of the shape of your pilgrimage gives you a framework for reflection and strengthens your imagination to grasp what it is you will do, are doing, or have done.

Sacred choreography: patterns through space

Pilgrimages the world over make the same patterns through space. The principal pattern is a linear one. For pilgrimages in which there is no intention of returning, such as the ascetic voyages of early Irish monks, or the wanderings of certain medieval pilgrims, the line extends up to the moment of death. More usual is the linear journey from A to B with a return by the same route, as along the Pilgrim's Way through southern England to Canterbury. Linear pilgrimages often take the form of processions, transforming the movement from an act of locomotion to a performance. The celebration of the Eleusinian Mysteries in Ancient Greece was preceded by a day-long procession, offering local produce at shrines along the way, each of which reflected some aspect of the story of the corn goddess, Demeter.

A variation on this is the massing pilgrimage. After leaving home from various starting points over a "catchment area," people converge on an assembly point and then proceed en masse to a shrine. One of the most striking examples of this variation is the pilgrimage to Pandharpur on the banks of the Bhima river, in Maharashtra, India. Myth and legend relate how Krishna, in the form of Vithoba, came to be at Pandharpur and how Pundalik, the mythological first saint or holy man of Vithoba's cult, also came there. Poet saints from Pandharpur and other places expressed their devotion to Vithoba by coming to visit his shrine and the tomb of Pundalik, singing on their way devotional songs composed as offerings.

The most famous among these devotees is Jnanesvar, a poet saint of the thirteenth century from Alandi, where he voluntarily entered a living tomb. His tomb, too, became a focus for pilgrimage, but also, soon after his death, his followers began venerating replicas of his feet, called *padukas*, and carrying them to Pandharpur, recreating his own pilgrimage there. Today, the

A Saint, a star, and a shell

In 1982, two 18-year-old boys and an adult guide set out from Belgium on a walk to Santiago de Compostela. The boys had been living in institutional care for a long while and were starting to be involved in criminal or otherwise unacceptable behavior. Their future in society looked bleak, and the journey to Spain along the sacred road to Compostela represented a kind of last chance to redeem themselves. The aim was to complete the four-month walk in good understanding and in good order, showing respect for the cultures through which they walked. Then, the youth judge in Belgium would let them go, to take their futures into their own hands and start an adult life.

The walk was a success, and the boys were able to find themselves a place in society, supported by a group of people who were ready to help them establish their lives. From this success was born an organization known as Oikoten. This Greek name means two things: "away from the fatherland" and "on own force, relying on own resources." The founders of Oikoten were inspired by Vision Quest in the United States, which organizes survival journeys, known as caravans of the last chance, for young people with heavy criminal pasts. Since 1982, Oikoten has guided about 160 youngsters of both sexes to Compostela.

In my journey to Santiago, I acted as a guide for the two boys who had spent more than six months in state-run education homes in Mol and Ruyselede. I focused primarily on their lives and paid little attention to the cultural aspects of the road, from Jaca over the Pyrenees to Santiago. Personally, I give great value to the influence of a path that has been walked by millions of pilgrims since early medieval times. The people we met along the way gave us great support in creating a climate in which changes and transformations could happen.

For me, this pilgrimage was part of a series of travels I had undertaken since leaving my job in a motorcycle garage in 1986. The travels helped me find direction and depth in my own life. Gradually, especially during the Santiago walk, I found

BRUXELLES ●
Werchter
St. Joris Weert
Cortil-Noirmont
Florennes
Fumay
Rethel
Reims
Méry-sur-Seine
Troyes
Tonnerre
Luzy
Clermont-Ferrand
Vic-sur-Cère
Entraygues
Albi

that this traveling never stops, never comes to an end. The meaning of such a pilgrimage is to experience physically what the whole of life is about: growing, being on your way, getting closer to beauty within. The real pilgrimage for me, as for both of the boys, continued after arriving in Santiago and returning home. Several years later, we still meet regularly, and I can tell that they came out of the pilgrimage in another state of mind, as stronger individuals with more self-respect and with a new sense of direction.

It was important not to stress the religious beliefs behind the pilgrimage to Santiago—this might have resulted in rejection from boys who viewed society defensively and negatively. Religiousness and the ability for contact with God lie inside ourselves, where pilgrims can truly meet—whatever their beliefs.

A pilgrimage really works when it is long enough to make it the "normal life" you are living. It is not an abnormal life from which you then return to normality. Arriving on a mountaintop after hours of hard work with those boys and looking into one another's eyes, where only for a part of a second infinity finds a mirror, was such a great experience that for me it was worth four months of strenuous effort.

Walter Lombaert

Practicalities

Legend has it that St. James the apostle fled persecution in the Holy Land and came to northern Spain. There, he preached the gospel until his return to Jerusalem, where he was martyred in 44 C.E. His remains were brought back and buried in Spain, where in the ninth century they were rediscovered in a field indicated by a bright star. *Santiago de Compostela* means literally "St. James of the star field."

Pilgrims and penitents have made the pilgrimage to Santiago—the most arduous in Europe—since medieval times, when they would gather at monasteries to travel in groups for safety. Four routes through France meet at the Spanish border. Pilgrims carry a shell, the symbol of St. James, as it is said that an early pilgrim who fled to the sea to escape vagabonds returned to land covered in shells.

tombs of the saints of Vithoba's cult are starting points for thirty or forty groups of pilgrims, called *palkhis*, from the Marathi word for the palanquin in which they carry to Pandharpur the *padukas* of their particular saint. These *padukas* were once stone and quite small, and were worn round the necks of individual pilgrims. However, since the early nineteenth century, these have been replaced by life-size silver replicas, borne on a palanquin by particular members of each *palkhi*.

Plotted on a map, the traditional routes of the *palkhis* run like tributaries of a stream to join at the tiny village of Wakri on the outskirts of Pandharpur for the great procession into the holy city. Rituals of joining are performed at the point where two *palkhis* meet: In one popular ritual, members from each group approach one another, and with arms crossed right over left, clasp hands and swing each other round in a circle.

"...the universe is a sacramental kind of place in which the material elements and bodily actions can speak of God."
J. G. Davies,
Pilgrimage Yesterday and Today
(1988)

Some pilgrimages themselves take a circular form, from the practical desire not to return by the same route (in tourist parlance, the round trip) and also from the deep satisfaction that the circle as a geometric shape gives the human mind. The thirteenth-century Christian theologian Thomas Aquinas said that the circle was the perfect whole, as a return is made to the beginning. The ancient Greek philosophers likewise held that the circle was the perfect figure and circular motion, the perfect motion. It is an appropriate figure for pilgrimage.

At the level of imagery rather than metaphysics and geometry, the circle is connected with the sun: the sun's shape, and the shape of its course through the day and the year. Clock faces are circular because they chart the round of hours through day (sun's presence) and night (sun's absence). The zodiac is the circle of the sun's apparent progress through the stars. Not only do Hindu pilgrims to sacred cities often follow a traditional circular pilgrim route round the city, the following of which in its entirety brings special merit, but they also move from one holy place to another in a rough circle, always moving around to the right, their right shoulders pointing inward toward some invisible center. It is a common practice, too, to circle individual shrines, keeping the shrine on one's right (*pradaksina*). This ritual movement is probably in imitation of the passage of the sun.

People worldwide assign a beneficent influence to sunwise (clockwise) movement, but maleficent to movement counter to the sun (counterclockwise). In British folk practice these are the directions called *deiseil*, or the sunwise turn, and *widdershins*, or *withershins*, a dialectal word meaning "contrary to the sun." The first is used in rites and charms of blessing, the second in cursings and blightings, most notoriously by post-Reformation witches. Still in Britain today, when processions circuit holy wells or perform the ceremony of Beating the Bounds or join hands to "clip" (embrace) the church at a Church Clipping as at Painswick in Gloucestershire, they move in a sunwise direction.

Rounds of pilgrimage on a broad scale may take the pilgrim on a journey encircling a landscape feature such as a mountain, as in the pilgrimage to Mount Kailash in Tibet, or an island, as in Shikoku, Japan. Here, too, the sunwise turn is found. The Shikoku pilgrimage consists of visiting 88 temples, following a circular route around the circumference of the island. Traditionally, pilgrims started from Ryozen-ji, temple number one, proceeding from there in a clockwise direction to the eighty-eighth temple, a distance of more than 900 miles from the start of their sacred journey. Many pilgrims, however, close the circle, by visiting Ryozen-ji again at the end of their pilgrimage before they leave the island, thus making it both their starting point and their goal.

Another common pattern of pilgrimage is the spiral, the path winding round and round until the goal is reached. In Christian art, the evolution of the spirit is often represented as an ascending spiral: Each step takes the soul farther from the material world and lifts it toward the divine. At the same time, the ever-decreasing spirals take the soul in toward a point on the apex of the climb. Jill Purce writes in *The Mystic Spiral*: "Movement along this three-dimensional spiral is at once aspiring and centering, going toward God without and God within." The spiral pilgrimage may take the form of a symbolic ascent, as among the Hopi of Arizona, who believe that they have already climbed from three previous worlds into the fourth one and will soon be entering the fifth. A labyrinthine design (see above) very like that of the Labyrinth of Knossos in Crete is their symbol for Mother Earth.

The spiral pilgrimage may also be an actual pathway to ascend a height: As

"To turn, turn, will be our delight, Till by turning, turning, we come round right."

Shaker Hymn

many holy places are on mountaintops, an ascent by spiraling around a mountain is common. The most dramatic illustration of the ascent toward God is the ninth-century minaret of the Mosque of Samarra in Iraq. A spiral path climbs to the top of this massive tower, whence the muezzin launches his prayers upward to Allah. Although circular rather than square, it is not unlike one of the ancient ziggurats of the same area, built as symbolic holy mountains.

When we think about sacred journeys, we think mainly in terms of horizontal space—here and there. But as we see from the spiral, there is also vertical space—up and down. Many living pilgrimages consist of an ascent into a high place. For example, in the mountains of southern Austria, people still ascend on foot to the crests of four mountains, traditionally to stave off the prophesied end of the world. But in prehistoric and early historic times, the search for the sacred often took the downward path into the underground caves where Paleolithic artists recorded their views on divinity and its intervention in human affairs.

Downward, too, was the movement in chthonic (Underworld) cults. The Mysteries of Eleusis, the secret rites of the goddess Demeter, insofar as they are known at all, included the *dromena*, a ritual drama, probably an enactment of Persephone's abduction to and return from the Underworld. In the rites' original home at Eleusis (modern Elevsis) in Greece, this drama was perhaps connected with a shallow cave known as the Plutoneon, a symbolic link between Earth and Hades, the Underworld. Underground, too, were the rites of the Persian god Mithras, Lord of Light, worshiped in subterranea known as *mithrea*.

Down is the direction of the Underworld, because world-wide, humankind has buried its dead in the ground. By natural imagery, down is the direction of the cults of death and resurrection. Down is the direction of the Earth Goddess, the Corn Mother, from whose womb (the earth) new life (corn) springs. It is the direction taken by the Pueblo Indian *kachinas* (the mythical ancestors of humankind) when they return to Shipap, the underground realm where (like Persephone) they stay for the half of the year when they are not on Earth. Shipap is also the home of Iyatiku, the Keresan Corn Mother, from whose subterranean dwelling humankind originally emerged, from which each new baby comes, to which the dead return.

Descents are often made through caves, real and symbolic, sometimes conceived of as the entrance to the Underworld, sometimes, as with the cave sanctuaries of ancient Crete, connected with the cult of the Mother Goddess and identified as the womb of Mother Earth. The cave is the entrance to the world of the dead, which is also the entrance to the world of the living. Cave-born deities and divine heroes include Romulus and Remus, raised by a wolf in the Lupercal cave venerated in Ancient Rome; Mithras, who was born from a rock and worshiped in artificial caves (the *mithrea*); and Zeus, said to have been born in either of two caves in Crete: one on Mount Ida, one on Mount Dikte. Caves, natural or artificial, also have historically provided tombs for the dead, often acquiring sanctity from those buried in them. Cave-born and cave-buried in cult if not in doctrine is Jesus Christ, in terms of influence on civilization the most powerful god of death and resurrection the world has yet seen. The descents provided by his cultic life cycle—cave to cave, womb to womb—are described later in this book.

Descents, whether physical or symbolic, engage our primal instincts and our atavistic fears and can be the most mind-altering of all sacred journeys. Whether we are bound for the caves at Mount Dikte or Bethlehem, the magnificent temple caves at Karli, Ajanat, and Ellora in India, or the caves of the Thousand Buddhas at Tun-Huang in China, we are tracing through space one of the most powerful patterns of them all.

"From the sea the ribbed floor of the cavern slopes high through deepening shadows back to the black mouths of a farther grotto: and all that slope is covered with hundreds of thousands of forms...little towers of stone and pebbles deftly piled up by long and patient labor.

'Shinda kodomo no shigoto,' my kurumaya [boatwoman] murmurs with a compassionate smile; 'all this is the work of the dead children.'...

Following after her, we...discover a very, very narrow passage left open between the stone-towers. But we are warned to be careful for the sake of the little ghosts: if any of their work be overturned, they will cry. So we move very cautiously...to a space bare of stone-heaps, where the rocky floor is covered with a thin layer of sand....And in that sand I see light prints of little feet, children's feet, tiny naked feet, only three or four inches long—the footprints of the infant ghosts."

Lafcadio Hearn on the Kyu-Kukedo-San (Ancient Cavern) Kaka, from *Glimpses of Unfamiliar Japan* (1894)

75

Sacred geography: The pilgrim's path

Pilgrim paths the world over tend to be well trodden, like the sacred routes established by early pilgrims such as St. Helena, mother of the Roman emperor Constantine the Great (*c.* 274–337 C.E.), who visited the Holy Land toward the end of her life. According to legend, the whereabouts of the True Cross was disclosed to her in a dream, as lying under what is now the Church of the Holy Sepulcher in Jerusalem. Her historical purpose was to discover and mark with a church as many as possible of the sites associated with the Gospel stories, and she also founded basilicas in Bethlehem and on the Mount of Olives. Others followed her example and discovered more relics, founded more churches, and established more sites (and sights), until a visit to the Holy Land became a living Bible.

The pilgrim path is dotted with stopping places. A pilgrimage to a single holy place often involves visiting points of religious significance on the way that symbolically mark the pilgrim's passage from the profane to the sacred world. They may also prepare him or her for the transition in other ways: The monastery at Sivananda Hill at Rishikesh, for example, prepares Hindu pilgrims both physically and spiritually for their punishing trek northward through the Himalayas to Badrinath or Kedarnath (or both).

Wherever the sacred journey exists or has existed in an organized form are found networks of sacred places and holy buildings. Adventurer pilgrims, such as Tom Coryat and Samuel Purchas in the seventeenth century, responded both to the dangers of the sacred journey and the richness of this tradition. The

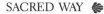

routes they followed were related from practical necessity, to highways, trade routes, and paths of refugees and conquerors and were marked by earlier pilgrims with way marks, rest stations, shrines, temples, tombs, stairs worn hollow by their feet, and objects rubbed smooth by their hands.

Not the least, there are the traditional "pit stops"—the caravansaries and the pilgrim hostels (in the old sense of this French word, ancestral to English *hostel, hospital,* and *hotel*), such as the George and Pilgrims Hotel at Glastonbury, England, whose fifteenth-century stone facade conceals the older lines of a Benedictine Maison Dieu. Even if you are making your way alone, there is "company" on the road from generations of pilgrims who trod the path before you.

In Northern Europe, the Protestant Reformation in the sixteenth century struck at the heart of pilgrimage, destroying many of the medieval shrines and causing the pilgrim paths to become lost and overgrown. But those ruins and those paths still possess a powerfully beckoning *numen.* At Lindisfarne in Northumberland on a bank holiday, a line of cars will form, waiting for ebb tide in order to cross the causeway to St. Cuthbert's Holy Island. Canterbury, Westminster, Iona, and Little Walsingham still draw enormous crowds. Comparatively few come as "simple" tourists.

Similarly, ancient sites of religions long since abandoned exercise an attraction that holds more of myth and magic in it than archaeology. In some places, there may indeed be signs of continuity of religious belief from the deep past. Two major Andean pilgrimages, one to Copacabana on the shores of Lake Titicaca, the other to Motupe in the coastal desert of northern

Peru, appear to have ancient pre-Christian roots—both regions having had major pilgrimage traditions before the Spanish Conquest. In Europe, Frontinus (c. 40–103 C.E.) was able to write of the wells that in earlier times had provided Rome's water supply: "The memory along with the sanctity of the wells still endures and is tended: they are thought to bring health to diseased bodies." In the same way, clear signs of medieval Christian practice linger to this day in local customs surrounding Irish and British holy wells.

Even where there has been discontinuity, all is not necessarily lost. The great pagan temple of Old Uppsala in Sweden was once visited by crowds of worshipers from all over the country, who came every nine years to a general festival lasting nine days. On each day, one man and eight male creatures were sacrificed to the gods, until by the end of the festival the bodies of 72 horses, dogs, and men hung in the adjoining sacred grove. A living man was then thrown into the sacred spring, and his failure to reappear taken as an omen that the people's wishes would be granted. The temple was destroyed in the twelfth century, its "idols"—Thor, Odin, and Frey—thrown down, the huge evergreen holy tree beside it felled. The sacred grove was cut down, the sacred spring desecrated. The whole site was nullified and defused by the building of a Christian church.

Soon after, the center of the Swedish kingdom moved elsewhere, leaving nothing but a row of three mighty grass-covered mounds. Although they are known as Odin's Howe, Thor's Howe, and Frey's Howe, they were almost certainly raised over the places where were burned the bodies of Aun, Egill, and Athils, three warrior kings of the sixth century, reported in early records to have been "howed at Uppsala." But for today's visitor this trace of the "glory days" of Scandinavian paganism is enough: The meaning of the sacred way comes from the history of the pilgrims on it and the imprint it takes of human belief in divinity.

Wherever it is found, the contemplation of holiness in its own place has meaning. It does not matter if we do not hold with human sacrifice or literally believe that it is the footprints of the Tibetan Buddhist saint Milarepa we see on Mount Kailash. It is not important that we suspect that the Jewish shrine known as the tomb of Esther and Mordecai in Hamadan, Iran, in fact contains the wife of King Yazdagird I (r. 399–421 C.E.). Hamadan (of old called Ecbatana), the summer capital of the early Persian kings, is not far from the excavated ruins of Shush, ancient Susa, called Shushan in the Bible, where in the Book of Esther, the story of Queen Esther and her uncle Mordecai may be read. The ruins of this once-great city, the dramatic and inspiring story, and local piety do their work: It is a hardhearted visitor indeed who, at the sight of the two sculpted ebony tombs of uncertain age, although of ancient appearance, is not moved to leave an offering.

"The faces of the people have an indescribable look of patient expectancy—the air of waiting for something interesting to make its appearance. If it fails to appear, they will travel to find it: they are astonishing pedestrians and tireless pilgrims, and I think they make pilgrimages not more for the sake of pleasing the gods than of pleasing themselves by the sight of rare and pretty things. For every temple is a museum, and every hill and valley throughout the land has its temple and its wonders."

Lafcadio Hearn,
Glimpses of Unfamiliar Japan (1894)

MOUNT KAILASH

A circular journey of renewal

Mount Kailash, or Kangrinpoche, where Shiva and Parvati lie together in bliss and where eternity meshes with time, lies hidden at the western end of the Great Himalayas. All of the pilgrim routes to the "precious jewel of eternal snow" cross at least one pass above 17,000 feet. Expect to suffer: Sickness, depression, dizziness seize the unwary foreigner at these altitudes. Expect to be joyful: You will leave your old life behind, and as you walk the *kang kora,* the pilgrim way, you will discover friendship, generosity, and beauty beyond wonder.

MOUNT KAILASH
• Lhasa

Kailash stands alone, behind the sea of mountains where Tibet and India meet, its four faces to the four directions, with a great river flowing from each: the Indus, Brahmaputra, Sutlej, and Karnali, a tributary of the holy Ganges. Here is the abode of Shiva, where the waters of heaven pass through the god's matted hair and become healing streams; the *tirtha,* the place where the waters meet, the focus of all Hindu pilgrimages. Some devotees say that Kailash is the Shivalinga; others that it is Mount Meru, the presence of the eternal in time.

Today, it is difficult for Hindus to get to Kailash. The Chinese government allows only a small number of licensed travelers to take the old pilgrim route from Kumaun in Uttar Pradesh across the Lepu Lekh. The permitted route is via Kathmandu and Lhasa, the tourists' and trekkers' trail, under the watchful eyes of the border police. Here are Buddhists, for whom Kailash is the center of Earth; and Tibetans following the Bön way of the spirits, the religion of Tibet before Bodhidarma crossed the mountains. Western pilgrims carry chocolate to share and pictures of the Dalai Lama, which Tibetans greatly prize, giving sunflower seeds in return.

The pilgrimage begins at Darchen, a straggling settlement of huts and tents beyond Lake Manasarovar, itself a place of pilgrimage. Pilgrims take three days to circle Mount Kailash, a walk of just over 30 miles. Every step is rich with the prayers and praise of those who have walked the way before—for more years than humankind can recall. This circular pilgrimage leads nowhere, and yet in the act of going, the old life is left behind; and the pilgrim returns renewed.

Ascending gently through thorn scrub and nettles, you see gifts of honey and coins at the holy places associated with gods and ascetics. The imposing north face of Kailash, 4,000 feet of sheer striated black rock topped with vast overhanging cornices, looms ahead. At the Drolma-la, the highest point of the path at over 18,500 feet, heaps of clothing lie beside the path, cast off symbols of the old life. Close by is the cave created by the Buddhist Milarepa in the contest for the mountain with Naro Bonchung and the Bön religion, and the rock impressed with Milarepa's footprint.

Just beyond the pass and below the trail lies a small icy lake, Gauri Kund, where braver travelers may take an invigorating plunge into new life. From the pass, the trail descends through a rocky gorge. Tibetans make three, five, or thirteen, or even more, circumambulations of Mount Kailash. Sometimes they prostrate themselves, rising to walk the length of one prostration only, then once again falling to the ground. To circle the mountain in this way may take up to four weeks of patient and meditative movement. These pilgrims may then turn and return, rapt in their awareness of the eternal. The way has no beginning and no end.

Patricia Stoat

Indus
Sutlej
Ganga
INDIA
Mt. Kailash (Kangrinpoche) 22,000 ft
Darchen
Lake Manasarovar

Drira Phuk Monastery
Drolma-la
vatshal cemetery
Thupke Dzingbu Lake
Mt. Kailash (Kangrinpoche) 22,000 ft
Zutrul Phuk Monastery
Darchen

Practicalities

To enter Tibet you must join a tour group either in China or in your own country and obtain a permit. You will also need a visa for China. It is recommended that you consult your government foreign affairs office for up-to-date travel advice for Tibet.

The best months to go to Mount Kailash are May, June, and early July to avoid heavy snow and the monsoon rains.

Lake Manasarovar

Tibet's holiest lake lies 20 miles south of Mount Kailash. Venerated in Indian mythology, it is a sacred bathing place for pilgrims. It takes four days to walk the traditional route around the lake, starting from the Chiu Monastery south of Darchen.

Our hearts, minds, and souls can expand and grow in the light of other people's beliefs. As Stewart Perowne observes in *Roman Mythology:* "About Apollo…whole books have been written, so many-splendored, so beautiful were his character and attributes. The visitor to Delos or Delphi can with…much profit meditate on the gifts of this god of light, the lord of all brightness in thought and form…."

The rise in the number of people visiting pilgrimage places worldwide in the second half of the twentieth century was partly due to the emergence of pilgrim tourists, people combining recreation with devotion, taking the opportunity to enlarge their information and experience while seeking their own personal encounter with the divine. This is a phenomenon of holy places in the East as well as in the West, and in neither is it new — it is merely emphasized by the great easing of travel. As we have seen, this principle underlay much medieval Christian pilgrimage — witness Chaucer's *Canterbury Tales* — and, transmuted by Zen, Basho's travels on *The Narrow Road to the Deep North*.

The secular and the sacred

On pilgrimage roads, the secular and the sacred are intertwined. To illustrate the richness of experience available to the pilgrim tourist, let me give you the example of a journey that I made with my husband and son to Mashad and the most sacred shrine in Iran, the mausoleum of the ninth-century Muslim saint, Imam Reza, the Eighth Imam. This journey was on the eve of the Islamic Revolution. Now as then, you can go by air or rail from Tehran to Mashad or take the northern highway by way of Gurgan, passing through spectacularly beautiful scenery. But, we took the southern Khurasan highway, following the old caravan route, the Silk Road to the East. The image is romantic, reality is otherwise. This *can* be one of the most hellish journeys in all Iran. Covering nearly 600 miles, much of it skirts the Dasht-i Kavir (Great Salt Desert), hot and dusty even in late summer and early autumn when the road is at its best. This is the time of year we chose to drive it in a Paykan, the locally made Hillman Hunter (no four-wheel drive, no air conditioning).

Leaving Tehran through Ray, the magic carpet of Iranian history unrolls before us: 48 miles to the "Caspian Gates" of classical literature; 150 miles to Semnan, an ancient town on the edge of the desert, once a staging post on the main caravan route to Central Asia; 221 miles to Damghan. The distances are great and seem greater. But already we have seen ruined *serais*, the wayside inns that served the camel caravans, and mosques, minarets, and shrine tombs *(imamzadehs)*. Via a dirt track off to the south we have visited Shar-i Qumis, now a series of great mounds on a baked mud plain; once, it is believed, what the Greeks called Hecatompylos, "City of 100 Gates," where Alexander the Great told his dismayed army that they were about to march to India.

Thanks to the inordinate kindness of a man on his way to his melon patch, who abandons his bicycle and comes with us, we have also found Gerdkuh, the famous Assassin castle perched on a mountain mentioned by Marco Polo. From here, the Assassins preyed on caravans until 1256 when the Mongols took the castle—some say after a siege begun by Genghis Khan that lasted 27 years. The besieged only surrendered when their clothes wore out. A pile of mangonel balls from that siege still sits at the foot of the cliff.

In Damghan we find probably the oldest mosque in Iran, founded in about 760 C.E., the Tarik Khana (Tari Khaneh) or Masjid-i Chehel-Sotun ("mosque of forty columns"). Its almost square courtyard is surrounded by arcades of tunnel vaults supported by squat brick piers nearly seven feet across. In its strength and simplicity, it is one of the noblest buildings we have seen in the Middle East. Its very beautiful, detached minaret was built in 1026–1029 to replace one that probably collapsed in a ninth-century earthquake: Even the repairs are old here. Other religious buildings include a Dervish monastery, but courteous children lead us to the tomb-tower of Pir-i Alamdar, built in 1021, around the inside of whose dome runs a painted Kufic inscription (Kufic being an early Arabic script).

A short diversion south takes us to the great, dusty tell of Tepe Hissar, the main levels of which date from around 3500 B.C.E. to 1700 B.C.E. Its baked-mud surface is still littered with fragments of pottery decorated in lively black line—someone's dinner service. The highway rolls on to Shahrud, a leafy town blessed for its shade, its great slab of ice for our icebox, its gas. It is the halfway mark between Tehran and Mashad. A farther short diversion north brings us to the walled village of Bistam (or Bastam). Probably founded during the reign of King Khusraw II in 590 C.E., it is the birthplace and shrine of the Sufi sheikh Bayazid-al-Bastami. Ever since he died in 874 C.E., his tomb has been a place of pilgrimage and hence, the proliferation of religious buildings. It is easy to get lost in this high-walled labyrinthine place: Mistaking a gap between houses for a lane, we blunder into someone's courtyard. A woman is hanging washing, unveiled, and her husband justifiably shouts at us—uncouth *farengi* (foreigners). Chastened and more careful, we discover Bistam's treasures, including a splendid fluted tomb tower built in 1313, known as the Kashaneh, and Bayazid's own conical-roofed tomb (which locals say he built himself), standing in a large courtyard, pleasant with trees.

From Shahrud, the road east for the next 100 miles was once known as the Stages of Terror. We can still see the small circular towers erected as defenses against Turkoman raiders. The bleak monotony of this route along the edge of the desert, little changed for the last thousand years, is broken at Miandasht, about 70 miles from Shahrud, by an enormous caravanserai built under the Safavid dynasty (1491–1722). We are grateful for the ruined *serais*, whose walls in this empty landscape often provide the only shade. We also thank God many times on this journey for the genius of Iranian motor mechanics with their ability against all the odds to keep Paykans running.

"So we arrived at the summit of the mountain (Nebo), where there is now a small church. Inside this church I saw a place slightly raised containing about as much space as is usual in a grave. I asked the holy men what this was, and they answered: 'here Holy Moses was laid by the angels, since, as it is written, "No man knows how he was buried," it is certain that he was buried by angels. For his grave where he was laid is now shown today. As it was shown to us by our ancestors who lived here, so do we point it out to you. Our ancestors said that it was handed down to them as a tradition by their ancestors.'"

St. Silvia of Aquitania (fourth century C.E.), *Peregrinatio ad Loca Sancta*

Walking with the saint

The pilgrim's way circles the Japanese island of Shikoku

Mount Koya
Shikoku

and leads to 88 temples in a journey of more than 900 miles. The temples perch atop the mountains or overlook the sea, with a wild and rugged landscape all around. Some pilgrims walk, some travel by bus in organized parties, others go by car. What unites them all are the clothes they wear and the faith they share in Kôbô Daishi, the Buddhist saint.

Pilgrims symbolically travel the path Kôbô Daishi trod to enlightenment. The route divides into four stages, which represent in turn the awakening of the Buddha mind, the ascetic practice required to develop it, the flowering of awareness, and eternal enlightenment. Pilgrims leave the everyday world and travel, accompanied by the saint, into the realms of death: They dress as the saint, in the guise of a wandering monk, and wear white—the color of purity and death in Japan.

A completed pilgrimage symbolizes rebirth and renewal, while death as a pilgrim is believed to confer immediate rebirth in the Pure Land. Those who have completed the pilgrimage may at death be placed in their coffins in their pilgrim's clothes with their pilgrimage journal, ready to make their final journey.

As the route circles the island, pilgrims return to the point where they started. In reality there is no destination, and many make a second and third journey. Some do it hundreds of times or even walk permanently with the saint in an incessant journey round the island.

I walked the pilgrimage in a cold and snowy early spring some years ago, not as a believer but as a foreign traveler and researcher. Although swathed in scepticism, I donned the traditional garb to identify with the pilgrims. As I walked, I found my identity changing, gradually at first, from self-conscious outsider to ardent walker, to pilgrim. As I hiked up steep mountain paths past moss-covered stone Buddha figures, I would come across stone markers erected by pilgrims of the past to help future fellow-seekers find their way, and I was grateful for their kindness.

Giving *settai* (alms) to a pilgrim is seen as giving a gift to Kôbô Daishi and allows the donor to share the merits of the pilgrimage. As I traipsed, freezing, through the winter snow, a car stopped, and a man handed me a hot drink—a gift to the saint that warmed the pilgrim.

As I stumbled wearily into temple courtyards, busloads of pilgrims would draw up, and energetic old people, their shirts spotlessly white, would bound out. I would be annoyed, for I had walked, and climbed mountain paths, and they had just sat on luxury buses. Was I not better, because of the arduous nature of my journey? And then, one of them would smile at me, maybe hand me something—*settai* from one pilgrim to another—and I would smile back.

And I would realize, yet again, that no one is better than anyone else, that what really mattered was the spirit in which the journey was done. And I would learn again and again the true meaning of *settai*: a spiritual gift—the gift behind the gift. All bear the same message: We are together—you, the saint, and me. In that message there is unity and equality: the rich pilgrim on the comfortable bus, the ragged pilgrim on foot, the local housewife giving a coin, the schoolchild who bowed to me and smiled one morning. All one, together, with the saint.

Dr. Ian Reader

(map labels)
Starting point
rine
e pilgrim route—
ockwise round the island

Mount Koya

Traditionally, the pilgrimage started here, at the tomb of Kôbô Daishi (774–835) in the mountaintop monastery he founded. In 835, the saint announced the date that he would die and led a prayer festival at the Imperial Palace in Kyoto before returning to Mount Koya to die on the day he had foretold.

The pilgrim's dress

The shirt bears a picture of Kôbô Daishi, and the ideograms, *dôgyôninin*, "two people one practice." The staff signifies both the body of Kôbô Daishi and the pilgrim's gravestone. The bamboo monk's hat, inscribed with a Buddhist poem about transience, protects against sun and rain but also represents the pilgrim's coffin.

Other *serais* and the Minar of Khosrogird, dated 1111 C.E., a beautiful brick minaret nearly a hundred feet high, ease our next six miles to Sabzevar. Then on again for 70 miles across a wide plain with patches of cultivation—a relief to the eyes—to Nishapur.

Destroyed and rebuilt more times than any other city in Iran, Nishapur has little to show from the days of its foundation in the third century. The Mongols devastated it so thoroughly that even the dogs and cats were exterminated, and the whole city was plowed into the ground. But what food for the imagination! Somewhere in the mountains to the northwest may be the shrine in which burned Adhar Burzin Mir, the sacred fire of the farmers, one of three perpetually burning fires of ancient Iran. In Nishapur itself was born the philosopher and astronomer Omar Khayyam (d. 1123). His mausoleum is a modern building erected in 1934 on the site of his original tomb. From the seeds of the roses that once grew on it came a rose planted in 1893 in Woodbridge, England, on the grave of Edward Fitzgerald. It was his loose translation, *The Rubáiyát of Omar Khayyám* (1859), that made Omar famous in the West as a poet. Descended from that one rose is every bush of the pink damask "Omar Khayyam" that blooms in British gardens today, keeping both of their memories green.

In Nishapur, we visit the shrine of Farid-ud-din Attar, a Sufi poet of greater fame in his own country than Omar. His *Conference of the Birds*, like Chaucer's *Canterbury Tales*, is a group of stories bound together by a pilgrimage. He was killed during the Mongol invasion of Iran in 1221, and (like some Christian saints) is said to have run for some distance after being beheaded by his captor. Filled with remorse, he built a tomb on the spot where the poet fell. The shrine we see is a seventeenth-century building restored in 1934, standing in a peaceful garden.

Sixty-nine miles remain to Mashad. From here on are constant reminders of the Eighth Imam. At Mahmudabad, a village of Sayyeds (descendants of the Prophet), is the shrine of Qadamgah, containing what are believed to be the Imam's footprints. We are discreetly dressed, my head is covered, and I have a *chador* for complete veiling if needed. May we come in? On this journey the answer is always yes: Only the shrine of the Imam himself is closed to us.

Closer to Mashad, a signpost points up a track. Here is the shrine of Khwaja Murad, "Fulfiller of Vows," the local name of Harsmat ibn Aiyin, who died in 832, only fifteen years after the Eighth Imam. We have read that local farmers bring a tithe of their harvest here as an offering. The tomb is built against the mountain, with a little garden in front of it, and here are pilgrims, mainly Baluchis, picnicking under the trees. Professional reciters of the Karbala are often to be found at this tomb because Khwaja Murad himself was one of the first reciters of the martyrdom of Imam Reza.

"If all of us could boast a spotless mind, Why should the prophets mingle with mankind?"

Farid-ud-din Attar (c. 1142–1220), *The Conference of the Birds (Mateq at-Tair)*

Continuity is a keynote of this land. Our third and last shrine before Mashad is the mausoleum over the tomb of Khwaja Abbasalt Haravi, said to have been present at Imam Reza's death. He died in about 851, and his tomb is much frequented by pilgrims.

At the River Toruk, which in Arabic means "crossroads," the trade routes from the Middle East, central Asia, India, and Afghanistan all met, and here are the ruins of many caravanseries. Violent times prompted the building of the now-ruined Ribat (fortified *serai*), on the outskirts of Mashad from which, at long last, we get our first glimpse of the golden dome covering the mortal remains of Imam Reza. It has been a long, hot haul in our little Paykan, but we have met with extraordinary courtesy and kindness on the way and seen extraordinary places. We complete the circle by returning to Tehran by the northern "scenic" route—start hard, finish soft is a good way for travelers.

Some might call this journey tourism, but for us it began to make sense of Iran, of the Iranians, of Islam. If shrines, Sufis, and *serais*—a people and their faith—are not the stuff of pilgrimage, what is?

CHAPTER 5

Adventures and Difficulties

Adventures and difficulties are often one and the same thing. We've all met vacationers newly returned from abroad whose account of the trip is a litany of woe. But listen to their voices, watch their faces: As often as not these horrific sagas are told with humor and with uncommon animation. Living to tell the tale is the headiest thing there is.

My grandfather, who as a young man at the beginning of the twentieth century worked his way (I mean this literally) from Toronto almost to Tierra del Fuego, had many tales to tell, but his favorite was how one day he and his mule met another man and a mule on a narrow and precipitous trail high in the Andes. With no room to pass, one mule had to lie down while the other stepped over. He recounted this in the 1950s as if it were yesterday. Of all he had seen and experienced (including World War I in France), this dice with death was most sharply etched on his memory.

Death is not normally something the pilgrim wishes to meet on the sacred journey, unless it is for cultural reasons — as in the case of old or mortally sick Hindus, for whom death at a holy place is the best of all possible ends.

Yet accidental death occurs almost every year on mass pilgrim journeys and in crowded pilgrimage places. Liminal experience—experience outside the normal frame of reference—means no safety net. Unless you are traveling within your own country or in an escorted party (and not always then), you may have to make adult and individual choices. Do you get onto a ferry already dangerously low in the water from the weight of passengers? Or, do you wait hours, perhaps a whole day, for the next?

"When I traveled, I saw many things; and I understand more than I can express." Apocrypha, Ecclesiasticus 34:11–12

Do you venture into regions where war has just been, is being, or might be waged? Not a few pilgrimage places are on "debatable ground," just as were Christian shrines in the Holy Land in the time of the Crusades. These are questions that only you can decide (except in cases where governments intervene and refuse visas).

Dangers don't necessarily come marked with a skull and crossbones. There are many decisions to be made that could turn out to be the wrong ones if made from a background of your own cultural assumptions. It might not occur to a traveler from Ireland, for example, used to a small island and a temperate climate, always to carry water in the car on long journeys (as it would to someone from Arizona) or snow chains in winter (as it would to a Canadian). Similarly, the European traveler used to long-distance walking may anticipate getting cold, footsore, weary, stranded at night in the rain but totally overlook the fact that, at first, simply breathing is hard at high altitudes in, say, the Himalayas or the Andes. It is especially easy to forget that some cities are at high altitudes, such as Cuzco (11,450 feet), Mexico City (7,400 feet), and Tehran (3,800 feet)—in any of which the world pilgrim might find him- or herself. Here, just as much as in open country, you will need time to adjust to the difference not only when moving about but also in cooking (water boils at a lower temperature).

Equally it may not occur to those through whose country you are traveling to warn you of local dangers that are so much a part of everyday life that they are taken for granted—what "every-one knows." When I lived in Virginia, my neighbors there warned me about poison ivy but forgot to mention the little ticks that spread Rocky Mountain Fever (which can be fatal).

Assuming the worst—or the best

The other possibility is that your cultural assumptions may make you see danger where there is none. How many times have we heard of the "mad" drivers of the Middle East? Look again. On the long, dusty roads of Lower Egypt, for example, you can see some of the most intelligent driving in the world, by profes-sional drivers who drive on the right or the left as turn serves, remembering and exploiting the condition of the surface. They drive extremely fast, terrifying Westerners, who on the whole drive defensively and always assume the worst. Assuming the best, these drivers collaborate with oncoming traffic (rather than compete with it). When the passenger calms down enough to watch this high-speed ballet, he or she will observe that the

CROAGH PATRICK

At the still point of the turning world

The figure in front of me looked familiar. His white robes flowed down to his feet. In one hand he held a staff, in the other a shamrock. Beneath a bishop's mitre his face expressed gravity—a reminder that the climb ahead was not to be taken lightly.

The statue of Saint Patrick guards the ascent of Croagh Patrick, the most sacred mountain in Ireland. Its gray cone overlooks the sea about two miles west of Westport in County Mayo. The Reek, as the mountain is known locally, has been a pilgrimage place since 441 C.E., when Patrick, during his mission to convert the pagan Irish, spent the days of Lent on its peak, fasting and meditating. Now, its popularity is such that every year on the last Sunday in July, up to 60,000 souls make the ascent, some in bare feet.

When I climbed the Reek in August, the weather was drizzly. I was thankful for my thick-soled shoes and back-pack containing chocolate and a thick wool sweater—precautions against fatigue and the fickle weather. Although the Reek was not high, I had heard the last stage of the climb was steep, and clouds could descend without warning.

Clew Bay

The first part of the climb was gentle. A rocky path snaked upward at a manageable angle. Soon, however, the mist began to thicken, so I stopped for a rest and turned to see pilgrims trudging up behind me. In the distance, as the mist cleared, I could see the shimmer of Clew Bay, studded with tiny islands. Sunlight drew a glittering silver finger across the water; then the mists blotted out the panorama.

Higher still, I climbed until I reached the spot where the path changes direction to the west. If the vapors had cleared I would have seen the hills of Connemara to the south. As it was, I followed the route to a mound of stones—one of the three stations around which Christians may perform penitential exercises—and the final ascent.

Here was the moment of truth. Through the toneless gray, I could see the path disintegrating into a sea of small rocks—only wraithlike pilgrims indicated any sort of track. With mist all around, I felt suffocated, desperate for a shaft of sunlight. But having come this far—two-thirds of the journey—I was determined to carry on. Step after step, I crept upward. Then, just as I thought the ascent would never end, I found the angle softening. Suddenly the ground was level: I was standing on the summit. Here, where Saint Patrick is said to have beaten off demon blackbirds and got rid of the snakes of Ireland, I now stood encircled by cloud.

Opposite me rose a small chapel, whose stark interior was a welcome haven from the wind. Outside again, as I looked northward into the mist, a porthole suddenly appeared, and for a fleeting moment, I saw Clew Bay rippling like gray satin before the cloud resealed itself. Yet, the revelation was heartwarming, a glimpse of a transcendent world. With that thought I set out on the downward journey. Buoyant, revitalized, I found myself unselfconsciously encouraging upward pilgrims, wishing to perpetuate the bonhomie this magical mountain engenders.

At the bottom, I made my way to Campbell's Bar—the traditional postpilgrimage hostelry—and there relaxed into a steaming cup of tea. In five hours, I had completed a journey that had taken me back to the time of Saint Patrick and inward to a sacred space. And I had stood, as T. S. Eliot expressed it, "at the still point of the turning world."

James Harpur

Westport

GH PATRICK
500 ft

Practicalities

The climb up Croagh Patrick, which rises to about 2,500 feet, takes three hours to go straight up and down or up to five hours with short rests and half an hour at the top. Transport from Westport, County Mayo, about two miles to the east, is provided for pilgrims on Reek Sunday—the last Sunday in July and the official pilgrimage day.

driver takes the same care as any Westerner and rather more than most when overtaking children walking to school or encountering the village ducks or someone's escaped donkey. Danger can only be judged by observing the local context.

Other people will also be making cultural assumptions: Once when (as often) lost in Iran, we asked a shepherd sitting by the roadside if a particular road led to the town we were seeking, he answered very courteously: "In my experience it has never gone there." We thought he was trying to avoid saying no (impolite in his culture). We took the road, just the same, out of curiosity, rather than taking the main highway, which he said was the way to go. It did lead to the town we wanted—although long, full of potholes, and devoid of *chaikhanehs* (teahouses). The shepherd had kindly assumed that, as foreigners, we would want to go from A to B by the fastest route in the greatest comfort. As it happened, it was our kind of road.

"I am here abroad,
I am here in need,
I am here in pain,
I am here in straits,
I am here alone,
O God, aid me."

Carmina Gadelica
(Charms of the Gaels)
Collected in the
nineteenth century

Sometimes the elaborately veiled no really means it. Once again in the 1970s, we were on our kind of road in Iran, driving north toward the (then) Soviet border. We were seeking the so-called Sad-i Iskandr (Alexander's Wall), probably built in the sixth century C.E. as a defense against central Asian raiders, but according to local tradition, a relic of Alexander the Great. It was described in our up-to-date archaeological guide and marked on our American map, although not apparently on local tourist maps. Up here there are no signposts. We knew we needed a police permit to go near the border, and when we eventually encountered signs of life, we asked a policeman. He sent us farther north to a militia outpost. They seemed quite excited by our map, and after poring over it sent us north again, to another outpost—this time the army's. We were taken to the officer, who appeared to be questioning two men whose heads were bloody. (Had they been in an accident? Were they prisoners?) The officer, guards, and "prisoners" were as interested in our map as were the militia. They said we could not go to the wall—the road had been washed away by a flood, it was impassable except by tractor. Where could we hire a tractor? They said even a tractor couldn't get through. They said, whatever it says in the book, the wall is gone, it's been gone a long, long time—ages. We realized that we would not see this wall: They would not let us within spitting distance of the border, but like the shepherd, were too civil to give us a plain no.

Austerities

Like any other traveler, the pilgrim going to foreign lands needs to know not only the physical conditions but the cultural background to be encountered. If the culture sets a spiritual value on hardship itself, pilgrims will sometimes be expected to follow a harder road than most. In both Hindu and Christian traditions, for example, difficulties surmounted add to the merit acquired by undertaking the sacred journey and also serve for the mortification and disciplining of the body. Fasting and self-flagellation are just two of the austerities practiced widely. South Indian pilgrims have, at various times, had themselves branded on both shoulders, pierced their cheeks and tongue with silver needles, and worn a mouth-lock to demonstrate observance of a vow of silence. Although seldom undertaken today, one of the best-known austerities is for the pilgrim to repeatedly prostrate him- or herself all along the route.

A few years ago, a BBC television documentary was devoted to Lotan Baba, which in Hindi means "Rolling Saint." He ran away from home as a young man to escape an arranged marriage and became a *sadhu*, an ascetic. Settling in Ratlam in central India he embarked on a series of inconceivably hard physical austerities, including standing in one place and eating nothing but grass, for seven years. The film by Naresh Bedi showed his pilgrimage, undertaken for Indian unity and world peace, by rolling from his village through Gujarat, Rajasthan, and Delhi to the shrine of Vaishno Devi, in Kashmir. It was a journey of some 2,500 miles along highways, across desert sands, through all the varieties—often pretty nasty—of the Indian land-scape.

No one expects this of an ordinary pilgrim, but hard physical conditions are an accepted part of some sacred journeys. In 1962, the Indian anthropologist Irawati Karve wrote of her pilgrimage from Alandi to Pandharpur: "There were hundreds of professional beggars and poor people. They ate whatever people gave them, spread their mats wherever they found room, and walked with the palanquin. They suffered if it rained. Fortunately this year there was not much rain...."

What is accepted with fortitude by the indigenous inhabitants may be too much for other pilgrims from other places. The great Ganges pilgrimage performed in May, June, and July, begins at Haridwar and covers more than 600 miles across northern India. Although transport is available to pilgrims for much of the way, a large part of the journey is done on foot—often in extreme conditions. *Man, Myth & Magic* (1971) records, without dating the event, that a Western youth who attempted this in bare feet had to have both of them amputated because of frostbite. Frostbitten feet also put an end to the

"When they had passed by this place, they came upon the borders of the Shadow of Death; and this valley was longer than the other; a place also most strangely haunted with evil things....But these women and children went the better through it because they had daylight, and because Mr Great-heart was their conductor."

John Bunyan, *The Pilgrim's Progress*,
Part II (1684)

"Gentlemen and you of the weaker sort, if you love life shift for yourselves, for the robbers are before you. ...Well, said he [Mr Great-heart], we are ready for them. So they went on their way. Now they looked at every turning, when they should meet with the villains; but whether they heard of Mr Great-heart, or whether they had some other game, they came not up to the pilgrims."

John Bunyan, *The Pilgrim's Progress*,
Part II (1684)

"Flying Guru" Swami Vishnu-devananda's 1986 retreat of several months to a cave at Gangotri in the Himalayas.

Rogues and villains

"I have seen some who have spoke very well of a pilgrim's life at first, that after a while have spoken as much against it," wrote John Bunyan in the seventeenth century, clearly not without reason. Historically, dangers have abounded. "Departing thence through Lycia, we fell into the hands of the Arabian thieves: and after we had been robbed of infinite sums of money, and had lost many of our people, hardly escaping with extreme danger of our lives, at length we entered into the most wished city of Jerusalem." Thus wrote Ingulph, Abbot of Crowland in Lincolnshire, England, who made the pilgrimage to Jerusalem in 1064.

Things were not much better in the sixteenth century, though by then the trouble came from a different direction. Laurence Aldersey, whose *Trip to Jerusalem* was published in 1581, was a Protestant who refused to do what the Franciscan friars controlling the Jerusalem "pilgrim trade" required of him, and so was ill-treated. A century or so later, the Quaker George Robinson on a trip to Jerusalem by himself likewise refused to do what the friars demanded, so they twice organized for him to be waylaid and robbed.

Today's pilgrims may not have to endure this kind of victimization, but those who follow established routes to crowded destinations may have pockets picked and wallets or passports stolen. Some airports are notorious among travelers: At Bangkok, you will see luggage covered with chicken wire and padlocks in an effort to keep the contents intact between unloading from one plane and loading onto another. A friend, who arrived in Bangkok from a year of globe-trotting with a backpack on which she had patiently stitched a badge from every place she had visited, got it back from Baggage Handling with every

> "But my husband was always ready when everyone else let me down, and...went with me where our Lord sent me; and all the while he trusted that everything was for the best."
> *The Book of Margery Kempe*
> (1436)

badge ripped off. In other words, you may have to deal not only with petty crime but with a much more difficult thing to accommodate—petty malice.

What you are more likely to meet is a kind of cheerful roguery. Mildred Cable and Francesca French tell in *The Gobi Desert* (1942) the story of their visit to an Islamic cave temple in the village of Tuyok, an oasis in the Gobi. Visited by pilgrims from all over Asia, the shrine was then kept by a tall, bearded, white-turbanned *hajji*, who was an artist among custodians— highly skilled in displaying the wonders of his grotto and in extracting rewards for his trouble. His greatest asset was his elderly mother, who had claimed to be one hundred years old on each occasion the travelers had visited the place, although "For a centenarian she was extraordinarily agile and ran out to meet us." Having pressed his and his mother's services on the ladies the *hajji* obliged them to sign his visitors' book. "We wrote our names and spoke of his hospitality, but added a discreet word that might warn others to accept it with caution, indicating that such privileges as reception by a Ma-ma of one hundred years might be followed by a bill proportionate to her exceptional age and her inexhaustible energy."

This is amusing, but rather British colonial: uptight and patronizing. One would hope that explorers today would pay with a better grace, not the least in return for the makings of such a travelers' tale. What a blessing, after all, that in that far place there *was* someone to show the shrine and provide hospitality. The pilgrim cannot necessarily rely on things being reasonable or "fair"—played according to Western rules. The people operating the other end of pilgrimages have their own agendas.

Guardian angels

The condition that creates the difficulty or potential danger is often the one that also creates the adventure. My travels throughout my life have mostly been secular, but as examples, they will serve to show that Providence, or what you will, is seldom idle.

If as students in the early 1960s we had not been too poor to sleep anywhere but on the beach after arriving in Crete off the ferry late one night, we should have missed being woken in the morning by concerned women, with breakfast and warm water for washing. We should have missed being invited to return at midday to a house cut into the cliff: simple, spare, and immaculate inside. We should have missed the biblical—and to four British girls, embarassing and humbling—experience of having our hostess wash our feet. We should have missed being put to bed between coarse but pure white sheets and waking to find every stitch we owned washed, dried, and ironed. We should have missed our chance for a relationship with that kind and generous woman and the knowledge that gifts of love can be made by strangers to strangers, without expectation.

"There are three acts in a man's life which no one ought either to advise another to do or not to do. The first is to contract matrimony, the second is to go to the wars, the third is to visit the Holy Sepulchre. I say that these three acts are good in themselves, but they may easily turn out ill."

Letter from Count Eberhart of Württemberg to Felix Faber (1493)

If in the late 1970s a flash flood had not hit the road on our way to the Iranian desert city of Yazd with its great mosque and its

"Towers of Silence"—towers on which the Zoroastrian dead were until comparatively recently returned to the elements—my family would never have met a guardian angel. In the *chaikhaneh* at the crossroads where our route began, everyone else shook their heads: "road closed." He waited until we had gloomily finished our tea, then pointed to his gas truck. We drove behind him for more than a hundred miles, through villages where water blocked the road, going at a run through the wake he created like the Children of Israel at the Red Sea crossing. Villagers turned out to watch. It was crazy, and masterly. When we parted he would scarcely take thanks, much less anything more tangible. It was all part of looking out for strangers. But, he did accept a souvenir for his wife: something by which to remember us and the adventure.

Speaking as an English Protestant, it seems to me a shame that the story of Tobias and the Angel is hidden away in the Apocrypha and is not part of the Authorized Version of the Bible. It is a tale of serendipity. Briefly, it tells how God answers two prayers, one offered up by Tobit in Nineveh (in modern Iraq), the other by Sara in Ecbatana (modern Hamadan in Iran). Both of them are so poor and wretched they want to die. Tobit suddenly remembers (why didn't he think of it before?) that he once lent some money to someone in Rages (Ray, just outside Tehran). His son Tobias must fetch it, but he doesn't know the way. "Seek thee a man which may go with thee,…and I will give him wages…. Therefore, when he went to seek a man, he found Raphael that was an angel. But he knew not; and he said unto him, Canst thou go with me to Rages?"

And so God's plan works itself out: Tobias, the angel, and Tobias's dog set off for Rages via Ecbatana, where Tobias marries

"O every shower and dew, bless ye the Lord:
   praise and exalt him above all for ever....

O ye fire and heat, bless ye the Lord:
   praise and exalt him above all for ever....

O ye frost and snow, bless ye the Lord:
   praise and exalt him above all for ever.

O ye lightnings and clouds, bless ye the Lord:
   praise and exalt him above all for ever.

O let the earth bless the Lord:
   praise and exalt him above all for ever."

Apocrypha, The Song of the Three Holy Children verses 42, 44, 50–52

Sara (solving her problem), and brings back the money (solving Tobit's). They try to reward Tobias' guardian and guide with half the money. "Then he took them both apart, and said unto them, '…I am Raphael, one of the seven holy angels, which present the prayers of the saints, and which go in and out before the glory of the Holy One.'" It is a satisfying parable by a master storyteller, who even remembers to bring the dog home (Tobit 11:4) to join in the happy-ever-after.

Above all, it is a good parable for pilgrims. God, Providence, life has an uncanny way of delivering us what we need when we need it (although we don't always recognize salvation when we see it) and of placing people in our paths who make a difference. Even if you have never traveled much beyond your own town, much less to distant places, your own memory will provide examples.

Building bridges

When you follow the pilgrim road, there will be people who, if you let them, will enrich your physical journey with their travelers' tales of other days and other places and their observations of things seen along the route. Landscape historians and naturalists make wonderful traveling companions but so does anyone with a keen eye for the beautiful and the odd. Others will enhance your intellectual journey as a human being, deepening your understanding of your own life and enlarging your horizons with their own experience.

Sometimes, this will be the shared experience of the like-situated, such as on the International Military Pilgrimage to Lourdes, which takes place every June. This carefully orchestrated three-day event—days of instruction, initiation (baptisms, confirmations, first Masses), and praising God—brings together about 20,000 soldiers from 20 or so nations in a spirit of reconciliation, to share their hopes and aspirations for their family and military lives, and also for the future.

Sometimes it will be a matter of contrast. Irawati Karve made her Maharashtrian pilgrimage in an organized party of Brahmins and Marathi. Although they were all approaching the same goal, on their journey toward it, they led more or less separate lives: cooking, eating, sleeping apart. "All of the people were clean, and ate their food only after taking a bath. Then why this separateness? Was all this walking together, singing together, and reciting the poetry of the saints together directed only towards union in the other world while retaining separateness in this…?" The question was in her mind the whole time, and she joined first one group for meals, and then the other, making friendships that spanned the social and racial divide, learning, and constructing her own mental bridge.

Miraculous and revelatory bridges come of such journeys. Not the least thing Malcolm X brought back from his 1964

105

AN AMERICAN
DESERT RETREAT

I was burned out. So dry I only wanted to be with other dry, half-dead things, with whom I wouldn't have to pretend to be alive. So I fled to the Sonoran Desert near Tucson to be among my own kind for a while.

The Desert House of Prayer northwest of Tucson, Arizona, is dedicated to silence and simplicity and offers hermitages on its grounds. A bleached green houselet named Bede Griffiths (for the twentieth-century Benedictine mystic) became my home. Although alone, I enjoyed the constant companionship of the tall saguaros. At sunrise, they opened their prickly arms as though to enfold me in their warmth. But as night fell, their silhouettes hardened into crosses.

I fell into the rhythms of desert life. Up at first light to meditate and hike, down to nap or read in the shade after high noon. This was a silent retreat. No radio, no television, no telephone, no talk. Yet the desert is a place of listening: for a curve-billed thrasher's *whit-wheet,* the *chi-ca-go* of the Gambel's quail, the shake of rattler coils, and sometimes, even the voice of God.

Desert House's horarium honors both Roman Catholic and Zen traditions, with group meditation at dawn, Morning Praise and Eucharist, Vespers, and on occasion, nightlong Adoration of the Blessed Sacrament. I hadn't planned to participate in these rituals, but somehow my daily discovery of strange cacti, crawlers, and birds made me want to praise God in formal ways. All nature took on a sense of the sacred. I began saying the rosary for the first time since my childhood and sought spiritual counseling from Desert House's founder, Father John Kane.

The Sonoran desert is rich in history. The Hohokam and Hopi revered nearby Safford Peak as a holy mountain. They left pictoglyphs on what are now called the Picture Rocks to mark their presence and honor the spirits. The Spaniards left missions. San Xavier del Bac, popularly called the Winged Dove because its sparkling white dome and side chapels look like a dove with outstretched wings, is a mission near Tucson that houses the relics of San Xavier. Even today he is credited with healings. I made pilgrimages to the Picture Rocks and the Winged Dove and reconnected with God, with others, and even with a younger self. The desert is a place of healing for the body and the mind and every kind of relationship.

Some days were dark, filled with too much dwelling on my own and others' sins and memories of a past I'd painted over. There were demons and monsters out there, not just scorpions. But, isn't that why so many have sought the desert—Moses, Jesus,

Muhammad, the eastern mystics—for the power of its inescapable light to reveal even that which we'd rather not see?

The day before I had to leave, there was an unexpected heavy rain. It was absolution and baptism, a sign that sins I'd examined while here were forgiven and that I was ready to live a new life. The *lectio divina,* close observation of nature and the silence made me feel as spiritually supple as an aloe vera shoot.

This part of the Sonoran is sometimes called high desert or green desert because at its higher elevation more plants flourish, and the paloverde trees and saguaros lend an aura of verdancy. For me it was green, with all the hope and life the color suggests. Maybe that's why I choose to return again and again.

Rita Winters

Practicalities

Desert House of Prayer is a retreat campus dedicated to silence and simplicity founded by Redemptorist Father John Kane in 1974. It is set in a place of intense spiritual vibration within sight of 10,000-foot Safford Peak, which is considered a holy mountain by Native Americans. There is no bad time to visit the Sonoran Desert or the Desert House of Prayer, although you may want to avoid the monsoon season, which starts abruptly at the beginning of July and runs through mid-September.

Mecca pilgrimage was a recognition of common spiritual ground between himself and white Muslims.

Learning and growing

Learning from others met along the road is a part of spiritual endeavor worldwide. Thus, the Akawaio trainee shaman often leaves his home village in Guiana and travels across the country, learning new ways of speech and observing new types of people for use in his seances—his spirit flights. On the other side of the world, and in a different religious tradition, the Right Reverend Peter Nott, Bishop of Norwich, England, prepared for the celebration of the nine hundredth anniversary of the founding of Norwich Cathedral by making a pilgrimage throughout his diocese—visiting parishes in every deanery in the county of Norfolk between May 1995 and Easter 1996. He arrived in the parishes by any transport offered—rowboat, canoe, lifeboat, British Rail diesel engine, narrow-gauge steam train, Sherman tank, pony and cart, glider, Automobile Association van, fire engine, horse-drawn wagon, pageant float, bean harvester, light airplane, tractor, and Demon three-wheeled cycle made by the manufacturer of Chris Boardman's Olympic "superbike." Sometimes less spectacularly, he came on horseback or on foot in the way of bishops of old. However he traveled, it was sufficiently out of the ordinary behavior for a bishop to attract people's attention to his journey and to build bridges. He wrote: "A Christian pilgrimage always involves two kinds of traveling, interior and exterior. The purpose of my [pilgrimage] is not only to meet people…but also that together we might make a journey of the spirit."

Of course, there is not always the opportunity for meeting and sharing exploration. Pilgrimage today is open to more people than ever before because of easier travel, but at the same time, there is often less exposure to other travelers. In 1838, a Muslim from Mauritania, called Ahmad—a pious, well-educated man who had the advantage over many of his fellow pilgrims of speaking a dialect of Arabic—set off for Arabia. His journey, recorded in *The Pilgrimage of Ahmad, Son of the Little Bird of Paradise,* took six years. It not only deepened his faith, but also brought him into contact with many of the learned and devout of the Muslim world, who shared with him both their learning and their books (he brought home more than 400, all acquired on his travels—many of them as gifts). Today, West African pilgrims fly to Jeddah, shuttle to Mecca to make the pilgrimage, shuttle back to Jeddah, and fly home. The byways taken by Ahmad through the holy places of Islam, and the contacts he made on the way, are not part of their experience.

But at their best, pilgrimage adventures can bring you to the people you most need to meet—those who can help you explain and enlarge the spiritual patterns unfolding around you. The anonymous author of *The Way of the Pilgrim,* one of the many Orthodox Russians who in the nineteenth century dressed in pilgrim costume and lived by begging as an imitation of Christ, gave his life to saying the Jesus Prayer endlessly. He decided to go to Siberia, thinking that in the forests and on the steppes he would travel in greater silence and, therefore, have less distraction from prayer. His ultimate goal was Jerusalem, but he seems to have rather lost sight of it, wandering instead from shrine to shrine—taking in among other sights the miraculous footprint of the Mother of God at Pochaev—and in the event, never leaving Russia. "Of course I fretted at first because I had not been able to carry out my wish to go to Jerusalem, but I reflected that even this had not happened without the Providence of God....And so it turned out, for I came across the sort of people who showed me many things that I did not know....If that necessity had not sent me on this journey I should not have met those spiritual benefactors of mine."

On your personal sacred journey, too, things may not turn out as you expect. You may not even like the outcome. That is the difficulty but also the adventure. Let John Bunyan have the last word: "Some also have wished that the next [nearest] way to their father's house were here, that they might be troubled no more with either hills or mountains to go over; but the way is the way, and there's an end."

CHAPTER 6

Midway: Going on or Turning Back

"*E*ven at night when I slept, I dreamt that I was walking and when I got up in the morning, I was surprised that I still lay at the spot where I had fallen asleep." So wrote Indian anthropologist Irawati Karve in 1962 of her participation in the Hindu Maharashtra pilgrimage. As on a long flight or a long train journey, movement becomes the norm: A degree of automatism sets in. If this is your physical state, it may to some extent help you. But, if this is your mental state, beware!

Midway on your journey is as critical a point for you as your first passing of the threshold. You are at that place of choice embodied in the Hindu word for pilgrimage, *tirtha*, meaning "a sacred ford or crossing," and applied to many different facets of an individual's spiritual life—a shrine at the end of a pilgrimage, parents, a devoted wife, a spiritual teacher, the scriptures, virtues. *Tirtha* is the middle place across which you move to reach a more ideal realm.

"Now when he was got up to the top of the hill, there came two men running against him amain; the name of the one was Timorous, and the other, Mistrust; to whom Christian said, Sirs, what's the matter you run the wrong way? Timorous answered that they were going to the City of Zion, and had got up that difficult place; but, said he, the further we go, the more danger we meet with; wherefore we turned, and are going back again.

Yes, said Mistrust, for just before us lie a couple of lions in the way...and we could not think...but they would presently pull us in pieces."

John Bunyan, *The Pilgrim's Progress*, Part I (1678)

The midway position at which you have arrived, is in effect your "final call." You can still choose to continue on your journey or turn back. Pilgrimage is a movement between two poles, which in outer pilgrimages are most commonly home and the place of the ideal. These are both normally fixed, but not always, as in the case of (for home) gypsies and Middle Eastern nomads and (for the ideal) mobile gods sought in pilgrimage by, for example, Trinidadian Spiritual Baptists.

Even where these poles are not fixed, and in inner pilgrimage between the poles of self and the divine, there is still movement, from problem to answer. The solution comes from crossing the space between, from moving from familiar to Other, imperfect to perfect, human to divine. You are now halfway across this space, and it is a time for reflection: to consider how far you have come, how far you have to go, whether you can (physically) continue along the pilgrim's way, and whether you need to.

Remember the Russian pilgrim in Chapter 5? He did not "need" to go to Jerusalem. In fact, he needed not to. If he had made getting to Jerusalem his imperative, he would not have met with the spiritual counselors that he did. He did, in fact, accomplish what he really set out to do. He had begun with a goal (Jerusalem) that was part of a larger purpose (growing in spiritual stature). He achieved the second although, or perhaps because, he bypassed the first.

Identifying goals and purposes

Clarity about goals and purposes is vitally important for the pilgrim. Often what sabotages effort is an unspoken desire, a hidden agenda to do something other than your declared purpose. Listen to your language. When you take up exercise, do you think of it as "getting in shape" or "keeping fit"? If the first, your hidden agenda is probably looks: You want to look like a supermodel or turn back the clock. Unless you are more narcissistic than most, this may not be a powerful enough motivation to keep you in training through the winter, when no one can see you muffled up in coats. What you want to do needs to be assessed from the point of view of what you are really trying to achieve by doing it.

Goals are small; purposes, large. If Alfred had only had goals, he would not be the only king the English have ever called

> "Now...looking very narrowly before him as he went, he espied two lions in the way. Now, thought he, 'I see the dangers that Mistrust and Timorous were driven back by.' (The lions were chained, but he saw not the chains.) Then he was afraid, and also thought himself to go back after them, for he thought nothing but death was before him. But the porter at the lodge, whose name is Watchful, perceiving that Christian made a halt as if he would go back, cried unto him, saying, Is thy strength so small? Fear not the lions, for they are chained."
>
> John Bunyan, *The Pilgrim's Progress,* Part I (1678)

"the Great." His life was hard and short: when he died in 899 C.E. he was only just over fifty years old. Despite chronic, often debilitating ill health, he spent a lifetime in warfare, trying to prevent Vikings from overrunning England. In brief intervals of peace, at a time when most kings were illiterate, he took pains to educate himself in order that he could educate others, reviving monasticism and its concomitant learning, both in decline when he came to the throne. He had a few successes, many reverses. "Yet," says his biographer Asser, who knew him, "once he had taken over the helm of his kingdom, he...struggled like an excellent pilot to guide his ship...he did not allow it to waver or wander...even though the course lay through...many seething whirlpools."

> "[W]hen the mind is divided between many things at once, it is less...effective....For...when a man loses the...constancy which he ought to have within him, his mind tempts him to a great many useless activities....He is like the man on a journey who is occupied with other affairs to the point where he no longer knows where he wanted to go."
>
> King Alfred's translation (c. 890) of Pope Gregory's *Pastoral Care,* Chapter IV

It was in this paramount quality of steadfastness that Alfred's greatness lay. The generations immediately following did not regard him as a high achiever: not like his grandson, Aethelstan, who trounced the Vikings and finally unified Anglo-Saxon England, nor his great-grandson, Edgar, whose reign saw a great flowering of Christian learning. But, historians looking back from the standpoint of the twelfth century could with hindsight see the true quality of the king they called *engle deorling*

114

(the darling of the English). He had failed in many of his goals, such as building a fleet to outsail the Vikings, but succeeded in his purposes: living his life as a Christian king and laying the foundations of a single, civilized Christian kingdom for others to build on.

To go on or go back

"Returning were as tedious as go o'er," says Shakespeare's Macbeth. His was a moral dilemma, but the words themselves have a spatial dimension. As any walker knows, halfway along a bad footpath is no time to turn back. You may as well continue and see what happens: Conditions might deteriorate even further, but equally, they might improve. At least you will have the distraction of different scenery.

More often than not the pilgrim confronted with physical difficulties does not have a fifty-fifty decision. Eric Newby, in *A Short Walk in the Hindu Kush*, tells of the time when, taking off his new Italian boots, he found his socks full of blood. Although he had only been walking for three hours and perhaps ten miles, his feet looked as though they had been flayed. "[T]he villagers made little whistling sounds when they saw the extent of the damage. All of them knew the value of feet in the Hindu Kush." His traveling companion, Hugh Carless, asked if he wanted to return to Kabul. Certainly, to go on seemed madness: There was no question of his feet healing, given the miles they needed to walk each day. Then, he fell to thinking of all he had done to get thus far: giving up his job, letting his apartment, and taking his children out of school, as well as the money already spent. If he returned to Kabul, Hugh's dream of climbing Mir Samir would be frustrated, as would his own of becoming an explorer. Having pondered all this, Newby concluded: "There seemed to be no alternative but to go on. The fact that there was none rallied me considerably."

Taking a lesson from Newby, if you are in difficulties (other than some medical emergency), consider what you have already done and how far you have come physically and/or spiritually. You are on a road, whether real or metaphorical, that many never dare to travel. Your heart may be faint and your spirits weak at what more must be undergone — more miles for your feet, more companionship or more solitude to endure, more effort to expend going inside yourself to find what you are looking for.

Like Newby, remember not just your immediate goal (in his case the mountains) but also your overriding purpose (in his case, the dream of becoming an explorer). Revisit your original decision, reconnecting yourself with the longing for the ideal that set you on this road in the first place. Is your purpose still running clear and strong, or are the waters becoming muddied and sluggish the farther they get from their source? Do you need to find greater clarity?

Clearing the mind: ways and means

People have different ways of mentally clearing the decks for decision making: a solitary walk, jogging, yoga, chanting, prayer, meditation — anything that calms, revitalizes, and helps them feel more purposeful and more focussed. Others may use techniques learned on a self-development course.

On pilgrimage, if all else fails, you can toss a coin. I mean this quite literally. What I don't mean is that you leave the decision to chance. Provided that you suspend disbelief and play the game "for real," as if prepared to follow through on the outcome, the fall of a coin can show you in the blink of an eye what you really don't want to do. Tails, go home. What me? All the rational arguments for and against are instantly bypassed, and your deepest desire comes boiling to the surface in the face of opposition.

Although people do use traditional divinatory devices as if they were an external authority (thus exporting the problem of decision making), at a deeper level these devices can be used to give clarity to the mind. Working in the same way as the ancient oracles of Delphi and Cumae, systems such as the I Ching and Tarot cards distract the rationalizing, problem-seeking half of your brain into trying to fathom some unfathomable statement or symbol. This distraction liberates the intuitive, creative problem-solving half to come up with answers. These answers always lie within. As Cassius remarks in Shakespeare's *Julius Caesar:* "The fault, dear Brutus, lies not in our stars but in ourselves."

This is where your pilgrimage diary comes in. Following Eric Newby's example, revisit your original reasons for making your sacred journey. Then, revisit yourself. Read your notes. You have written them day by day, and they will not lie to you (as your mind may by this time, as a result of what has been happening to you). You may see yourself opening to the discovery of an unusual lightness of heart, a gradual loss of fear of the

117

unknown, and an increased ability to live in the here and now. You may be astonished by the strength of your response to the world around you, by powers of observation and expression you did not know you had, and by your ability to learn as you go from other places and from other people. If you had expected your sacred journey to be solemn, painful, and solitary, you may be surprised to catch yourself experiencing joy and pleasure in the enforced companionship of the road.

You may, on the other hand, discover a self in your pages who is losing his or her way, lonely whether in a crowd or alone. This self may be feeling an idiot (What am I doing here with this awful bunch/sitting here by myself waiting for miracles?), disappointed ("Sacred way"? This is a four-lane highway/"Inner journey"? So far so boring), frightened (Where is my baggage?/Are there bears?), shocked (What kind of religion peddles kitsch?/Why do I keep thinking about food when I'm meditating?), or just physically miserable (My feet are killing me/Why don't these people stop talking?). If this is what your diary is telling you, it is time to take stock not of where but of who you are.

St. Teresa of Avila wrote: "I ask those who have not begun to enter within themselves to do so; and those who have begun not to let the war make them turn back." The war is with ourselves. Now is the time to finally let go of your expectations and their concomitant—judgments. This may be the most unexhilarating, the most boring, the most frustrating, the most aesthetically null and void journey you have ever made, but you cannot possibly know that it will not lead to God. Your doubts and hopes are battling it out at this stage of your pilgrimage. We shall return to them.

Turning back

Suppose that you have made the decision to give up and go home or to turn aside and become a simple tourist or to seek a different pilgrimage goal. You will need to come to terms with the fact that you are abandoning a "sacred" journey, one that you have invested with a great deal of special meaning.

"Do not spend the night fearful of the morrow. At daybreak what is the morrow like?" *The Instruction of Amen-em-Opet,* British Museum papyrus 10474, possibly seventh to sixth century B.C.E.

Turning back may be a particular problem for Westerners, brought up to believe that they can do whatever they set out to do, in the spirit of "There's no such word as *can't.*" Whereas others may accept reverses philosophically, indeed, as sometimes inevitable, for Westerners abandoning plans is counterculture. They may have feelings of guilt, failure, disappointment, and anxiety over what to say to friends, family, and advisors. They may also experience a need to justify their decision—to find acceptable "excuses" so that they are not blamed. The problem is that you cannot be certain that you are making the "right" (defensible) choice until after the event. You cannot know how things will turn out until they do.

An example of decision making right at the cutting edge, on precisely this issue of turning back, comes from the life of the British climber Alison Hargreaves. In May 1995, she became the first woman to reach the summit of Mount Everest without oxygen and completely unsupported. Just three months later, on August 13, she was blown to her death off the Abruzzi ridge on her way down from the 28,250-foot summit of K2.

119

The weather had frustrated two attempts at the summit, and Alison had written to her husband on Saturday July 22 that on August 6 she would begin her trek back to catch her airplane home on August 13. Her flight from Islamabad was arranged. Why was she on the mountain that day instead of safely on the plane?

According to New Zealander Peter Hillary, she like others of the group, had fallen prey to "summit fever," becoming obsessed with making the ascent no matter what. Her husband does not believe this: Only a year before she had aborted of her first solo attempt on Everest just 1,312 feet short of the summit because the cold had started to eat into her hands and feet. "[N]ot only was Alison one of the greatest climbers in the world, she was also one of the most careful."

In her diary on August 5, Alison recorded that she was exhausted, mentally and physically. "It eats away at me—wanting the children and wanting K2—I feel like I'm being pulled in two." She decided to go home but lay awake that night, worrying that she had made the wrong decision. On August 6, the weather looked more promising, and she changed her mind. "I feel like a lead weight has gone from my shoulders...I feel much more content, restful, and happier."

When your motives are unclear and your desires are pulling you in different directions, it is no time to make decisions. But, the physical sensation of a weight lifted is a sure sign of no longer being "in two minds": That decision was for Alison, then, as a professional climber, a clear one. It was the same decision as that of a five-man Spanish team also attempting the ascent, who that morning judged the weather perfect for climbing, although bitterly cold. But, weather conditions on K2 are notoriously fickle. At 6:17 P.M. a radio call reached base camp saying that Alison, the American Rob Slater, and the New Zealander Bruce Grant had reached the summit; shortly after 7:00 P.M., a sudden icy gale (reports said 100 mph plus) destroyed Camp 4 on the route. The same wind blew Alison off the ridge.

The truth of this event is that a set of climbers made individual choices about going on or turning back, none of which had wholly predictable consequences. Of the Spanish team, three died and two survived. Of Alison's group, one turned back early and survived; one turned back later and died. Three went on and died. These three alone conquered the summit. They each made their choice, attained their goal, achieved their purposes—except for coming back alive. People in dangerous professions regard this risk as the trade-off. Alison's husband writes: "A climbing death is not a tragedy."

> "Once in the Valley of Bewilderment
> The pilgrim suffers endless discontent,
> Crying: 'How long must I endure delay?
> Uncertainty? When shall I see the way?"
>
> Farid-ud-din Attar (c. 1142–c. 1220),
> *The Conference of the Birds*
> *(Manteq at-Tair)*

Someone once said: "There are two choices, and neither of them good." When there is a "lesser of two evils," decision making is not hard. But, suppose retreat is just as unpleasant a prospect as advance? Tim Gallwey, author of the *Inner Game* series of books on realizing individual potential, gives an example of making such a decision. One cold winter night, when he was driving from northern Maine back to New Hampshire, his car skidded and embedded itself in a snowdrift. It was about 20

SAINTE-BAUME

The Holy Mountain of Provence

It is May 19, 1997, and we are singing. For two lifelong nonsingers, this is remarkable in itself. Even more remarkable, we have just climbed for an hour through woods and toiled up a flight of 150 stairs—something of a feat, as we come from an English county as flat as Holland. We were glad to find seats in a place already nearly full, although the main event does not start for an hour.

Meantime there springs into action a small, neat figure in a white suit, foreshadowing the white habits of Dominican monks who will join us later. This is the choir mistress, Marie-Noelle. She divides the assembly into two halves, to practice antiphonal chants. Both she and the acoustics are inspirational. By the time the Dominican brothers and the Archbishop of Aix and Arles arrive to celebrate mass, we are in full voice for the opening hymn: *"Marie...annonce la nouvelle, Jésus le Christ est ressuscité, Alleluia!"*

This is why we are here, on the Whitsun "Pèlerinage de Provence" in honor of Mary Magdalen, to whom the risen Christ first appeared (Mark 16:9, John 20:11–17). Our *alleluias* echo—for we are in a vast cave. It is also damp: There is a spring at the back of the sanctuary, and the walls and roof are discolored by the seepage of water, which from time to time drips down our necks. They are stained, too, from the smoke of the many candles that have burned here in the past and burn today, alongside the *ex votos*.

The cave is high up in a limestone massif 7.5 miles long, running east to west and rising abruptly from the plain in Var, Provence. Up to 3,415 feet high, this is the Chaîne de la Sainte-Baume, which takes its name from the cave: *sainte* meaning "holy," and *baume* (from Provençal *baoumo*) meaning "cave."

But why a cave? Why do we honor Mary Magdalen here? It is part of the old legend of the Three Marys (see p. 40). Leaving the others at the town named after them, Les Saintes-Maries-de-la-Mer, Mary Magdalene is said to have led the evangelization of Provence. Her sister Martha went to Tarascon, where she subdued a fearsome monster called La Tarasque, converted the town, died, and was buried. Their brother Lazarus went to Marseille, and St. Maximus, one of their companions, to Aix. Mary herself retreated to an inaccessible cave high on the Chaîne de la Sainte-Baume to spend the rest of her life as a penitent. She lived here for thirty years, clothed only in her hair. Each noontide she ascended to the peak of Saint-Pilon (3,261 feet) to pray and was raised into the air by angels. When she felt the approach of death, she came down from her mountain solitude to spend her last hours with St. Maximus. A fourth-century sarcophagus, said to be hers, can still be seen in the church he allegedly founded at St. Maximin La Sainte Baume.

The age of the pilgrimage to the grotto of Sainte-Baume is unknown. But, the massif has long been a special place. Archaeological evidence suggests that it has been thought sacred from ancient times, partly because of its association with life-giving water in an arid land—everywhere water seeps out of the rock, for this is the main reservoir for lower Provence, the source of the Huveaune, Peruy, Caramy, Issole, and other rivers. Perhaps here the Celto-Ligurians honored their god of springs, Borvo. But partly, too, its sanctity resides in the dark, mysterious forest that clothes its northern flank. Here the shelter of the massif has created a microclimate: In the cool atmosphere, mighty oaks flourish at the lower levels; higher up are huge beeches. Great yews can be found, locally said to be more than a thousand years old. It is the kind of forest one expects to find in the Ile de France but not in the sun-baked South. It is curiously hushed: Hardly a bird sings among these trees, and animal tracks and droppings—let alone animals themselves—are conspicuous by their absence.

Because of the difficulty of reaching the massif along tortuous mountain roads, and then climbing up, it long ago attracted hermits. There has been a monastic presence near the cave since at least the fifth century: first Cassianite monks and nuns; then, from the beginning of the eleventh century, Benedictines; and since 1295 Dominicans. When the pilgrimage itself began is unknown, but popes Stephen IV (816–817) and John VIII (872–882) both visited the cave, and in 1254, St. Louis, king of France, made a pilgrimage here on his return from the Holy Land.

Then in December 1279, Prince Charles de Salernes, the nephew of St. Louis, claimed to have rediscovered the body of Mary Magdalene, hidden for fear of Saracen invasion in the Gallo-Roman crypt of what is now the basilican church of St. Maximin La Sainte Baume. In 1295, when he became Count of Provence, he built the basilica and appointed Dominican monks as guardians of the pilgrimage to the cave. Soon the pilgrimage became famous throughout Western Christendom. Once Provence became part of the kingdom of France, the French kings made a pilgrim-age there from Nans-les-Pins on what is now called the Chemin des Rois (or Royal Road). Saints came here, too: St. Vincent Ferrier, St. Catherine of Siena, St. Brigitte of Sweden, and St. Vincent de Paul, among others.

In 1793, the shrine and monastery at Sainte-Baume were pillaged and burned to the ground by revolutionaries. It was rebuilt little by little in the early nineteenth century, and in 1859, monks of the Dominican order were restored as guardians of the shrine. In the nineteenth century, too, a hôtellerie was built at the edge of the forest to house pilgrims. So much is history.

When we return to Sainte-Baume in 2001, we learn that a massive rock-fall has cut off the grotto (although the interior is unharmed, we are told). Public access to the cave is prohibited until it is restored. There is no mass in the cave for the Whitsuntide pilgrimage nor for Mary Magdalene's feast day on July 22 and no procession through the dark forest to midnight mass on Christmas Eve.

But although, temporarily, you cannot climb the stairs that lead to the cave itself, you can still ascend the Chemin des Canapés, a steep path from beside the Hôtellerie leading up through the magical—some claim druidical—woods to where it is met by the easier Chemin des Rois. This route begins at the crossroads of Les Trois Chênes, where the D80 from Nans-les-Pins joins the D95 running through Plan d'Aups. It is a broad route leading past the source of the river Nans and is lined with oratories built by Monseigneur Jean Ferrer, Archbishop of Arles and Aix, in 1516. From the point at which the two paths meet, you can ascend to the crest of the massif and visit the chapel of Saint-Pilon, where according to a nineteenth-century martyrology "at each hour of prayer the angels descended from heaven and raised her [Mary Magdalen] into the air."

Jennifer Westwood

Practicalities

Stay at the Hôtellerie de la Sainte-Baume, 83640 Plan d'Aups Sainte-Baume, presently run by Les Soeurs Bénédictines du Sacré-Coeur de Montmartre. It is simple and quiet, with clean sheets, hot showers, plain but well-cooked food, and potable wine. There is good fellowship here—you will eat at long tables with pilgrims and long-distance walkers. Services are held in the chapel, which is also a place for private contemplation. There is a good café-bar (with souvenir shop) next door and a museum opposite. To reserve, call: 011 33 4 42 04 54 84, or fax: 011 33 4 42 62 55 56.

Although the cave is closed until further notice, pilgrims and other visitors can discover the cultural and spiritual heritage of the Sainte-Baume monastery at the House of Mary Magdalene (Maison Marie-Madeleine) opened by Brother Philippe Devoucoux, the Dominican guardian of the Sainte-Baume, and the "Fraternité Sainte-Marie-Madeleine," at Nans-les-Pins. Tel./fax: 011 33 4 94 78 69 24.

degrees below zero outside, and he had only a jacket. He would freeze if he stayed in the stationary car, but there was small chance of being picked up by another motorist: It was around midnight, 20 minutes since he had last passed through a town, and he had seen no farmhouses. He possessed no map.

He had to choose between going forward into the unknown or back to certain help fifteen miles or more behind. He started forward, but after about ten steps turned back. After a few minutes, he started running to keep warm, but the bitter cold soon drained his energy, forcing him back into a walk. Two minutes of this, and he was so cold he had to run again. So he went on, walking and running, walking and running, for shorter and shorter periods. Presently the recognition that he might well die brought him to a full stop.

After a minute's reflection, he found himself saying aloud and really meaning it: "Okay, if now is the time, so be it. I'm ready." Then, he stopped thinking about his problem and began walking down the road, suddenly aware of how beautiful the night was. He found himself running. Forty minutes later, he stopped and then only because he saw a light burning. Where had the energy to keep running suddenly come from?

> "A merry heart doeth good like a medicine: but a broken spirit drieth the bones."
> Proverbs 17:22
>
> "The courage of his choice will honour those Who taught this pilgrim everything he knows"
> Farid-ud-din Attar (c. 1142–c. 1220), The Conference of the Birds (Manteq at-Tair)

"It happens when one lets go of attachment to the results of one's actions and allows the increased energy to come to bear on the action itself." Whether you are on a real road as he was or on an inner journey, silencing fear and self-doubt will release in you energies and capabilities you never knew you had.

Aligning action with purpose

There is nothing intrinsically unworthy about turning back or changing your goal. Indeed, sometimes it is the only sane thing to do. Mythology worldwide teaches that, as the world changes, so sometimes must we. A popular version of the Hindu myth explaining how Krishna came to be honored (as Vithoba) at Pandharpur says that, when he was king of Dwarka and married to the goddess Rukmini, he was one day visited by a vision of Radha, the love of his youth. She said that he should leave his home and kingdom, and go on a pilgrimage to find her in the great forests of Maharashtra. Krishna set out on his quest but only reached the banks of the River Bhima, where he came upon a hut in which a young man, Pundalik, was devotedly massaging his father's feet. So absorbed was Pundalik that he did not notice Krishna, who began to shine so fiercely that Pundalik of necessity became aware of his presence. Nevertheless, Pundalik's devotion to his father was so intense that he would not let himself be distracted from his task. Not wanting to show discourtesy to the guest waiting at his door, without stopping what he was doing, he picked up a brick and tossed it behind him for Krishna to stand on, out of the mud. Krishna was so impressed with this example of filial devotion that he decided to remain there. Abandoning his quest, he sent for Rukmini to come and join him on the brick, just as their cult statues at Pandharpur stand to this day.

126

Chimayó, New Mexico

The Basilica, Sainte Anne
de Beaupré, Canada

Hagia Sophia, Istanbul

Benares (Varanasi), India

Procession in Les Saintes-Maries-
de-la-Mer, France

The Cathedral, Chartres, France

The Tor, Glastonbury, England

The Western Wall, Jerusalem

Shwe Dagon, Rangoon, Myanmar

Mount Athos, Greece

Stonehenge, England

What this story says is that even gods may abandon quests if life throws at them some event or some person that leads them to reappraise their own purposes.

Your decision to go on or go back also depends on your view of the divine. So far, I have assumed that you do not belong to a traditional pilgrimage culture and are not bound by vows, unlike, for example, pilgrims on *romarias* in Portugal, who will have made a vow to the saint of the shrine. They offer homage by enduring long journeys on foot to the shrines, or crawling on chafed and bleeding knees around a church or holy image, and in return, receive assurance of protection and help in critical situations: accidents, journeys, problems in love, examinations, thefts, natural disasters, business affairs, or health. If your belief system *does* include this transactional relationship with deity, your decision will involve more than practical considerations or self-image.

If your pilgrimage is time specific, making your decision is especially hard. Pilgrims to Ballyvourney, in Ireland, can go there at any time of year and perform the *turas*, or "rounds," praying at each sacred site at the shrine complex of Saint Gobnat. But only on Gobnat's feast day, February 11, can pilgrims buy blue silk ribbons which are measured along and around the thirteenth-century oak statue of the saint. These ribbons, known as "Gobnat's Measures," are thereafter kept to use against illness, by "measuring" the ribbon around the affected part.

For everyone, the decision comes down to aligning action with fundamental purpose. In *A Jewish Pilgrimage* (1956), Israel Cohen tells how, before setting off on a fundraising tour in aid of the Jewish national cause in 1920, he decided to make a pilgrimage to the Holy Land. But, news reached him of the persecution

127

of Jews in Budapest, Hungary, so he made a detour. Although he later continued his pilgrimage, his purpose in going—to strengthen his will to help found a Jewish homeland—had already been partly accomplished in Budapest.

By contrast, Mukul Dey, in *My Pilgrimages to Ajanta and Bagh* (1925), speaks of his struggle as a young artist in Calcutta to see the Buddhist cave paintings at Ajanta, in western India. Having endured poverty, ridicule, a 1,000-mile train journey, and a carriage drive through country infested with tigers, snakes, and bandits, he arrived at the village near the caves just before sunset.

His driver advised him to find lodgings; officials told him it was too late in the day to visit the caves; and a party of pilgrims invited him to join them. Despite these well-meaning attempts to deflect him from his purpose, Dey went to the caves and was rewarded with something he would not have seen had he waited until morning: As dusk fell, the paintings became clearer. For as the sun set, its light was reflected from the hills so that the caves became briefly radiant with light.

Once action and purpose are aligned, both flexibility and dogged persistence may bring unexpected rewards.

CHAPTER 7

Doubt and Hope

You are past the turning point, moving closer toward your goal. You started in the hope that the journey itself or the holy place you are heading for will perhaps confirm your beliefs or loose wellsprings of faith hidden within you.

But, on the road you will meet others heading the same way, either from different religions or from nominally the same religion but with beliefs seemingly far removed from yours learned in churches or synagogues or mosques or temples. Confronted with these different versions of "truth" you hit sudden turbulence: Your mental baggage is turned upside down as you react to the beliefs of others and question your own.

The more we learn, the more we doubt. Is your faith only fantasy—just a hope that there is something more to life than what we are stuck with? Pilgrimage tests like nothing else not only your physical endurance but also the sturdiness of your spiritual roots.

Faith

"[F]aith," said the sixteenth-century religious reformer John Calvin, "cannot be acquired by any miracle." He taught that faith comes first: Miracles are its confirmation. But on a sacred journey, faith can be sorely tried. Just as it takes us physically into the unknown, so pilgrimage often takes us beyond the teaching of our religious leaders into marginal territory. Out here, we may witness practices that belong to folk religion rather than the mainstream. We may encounter beliefs that are survivals of archaic ways of thinking, an embarrassment to orthodox religion trying to remain valid in an ever-changing world. Hitherto, we may have accepted the explanations of such things as anomalies or symbols. Seeing faith in action on a pilgrimage may come as a shock.

"My path is lost; my wandring steps do stray;
I cannot safely go, nor safely stay;
Whom should I see but Thee,
my Path, my Way?"

Francis Quarles (1592–1644)
from "Why dost thou shade thy lovely face?"

Perhaps the most challenging pilgrimage to take is not one of a totally different faith—in which everything is new and exciting—but one of a different "brand" of our own religion. As a Protestant educated at a Catholic school, I am comfortable with holy water, genuflection, lighting candles, and the Stations of the Cross. But, I hit my own belief boundary in Les Saintes-Maries-de-la-Mer, France, when I saw pilgrims touch the statues of the Marys and Sara. Their faces were ardent with the belief that through that touch blessing was transmitted. With four hundred years of Puritan ancestors behind me, when I touched the saints it was purely symbolic.

Your sticking point may come when you least expect it. According to an apocryphal story, Martin Luther, when in Rome, crept up the structure known as "Pilate's Staircase" on his hands and knees, this being a penance for helping souls out of Purgatory. Luther was doing it for his dead grandfather, but when he got to the top, stood up and asked himself (roughly speaking): How can this be true? Especially if we have had an education that places emphasis on rationality, we shall see and hear things on our pilgrim road that challenge us: How can this be true?

Many of us have been lulled into thinking that a pilgrimage is all about healing. Some of the most famous Christian pilgrimages founded in the past two centuries have been for healing—among them Lourdes in France, Fátima in Portugal, and Beauraing in Belgium. In the past few decades, pilgrimages for the sick have been introduced even at shrines with no previous reputation for cures. Familiar with the concept of "mind over matter," we can fit healing shrines into an acceptable psychological and scientific framework. The church disarms critics further by placing less emphasis on miracles (although acknowledging that sudden and unpredicted cures do take place) than on the general therapeutic benefit pilgrimage confers on the sick and the terminally ill.

But, pilgrimage is an ancient strategy for coping with all sorts of life's hazards, not just sickness. Shrines have been founded in response to invading armies, environmental dangers, accidents, famine, bad harvests, and supernatural threats. Some are created from inspiration or eccentricity, depending on the point of view. In the 1960s, a Yogi established himself in a hut inside the premises of the Government College of Chandigarh, India. Beside it, he built a mud structure, which he claimed was the grave of his ancestral guru, marking an ancient sacred site. Officialdom attempted to evict him, but he serenely maintained that he had had a dream that someone "from abroad" would help him. It was not long before local residents were coming to the "grave" to pray.

I don't know what happened next—whether history judged the Yogi a madman, a charlatan, or a holy man. But, S. M. Bhardwaj, reporting this event in *Hindu Places of Pilgrimage in India* (1973), remarks that if the Yogi found financial support from abroad, it is "entirely possible that there may one day be a shrine of allegedly ancient origin in the modern city of Chandigarh." The point of the story is that a pilgrimage may hinge wholly on one person's credibility.

Many pilgrims never question the basis on which the place they are going is supposed to be holy. But if we are heading for a reputedly miraculous shrine, now is a good time to ask: Do we believe in miracles? Not just a vague hope that deity will answer our prayers but an explicit belief in the possibility of overturning natural laws? We may accommodate miracles provided that they are remote, performed long ago—say, Christ's turning of water into wine—or far away—say, the superhuman running powers sometimes attributed to Tibetan lamas. Our faith may wobble, however, the closer we get to our own society and modern times.

Perhaps a million pilgrims every year visit Juazeiro do Norte, a city in northeast Brazil, on account of a Catholic priest, Padre Cicero Romao Batista (1844–1934). In his lifetime, he was credited with miraculous powers, and stories of them abound.

One tells how, when one man went to Juazeiro to see him, Padre Cicero greeted him warmly, but said: "My son, why did you leave your dagger by the *jua* tree?" On the way home, the man found his golden dagger where Padre Cicero had said, lying under the tree where he had slept the previous night. Do we believe this? Or that Padre Pio (1887–1968) could bilocate? According to General Cadorna, the Italian Army Chief of Staff, the padre appeared in his tent after an Italian defeat in 1917 and saying "Don't be so stupid!" prevented his suicide.

Do we believe in the powers of relics? More than any other feature, the physical remains of martyrs and saints were the focus of early Christian pilgrimage. Although often explained today as a focus for piety only—a reminder of the person we are praying to—this is not how they were originally thought of nor what many present-day pilgrims believe. If you look at medieval shrines, such as the recently restored shrine of Saint Melangell at Pennant Melangell, Llandgynog, in mid-Wales, you will see that the reliquary containing the bones of the saint is supported on arches. Under these arches, pilgrims would lie, to be as close to the saint as possible. Watch pilgrims at the shrines of saints reaching out to touch their tombs or the reliquaries holding their remains. Underlying what they are doing is belief in the physical presence of the holy. At saints' tombs, pilgrims came into direct contact with the saint, simultaneously present here on Earth and in Heaven.

A saint's potency was believed to be transmissible. This is why in Rome, at the shrine of St. Peter, pilgrims thrust their heads through a small window above the tomb to address their prayers directly to Peter and lowered onto it little cloths, which

CHACO CANYON

Peñasco Bla

Ancient life in the desert

Often it's the simple pleasures in which memories are embedded: leaning against the cool walls of impeccable stone masonry, seeking relief from the summer heat as the Anasazi had 1,000 years ago. Alone in the *kiva,* an underground ceremonial chamber, I try to imagine the prayers of the ancient ones, the predecessors of today's Pueblo Indians of the American Southwest.

At a time when Europe was emerging from the Dark Ages, a New World civilization was flourishing in what is now called the Four Corners region of New Mexico, at the state boundary with Arizona, Utah, and Colorado. Chaco Canyon was the political, economic, and spiritual center of the Anasazi culture, with an extensive network of long straight roads radiating like spokes to at least 70 regional settlements. Covering three acres and originally containing more than 600 rooms, this beautiful village is the largest excavated prehistoric ruin in North America. As many as 400 smaller villages are located in the canyon and the surrounding plateau. The underground sanctum in which I sit is one of 40 such *kivas* within Pueblo Bonito.

The presence of so many *kivas* in the canyon indicates their importance in daily Chacoan life. The largest of them may have been used for great communal gatherings, ceremonies, education, and other functions serving to join the communities.

It is a difficult journey to come here. Chaco Canyon is in a remote area of northwestern New Mexico. Clay roads, impassable when wet, provide the only access. There are no services, meaning no gas, no food, no lodging. The discomfort of the searing heat is only amplified by the dry winds in a desert landscape that hardly seems suitable for lizards, let alone a once-thriving center of 6,000 people. Rainfall is marginal; the growing season short. Winters are long and cold. Yet there is something about this land that beckons the soul.

Charles Fletcher

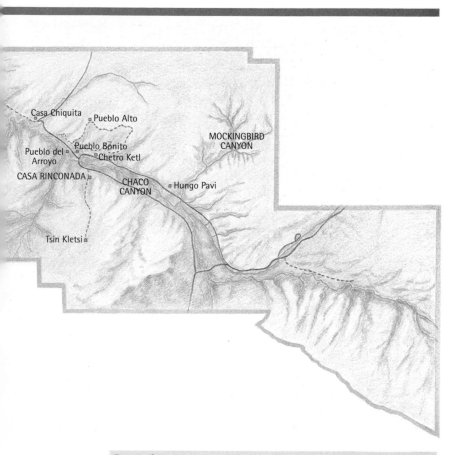

Practicalities

Chaco Culture National Historic Park runs along 12 miles of Chaco Canyon, inhabited by the Anasazi until the twelfth century. Research has suggested that climate change may have forced these ancestors of the Pueblo people to leave the canyon, which is now arid desert.

they drew up charged with his sanctity. This is why pilgrims to Assisi today give the attendant nuns articles to touch to St. Claire's preserved body.

Away from the tomb, small fragments of the saint's remains were thought still to contain their full potency. However, Protestantism rejected relics and pilgrimages to places where they were enshrined, at the same time as it rejected wonder-working images and on much the same grounds. Thomas Hobbes wrote in *Leviathan* (1651) "to worship God as inanimating or inhabiting...an image or place, that is to say an infinite substance in a finite place, is idolatry."

This belief in the powers of relics is not confined to Christianity. They form part of a wider cult of "traces," which exists even within Buddhism, although according to orthodox Buddhism, the Buddha, having achieved *parinirvana*, is permanently gone from the world and cannot be accessed. By the time the Chinese pilgrim Hsüan Tsang went to India in 629 C.E., a great range of objects had been preserved for the veneration of pilgrims: remnants of the Buddha's cremation; hair and nail clippings collected in his lifetime; his begging bowl, water pot, and staff; and bits of his robe. Also preserved were the sites of his birth, enlightenment, first sermon, and *parinirvana*; as well as physical traces, such as his footprints embedded in rock, and trees supposedly rooted from sticks he had used to clean his teeth (much as Joseph of Arimathea's staff became the Holy Thorn at Glastonbury).

"Martin in heaven here shines forth in the tomb"
Inscription on Tomb of Martin of Tours

136

In Buddhist societies, the Buddha's footprint is venerated as symbolizing his "setting forth"; and temples, monasteries, and shrines in Thailand not infrequently include representations of it (*phra bat camlaung*, or "holy footprint copy"). But also in Thailand several depressions in rocks are revered as "real" Buddha footprints. When the meditation master Luang Phau of the monastery of Wat Phra That Naung Sam Meun wanted to construct four "holy footprint copies," one each for Gautama Buddha and his successors Kokusandha, Konakomana, and Kassapa, he remembered that in northern Thailand he had once seen what local people believed were the genuine footprints of the four Buddhas. In May 1972, he led an arduous pilgrimage by bus, then by truck, then on foot, to collect detritus from the surfaces of these footprints and chip off small flakes of rock. These relics were then incorporated each under its appropriate "footprint copy."

For some pilgrims, the "footprint copies" are symbolic; for others, they are charged with the sanctity of the originals. Such transfers of sanctity worldwide have allowed sacred places to change location and copies of places and buildings to function as if they were the

"Now there was not far from the place where they lay, a castle called Doubting Castle, the owner whereof was Giant Despair, and it was in his grounds they now were sleeping: wherefore he, getting up in the morning early, and walking up and down in his fields, caught Christian and Hopeful asleep in his grounds. Then with a grim and surly voice he bid them awake, and asked them...what they did in his grounds. They told him they were pilgrims, and that they had lost their way....The giant therefore drove them before him, and put them into his castle, into a very dark dungeon."

John Bunyan, *The Pilgrim's Progress,*
Part I (1678)

"real" thing. At least 15 out of the 88 pilgrimage places on Shikoku in Japan have been moved. In western Japan, Imochigaura Lourdes on Goto Island is the outcome of a transference of sanctity from Lourdes in France. Loreto in Italy allegedly was created by a transference from the Holy Land.

For many of us this is an unaccustomed way of thinking: We set great store by the "genuine," and it matters to us when we arrive at a sacred site and discover that it is no longer on the spot where the irruption of the divine into the mundane (that we have come to celebrate) took place. It makes us uneasy to learn that the special blessing available at some holy place or shrine derives from something in which we simply cannot believe.

"Now a little before it was day, good Christian, as one half amazed, brake out in this passionate speech: What a fool, quoth he, am I, thus to lie in a stinking dungeon, when I may as well walk at liberty. For I have a key in my bosom called Promise, that will, I am persuaded, open any lock in Doubting Castle.... Then Christian pulled it out of his bosom, and began to try at the dungeon door, whose bolt (as he turned the key) gave back, and the door flew open with ease."

John Bunyan,
The Pilgrim's Progress, Part I (1678)

While we labor under doubts that separate us from our fellow pilgrims, the way is blocked for the flow of synergy that comes from being at one with others. The struggle with our beliefs also inhibits the operation of synchronicity, that apparently random falling into place of the answer to our question, that vital but elusive piece of the jigsaw. Doubts stultify: The way through them is hope.

Hope

We easily enter into the hope of those who long for bodily health and spiritual wholeness. We may not be so sympathetic, when we meet it in the flesh, to aspirations that cut across our views of what is spiritual and "right." What of those whose beliefs seem to us alien, primitive, superstitious, wrong, or even wicked?

If we are truthful about our reservations, we may find that deep down they are rooted in fear that other people's beliefs somehow threaten our own value system. If you are a Christian or a Muslim reading these words, how do you feel about the arrival in Portugal of Iranian pilgrims who believe that the shrine of Our Lady of Fatima is a christianization of one dedicated originally to Fatima, the daughter of Muhammad? Are you comfortable with syncretic religions in which your own faith has been merged with something else? What about the religion of the Macha of Ethiopia, in which Muhammad, the Virgin Mary, and a number of Islamic and Christian saints are all reverenced as *asayanas*, subsidiary manifestations of the central deity Waka? Or *Candomblé* from Brazil or *Vodou* from Haiti, blendings of Catholicism and African native religions?

> I am a man
> and account nothing human
> alien to me.
>
> Terence (c. 195–159 B.C.E.)
> *Heauton Timoroumenos*

Consider the villagers of Chumpón in Mexico, who venerate a miraculous cross that communicates its wishes through signs—if disobeyed or offended expressing its wrath by means of drought and epidemic. Can this be a Christian cross? The Maya of Chumpón believe so. It is the descendant of a series of crosses, which from 1850 until well into the twentieth century, both

139

ST. CATHERINE'S MONASTERY

A jewel in the desert

I grew up in St. Catherine's Valley, a steep cleft in a Cotswold ridge on the edge of Bath, England. In my late teens, I spent hours alone in the village churchyard, wondering each time I passed it at the medieval carving of the patron saint and her wheel that stood over the porch. I wondered how her fame could have spread even to this hidden valley in the depths of England from some remote desert far away; so that, even then, seven hundred years later, a boy should grow up there in the shadow of her name.

St. Catherine's in the Sinai: bastion of old Byzantium, far-flung jewel of a once Imperial crown, survivor through fifteen centuries of changing fortunes, the coming and going of civilizations, religions, conquerors, and vanquished. I had always wanted to go there. I wanted the living truth behind a childhood dream.

Now here I was, one November morning thirty years later, in the Eastern Standard Bus station in Cairo. A sleek bus, with shiny aluminium flashes down the sides and video entertainment already beginning, was about to leave directly for St. Catherine's. Sailing to Byzantium in a video bus: It just didn't fit. Another, shabbier bus stood alongside. Destination: Nuweiba on the Sinai coast of the Aqaba Gulf. I would go to Nuweiba, and find a guide there to take me on the seven-day walk through the desert to the monastery. I wanted to arrive at the monastery gates in the way that travelers and pilgrims had done for centuries.

I spent much of those seven days on the back of a camel, dipping up and down over a vast and empty expanse of black stones and yellow dust, through colored canyons and dun-colored mountains. On the fourth day, though, I followed Sliman, my guide, clambering up precipitous rock faces while his assistant led the camels the long way round. I wished I had gone the long way. We eventually reached a broad, flat sand plain, 1,500 feet up. It was bitterly cold, a strong wind suddenly in our faces; we trod on for hours beneath a sullen sky.

Was this what I wanted? My feet were sore, my legs were aching, the wind was whipping through me. I seemed to be plodding head down through this bare and featureless land for no other reason than for the sake of it. Fear hovered over me. I imagined St. Catherine's suddenly, a jewel in the desert and found myself moving toward it now—and me, not even a practicing Christian—with the old Orthodox prayer "Lord have mercy" on my lips.

Practicalities

St. Catherine's Monastery, in a narrow valley below Mount Sinai, was founded in the sixth century as a fortification of the site where, according to the Old Testament of the Bible, Moses saw the Burning Bush.

The best times of year to visit St. Catherine's are April or October, when it is not too hot. The monastery is open to visitors between 9:00 A.M. and noon daily, except Fridays and Sundays. A hostel is located next to the monastery, and hotels are in the nearby village.

St. Catherine of Alexandria

The monastery holds the skull of St. Catherine, a fourth-century martyr. She was persecuted for her Christianity and her refusal to marry the emperor because she considered herself a Bride of Christ. Her punishment for successfully arguing her case against anti-Christian philosophers was to be broken on a wheel and beheaded. In medieval Europe, a cult developed from this legend, and the monastery became a pilgrimage center.

Nuweiba

ST. CATHERINE'S
MONASTERY

We pushed on for hours, until finally we reached the other side of the plain to find Selman, Sliman's assistant, crouched by a fire among some rocks below. We climbed down to join him, my legs barely holding. I threw all the clothes in my bag onto my back and lay down by the flames like a child, teeth chattering, vital force gone. Sliman took his only blanket and covered me with it.

The next morning the world had righted itself again, and for three more days, we trod on through the desert silence, until at last I stood before the tall fortress walls that still protect the monks, the relics of St. Catherine, and the ever-flowering Burning Bush from which God is said to have spoken to Moses. I had arrived; yet those days in the desert had shown me that the way is as much the end in itself as the apparent destination. I returned home to England with two souvenirs of my journey, each as significant to me as the other: a copy of the Byzantine icon of Christ Pantocrator and a rock from the Sinai desert.

Roger Housden

spoke and issued written instructions governing the life of the Maya, who after an unsuccessful revolt retreated into the largely uninhabited forests of the present state of Quintana Roo. The Holy Cross of Chumpón—born of a fusion between Christianity and Mayan cosmology—still focuses the Maya's hope of preserving their cultural identity.

Consider also a pilgrimage in 1996 that brought Rastafarians to southern Ethiopia to celebrate the 105th birthday on July 23 of the former emperor, Haile Selassie. Dressed in red, yellow, and green—the Rastafarian and Ethiopian colors—with images of the emperor hanging round their necks, they gathered to consecrate their new tabernacle at Shashemane.

In 1937, in support of the American Back to Africa movement founded by Jamaican-born Marcus Garvey (1887–1940), the Ethiopian Emperor Haile Selassie donated land where people of African descent could be repatriated. Rastafarianism grew from this movement, the name coming from *ras*, meaning "prince," and *tafari*, the Emperor's title before his coronation in 1930. Haile Selassie, who ruled Ethiopia until the Marxist revolution of 1974, belonged to a royal dynasty that claimed direct descent from King Solomon in the Bible. It was this charismatic tradition that made my mother take me as a child on a long train journey to London to see him. For us and thousands like us lining The Mall as he rode by in an open carriage to Buckingham Palace on his State Visit, he was a living legend.

To Rastafarians he is divine—the fulfillment of the Revelation of John 5:5: the "Lion of the tribe of Juda." Although interpretations differ, many believe he is not dead and will return. The Welsh and the Bretons in the early Middle Ages believed this of Arthur, the Once and Future King. Oppressed peoples the world over yearn for a savior.

Rastafarians generally have a bad press: Dreadlocks, smoking of *ganja*, and sporadic violence provide better newspaper copy than the facts that strict Rastafarians do not eat meat or drink alcohol and are mainly pacifist. Although Rastafarianism is commonly labeled a "cult," if we listen with pilgrims' ears to the songs of Bob Marley (1945–81), who articulated its hopes of a fairer world, we begin to understand why the Catholic Commission for Racial Justice in 1982 recommended that "Rastafarianism should be recognised as a valid religion."

Pilgrimage gives us a unique opportunity to try our faith, to push on our personal boundaries, and to look through the differences that divide us to the hopes that unite. From here, it is but a short step to that overflowing of compassion and respect that Christians used to call *caritas*, or charity, but nowadays simply call love.

Love

Remember on our pilgrim road the supreme parable of the triumph of love over difference, "The Good Samaritan" (Luke 10:29–37). As pilgrims, we are required not necessarily to approve others' hopes but only to recognize that all humankind is needy: not only sick people who long for health, but heretical Catholic devotees of a Wisconsin shrine who believe that only they will be saved from eternal damnation; Maoris, Maya, and Rastafarians who each see pilgrimage as a way of asserting themselves against an uncaring society; Sikhs and Hindus, Theravada

Buddhists and Tamils, Muslims and Jews; all battling it out in different areas of the world to possess a square foot of sacred ground.

Pilgrimage gives us the chance to meet, at the very core of our beliefs, our own humanity. The road may be hard and painful. Find your way through the labyrinth of doubt by following the advice of author Carlos Castaneda's Don Juan: "Look at every path closely....Then ask yourself...one question....Does this path have a heart?"

"Peace and love are always at work in us, but we are not always in peace and love"

Mother Julian of Norwich, *Revelations of Divine Love* (c. 1393)

CHAPTER 8

Drawing Near: Anticipation

You are drawing near. Although physical hardship possibly, and spiritual doubts almost certainly, are not entirely behind you, you are carried forward by a mounting suspense. The road that yesterday was just a road to a far place is now bringing you within the ambit of the sacred.

As you draw close, the landscape becomes dense with cosmological and symbolic meaning: clusters of shrines, holy wells, caves, trees, and other features of sacred topography that prepare you for the encounter that is the purpose of your journey.

There are still practicalities to consider—the most urgent at this point being whether your arrival will be at the appropriate moment in the religious timetable. If you are behind schedule, and there is something you can do about it, then do it. As with much else with pilgrimage, you will not know what "missing" something means to you until after the event.

Now is the time to begin actively preparing for the climax of your journey, reminding yourself again of what it is you seek.

Now more keenly than ever, you may feel yourself to be part of a historical process. You are a member of that community of seekers, which, by making them their goal, has brought into being and activated the many thousands of pilgrimage sites and shrines all over the world. During the Middle Ages, there were a hundred and more well-attended pilgrimage destinations in England and Scotland alone.

"How I long to see among dawn flowers, the face of God."

Haiku by
Basho (1644–1694)

You may develop strong feelings of the *communitas* we spoke of earlier, the spiritual "togetherness." In the 1970s, the anthropologist Victor Turner suggested that this togetherness was the core experience of pilgrimage, the response of people used to a structured and unequal society, who find themselves on pilgrimage in an unstructured community of equal persons. Turner writes: "Pilgrimages seem to be regarded by self-conscious pilgrims both as occasions on which *communitas* is experienced and journeys towards a sacred source of *communitas*, which is also seen as a source of healing and renewal."

The experience of oneness is perhaps sharpest at sacred sites where there is no appreciable tourist element, as at Fatima, in Portugal. The devotion to Our Lady of Fatima began at a time of crisis, when Europe was involved in World War I, and Portugal itself was in a difficult social and political situation. Three shepherd children, Lucia Santos, and Francisco and Jacinta Marto, saw three apparitions of angels in the spring, summer, and autumn of 1916 in and around the village of Aljustrel. There followed six appearances of the Blessed Virgin Mary on May 13, June 13, July 13, August 19, September 13, and October 13, 1917, all except that of August 19 taking place in a semicircular hollow, the Cova da Iria, one mile west of Aljustrel, and near which the sanctuary is now situated. The second apparition of 1917 in the Cova da Iria was witnessed by about 50 people; the third by perhaps 4,000; the fourth by 5,000. No fewer than 25,000 people were present during the fifth apparition and at the last, in October 1917, 70,000 people were present. Not unsurprisingly in view of this mass witness, devotion to Our Lady of Fatima grew, and in 1929, the first foreign group of pilgrims arrived from the German city of Munich. Today, organized parties come from many countries, their purpose not to "see the sights" but to participate in the miraculous nature of the place.

But on many pilgrimages, cohesion is far less than you might expect. Theravada Buddhist pilgrimages in Thailand unite pilgrims spatially, but anthropologists have observed that there is no social mixing of one group of pilgrims with another or between individual pilgrims of different regional and economic backgrounds. Among Indian and Nepali pilgrims interviewed by Barbara Nimri Aziz in 1987 their accustomed social structures were often maintained—pilgrims traveled with family and friends and did not mix with outsiders.

"Togetherness" is less than universal where some religious taboo also comes into play. As mentioned in the last chapter, in recent years, Muslim pilgrims from Iran have also come to Fatima, although neither the Christian nor Muslim communities of Portugal give them support. *Communitas* clearly has limits.

Irawati Karve, whose Maharashtra pilgrimage was described in Chapter 5, was so moved by the experience of *communitas* within her *palkhi* group on the pilgrimage that she could not bear the subdivision into smaller groups by caste. After taking a meal with the Maratha women (there are strong taboos in

SODO

HAITI

SAUT D'EAU
Port-au-Prince

Gifts from a cool goddess

Sodo is the popular name for an annual pilgrimage to the Haitian village of Bonheur (Happiness) and its adjacent waterfalls, Saut d'Eau. At this mountainous site, sixty pot-holed and cork-screwed miles from the capital city of Port-au-Prince, the Miracle Virgin (Vierj Mirak) is honored each July 17, feast day for Our Lady of Mount Carmel. She is said to have manifested herself there in the nineteenth century and during the American military occupation from 1915 to 33. According to local tradition, the first sighting took place on July 16, 1841. A man named Fortuné, searching for a lost horse, came to a palm grove. He looked up and saw a beautiful woman in a palm tree. Soon afterward, pilgrimages to the site began.

Every year since Fortuné's vision, 20,000 or so pilgrims have set out by foot, donkey, or rickety public transport for Bonheur. Their immediate focus is the church built to commemorate his apparition. Roiling crowds of pilgrims now lend Sodo the look and feel of a Caribbean Atlantic City on a summer weekend. Ecstatics, beggars, vendors, nuns, gamblers, penitents, hookers, army officers, journalists, anthropologists are God's plenty in Haiti. They have come with many purposes: to seek a cure, to fulfill a vow, to pick a pocket, to escape the city heat, to eat fresh fruit, or to take a cool bath. Bonheur wishes all its pilgrims well.

Few travelers remain for Mass. Most head for the waterfalls a mile or so away to immerse themselves in torrents sacred to Ezili, the Vodou goddess of love, and to her serpent lover Danbala, the patriarch of the Vodou pantheon. Water is a divine element, and many pilgrims become possessed by these aquatic deities while standing under the falls. Pilgrims feel no contradiction in their dual devotions to the Vierj Mirak and the water gods. For in their Vodou practice, Mary and Ezili are different aspects of the same divinity. Many clergy are not happy with this assimilation. One bishop complained, "We have not Christianized the people. They have made superstitions out of us."

"Voodoo"

An amalgamation of several traditional African religions, "Voodoo" has also borrowed freely from Roman Catholic and Freemasonic rites first introduced by eighteenth-century French slave holders.

Although in Euroamerican folklore "Voodoo" is usually protrayed as a mixture of malign superstitions, it is the national religion of Haiti and a vital part of its Creole culture.

I journeyed to Sodo in 1986, the year the parish priest decided to take the pilgrimage back. He stripped the church interior of the saints' images, which were being revered as manifestations of the "Voodoo" gods. For the same reason, he cancelled the procession through Bonheur of the plaster statue of Our Lady. He did, however, bless a group of his parishioners intent on carrying a wooden cross from the church to Sodo. Along the way they prayed the rosary, planning to confront Ezili with Christ, as Paul had done to Diana in her own temple at Ephesus. But, the confrontation never occurred. The pilgrims with their cross simply vanished into the ecstatic spume and thunder of devotions at the falls.

Failure to vanquish these popular devotions is an old story. When the Miracle Virgin appeared again on top of her palm tree in 1915, the parish priest asked a captain from the occupying U.S. Army to cut down the tree. As the captain did so, the vision moved from tree to tree, until the woods were destroyed. As the last of the palms fell, the vision changed into a pigeon. From what the townspeople say, the bird remained close to Bonheur for several days and then flew to Sodo, where it disappeared into the iridescent mist. What a splendid metaphor both for the pilgrimage and for "Voodoo" as a religion of tolerance and endurance. The pigeon in the palm tree links Church and Falls into one holy site, sanctioned only by the devotion of the Haitian people. Miracles will no doubt continue to occur there, gifts from a cool goddess in a hot season.

Donald Cosentino

Hinduism against eating with other castes), she found they were more friendly toward her, a Brahmin. "Toward the end, they called me 'Tai,' meaning 'sister.' A few of them said, 'Mark you, Tai, we shall visit you in Poona.' And then one young girl said, 'But will you behave with us then as you are behaving now?' It was a simple question, but it touched me to the quick. We have been living near each other for thousands of years, but they are still not of us, and we are not of them."

There is a dilemma here. Pilgrimages by their nature as convergences of human beings at a center would seem necessarily to engender feelings of unity, but they are constricted by the religious systems to which they belong. Division runs all the way down the scale. The *hajj* to Mecca and Medina unites Muslims from all over the world but separates the Umma (nation of Islam) from all other faiths. The Maharashtra pilgrimage temporarily unites Hindus spatially but maintains the barriers between castes.

The complexity of the situation is epitomized by Malcolm X, said to be the first Black Muslim to go on *hajj*. Recalling his experiences in Cairo, Jedda, and Mecca, he wrote: "Everything about the pilgrimage atmosphere accented the Oneness of Man under One God" and "Never have I witnessed such sincere hospitality and the overwhelming spirit of true brotherhood as is practiced by people of all colors and races, here in this Ancient, Holy Land." But, the truth is that if Malcolm X had been a Christian or a Jew, this "spirit of true brotherhood" would not have been extended to him. And, his announcement in the United States that his revelation of brotherhood in Mecca extended also to white Muslims may well have led to his assassination by racists soon afterward.

Such considerations lead some to avoid structured pilgrimage. But within the limits of its religious framework, pilgrimage gives the individual pilgrim the choice, like that of any other traveler, of transcending the constraints on social behavior that operate at home and presents for him or her, however imperfect, a living model of human brotherhood. This is something to be going on with in a far from ideal world.

"[By] this time the pilgrims were got over the Enchanted Ground, and entering into the country of Beulah whose air was very sweet and pleasant."

"[N]either could they from this place so much as see Doubting Castle. Here they were within sight of the City they were going to."

John Bunyan, *The Pilgrim's Progress*, Part I (1678)

Holier than thou

As you see other people going about their business as pilgrims, you may find yourself judging the way they are doing things. Although the classic way to perform the Shikoku pilgrimage is to begin with the Ryozen-ji temple and follow a circular route round the island, many Japanese pilgrims today begin their journey with other temples, visit the sacred sites out of the "right" sequence, or only visit one or two. You may see this as a falling short, a lackadaisical approach to the spiritual. Ian Reader, in his personal account of the Shikoku pilgrimage on pages 86–87, records his first reaction to pilgrims arriving by bus: "I would be annoyed, for I had walked, and climbed mountain paths, and they had just sat on luxury buses. Was I not better, because of the arduous nature of my journey?"

The answer is, who knows? Pilgrimages were necessarily arduous in days when most were made on foot. Religion has justified that hardship by fostering the notion that the greater the difficulty, the more merit the pilgrim earns. Crusaders were told that if they perished on the Crusades (which were essentially military pilgrimages) all their sins would be forgiven. This belief was shared by Muslim pilgrims to Mecca, who if they died along the way, expected to go straight to heaven. Pilgrimages in many religions today are still considered particularly worthy if made the hard way.

But, there are horses for courses. Pilgrimage as an austerity is bound to the ascetic tradition of the wandering Hindu or Buddhist sadhu, or Christian mendicant. Austerities practiced today at St. Patrick's shrine at Lough Derg in Ireland, for example, are possibly an inheritance from ascetics in the days when it was a monastic center. However, in most pilgrimage traditions, a distinction is maintained between ascetics who have renounced the world and spend their whole lives in pilgrimage, and lay people for whom pilgrimage is an exceptional happening.

> "Suspense, suppressed excitement, the feeling of a profound experience soon to come, throbbed in every pilgrim heart as we neared Jeddah....For the first time, as the white-garbed faithful lined the rails (of the boat), I heard the immemorial pilgrim chant, to be repeated again a thousand times during my stay there: 'Labbayk, Alla humma, Labbayk!' ('We are here, O Lord, we are here!')."
>
> Idries Shah, "The Red Sea Journey" in *Caravan of Dreams* (1968)

In Japan, one of the most rigorous sacred journeys carried out by Buddhist priests in training is the ancient Kaihogyo pilgrimage of Mount Hiei, performed over one thousand days, broken into ten terms of one hundred days each, and spread over seven years. It includes a nine-day period without food, water, sleep, or even lying down, and, in the earlier years of training, a 25-mile circuit of the mountain each night; in the last two years, a 37-mile circuit. Very few complete it, but lay people can earn proportionate merit by performing a much shorter version.

If distance were all that counted, one of the greatest pilgrimages on record would be a journey made between 1935 and 1936 by Mary Augusta Mullikin and Anna Hotchkis, two artists who despite advancing years—Mary Mullikin was more than 60—the threat of political unrest, and the ubiquitous brigands, undertook a tour of China's nine sacred mountains. Traveling by horse, mule, train, and other means, painting and sketching as they went, they visited every one of the nine mountains, whereas Buddhist pilgrims rarely achieve more than two.

They covered vast distances—Heng-Shan in Northern Shansi is more than 1,000 miles from Heng-Shan in Southern Hunan Province. In the nature of things, there must have been hardship, although the only "austerity" they really complained of was the vegetarian diet in the monasteries. But although they encountered many pilgrims, such as a man who kowtowed every second step, knocking his head against the stones, and a young man who was carrying his mother up and down a mountain to acquire merit, they themselves remained "travelers."

Lay pilgrims within traditional societies are nothing if not pragmatic: Bess Allen Donaldson wrote in *The Wild Rue* (1938) of pilgrims in Iran: "Since the coming of the automobile most pilgrims on the highways now travel by that means. Some claim

OUR LADY OF GUADALUPE

Awakening the hidden faith

My Mexican grandmother Josefa poured her Catholic faith into my mind and my bones until her beliefs became my own. The other side of my family, the Tarahumara Indian part, agreed with her on the essence of our religion: adoration of Our Lady of Guadalupe. Grandmother Josefa often urged me to make a pilgrimage to Our Lady, saying it would be the most special day of my life. At the age of fifty, after years in the United States, I fulfilled my grandmother's wish and traveled to Mexico City for the feast day at Our Lady of Guadalupe's shrine on December 12. I had expected the pilgrimage to be wonderful, moving. But, nothing had prepared me for being catapulted to a depth of faith as enriching as my grandmother's.

Guadalupe pilgrims seem to be of four kinds: tourists with cameras, Mexicans and *mestizos* (people of mixed blood like me), trained sacred participants, and American Indians. What moved me was the sacrifice and trust of other believers, in particular the soul-baring devotion of the Indian pilgrims. They entrust their lives to the *mestizo* divinity who said: "I am the Mother of all of you who dwell in this land."

Grandmother often told me how Our Lady of Guadalupe appeared to the Indian Juan Diego on Tepeyac Hill in 1531, ten years after the Spaniards had devastated the Aztecs. The Lady spoke in Nahuatl, the Aztec language. Her message was not one of bloodshed but of love and compassion, the feminine face of God. Her image was miraculously imprinted on Juan's *tilma* (his cloak): Her face is darkly *mestizo,* her garment is European, and she wears the Indian woman's sash to show that she is with child. Grandmother instilled in me that this healing, loving mother gave birth to a new race and a new church, merging Spaniards and Indians as no military force could.

All over Mexico, people pray to her daily and promise that they will make the pilgrimage if she grants their pleas. They walk for days from tiny villages to one of the largest cities on Earth and on to Tepeyac. Holy banners, flowers, music, and hymns accompany the pilgrims. Many have no shoes. At night they clean cuts from family members' feet, oil and bind them with rags. Babies and food must be carried. I watched this holy host of countless thousands as they came from every direction, their footsteps echoed by drums.

All day, I saw groups climbing the hill, some on their knees, bringing profuse gifts of flowers to her miraculous image on the *tilma* in the new basilica. I joined the crowd to approach the pinnacle of the pilgrimage and pushed into the church. There,

Tepeyac Hill, the site of the basilica, is in the north of Mexico Distrito Federal (the Mexican name for Mexico City).

There are always large crowds at the shrine, but particularly on the feast day, December 12, the anniversay of the second apparition of Our Lady to Juan Diego. Hundreds of thousands come both in a devoted pilgrimage and to celebrate with singing and dancing.

Visitors to the holy shrine should dress modestly, with arms and legs covered, or they may be denied entry to the basilica. Altitude sickness may cause headaches:—the city is 7,000 feet above sea level. Also, the high pollution levels may exacerbate respiratory conditions, such as asthma.

we adored our Lady's image preserved on the cloak. I waited in a crowd to attend the next Mass, then climbed to the old basilica to pray at Juan Diego's tomb. I felt fulfilled and glad that I had come.

On the plaza, Aztec dancers offered their vigorous sacred movements all day, after having kept vigil before Our Lady's image the night before and danced all the previous day at a nearby village. But, their physical hardship could not compare with the suffering of an Indian family I saw there. The father on his knees, carrying a very sick child, looked as if he had crawled from the ends of the Earth. His wife and his mother placed a ragged foam pad under his bloody knees. His pain was immense, his exhaustion total. Overcome with empathy and humility, I knew in that instant my life had changed, my faith had come alive. Our Lady of Guadalupe, healer and guide, had transferred her blessing from my Grandmother to me.

Enrique Reza, as told to Dr. Maya Sutton

that much of the merit is lost by covering the distance so rapidly; others argue that the discomfort of being packed into a truck or bus, breathing fumes of gasoline, dust that swirls up, make the hardship no less than before—only over quicker."

In modern industrial societies, such as Europe, Japan, and the United States, the arduousness of pilgrimage has generally decreased or disappeared. Thanks to modern transport, a pilgrimage journey that previously took weeks, months, or even years to accomplish may be made in hours or days. In this way, one historical aspect of pilgrimage has undergone a change, no more. Except where religion prescribes penitential behavior, you have no sound reason to judge either others or yourself badly if the sacred journey takes no longer than going to the supermarket. As with meditation, it is not the time that it takes that is important, but the quality of the experience it provides.

> "[A]lthough your original purpose may seem largely frustrated, do not be distressed and angry with yourself or impatient with God because he does not give you feelings of devotion and spiritual joy that you imagine He gives to others. Recognize in this your own weakness...firmly trusting that our Lord in his mercy will make it good and profitable, more than you know."
>
> Walter Hilton (d. 1395),
> *The Ladder of Perfection*

Ebb and flow

The anthropologist Colin Turnbull published in 1987 a remarkably illuminating account of his Indian pilgrimage to Badrinath, Jumnotri, and Gangotri. It illustrates interaction with and reaction against other pilgrims, clashes between one's own perception of what a sacred journey "should be" and what it is for others, the promise of personal discoveries and revelations, and the movement in and out of *communitas*. He had set out with Mohan Kumar, a young Brahmin official from the Birla Manda (temple) in Delhi, and by train and then ancient bus, reached Badrinath high in a valley only a few miles from the border with Tibet. It was October, very cold and windy, but as yet there was no snow. Here, they performed *puja* (worship), but for Turnbull this was a nonevent. "I might have been more moved…but for the fact that a short distance away a number of pilgrims were clustered around a radio that was blaring a broadcast of a championship cricket match being played in Calcutta." For him, the incident struck a false note. "Mohan Kumar laughed and said that if I were really a pilgrim, then I would not have even heard the radio, let alone been distracted by it."

Mohan Kumar was himself critical of Turnbull for not having joined the other pilgrims in the ritual bathing in the hot spring that runs into a pool just below the temple. "I had offended him…because I was not getting my money's worth, not taking advantage of all the attractions available to me."

Turnbull could not escape the feeling that he had come to a deservedly unfrequented tourist resort, and he had to walk off into the hills for several miles before he felt he was on a sacred journey and not just a vacation.

None of his fellow pilgrims at Badrinath had any interest in continuing the pilgrimage all the way to the source of the Ganges at Gaumakh, beyond Gangotri. Mohan Kumar, "believing in the merit of right effort," however, agreed to go as far as Jumnotri. Hiring a car complete with driver, Lal Bahadur, they drove to within a day's walk of Jumnotri, then followed the narrow and perilous trail to the natural shrine. On the near side of the bridge leading to the shrine across a pine-clad gorge, some highly colored laundry was flapping on a line, and four Europeans on a climbing trip, wearing bright plastic rainwear, squatted on the ground playing cards. Turnbull was offended by the "visual pollution" and shocked to learn that in two days the climbers had not bothered to cross the bridge to the shrine, not even knowing that they would find hot springs there in which they could cook and wash. Kumar took a more tolerant view: "They may think they are just on holiday, but if they enjoy climbing so much, why have they wasted two days here unless they are getting something else? Perhaps, for them, this side of the river is sacred."

In the sacred cave at Jumnotri, each of the three (for Lal Bahadur came with them) discovered something. Kumar, encountering the holy man of the cave, realized that it was a sacred person rather than a sacred site that he was seeking. Lal Bahadur, a Buddhist, joining them out of general interest, found stones worn smooth by generations of worshiping pilgrims and joyously rang the bells hanging outside the cave. Turnbull discovered an unexpected natural shrine. When he had been there thirty years before as a student, prudery had prevented him joining other pilgrims bathing in the warm pools. But suddenly there he was, standing naked in the icy wind with the other two, ready to plunge into the hot water. After immersing themselves the ritually correct three times, they found the holy man's disciple in the temple at the edge of the pool, blessing them with song and incense.

"And there were the three of us, a Hindu Brahmin, a Nepali Buddhist, and an Anglo-American agnostic, all equally naked and all equally blessed. The exhilaration was more than just the combination of altitude (about 11,000 feet), cold air, and a steaming-hot outdoor pool provided by nature. The nakedness had something to do with it, banishing the last illusion of distance and difference."

But nothing, perhaps especially not the experience of oneness and brotherhood, lasts forever: Neither Mohan Kumar nor Lal Bahadur wanted to face the long walk to Gangotri, where the temples were already closed for the winter. Turnbull, determined to experience probably the most inaccessible and most powerful of India's natural sacred places, had to continue alone.

"Happy
those early dayes! when I
Shin'd in my Angell-infancy...
When yet I had not walkt above
A mile, or two, from my first love,
And looking back (at that short space,)
Could see a glimpse of his bright face...

O how I long to travell back
And tread again that ancient track!
That I might once more reach that plaine
Where first I left my glorious traine,
From whence th'Inlightned spirit sees
That shady City of Palme trees..."
Henry Vaughan (1622–95),
"The Retreate"

Aloneness

The feelings that pilgrims report vary greatly from person to person. Sometimes, a pilgrim who feels at one with others on one pilgrimage may the next time he or she goes to the same shrine or on a pilgrimage elsewhere experience something quite different, more distant, more separate, more individual.

Be prepared for a falling apart rather than a drawing together of your group as you move ever closer toward the sacred center. Among Indian and Nepali pilgrims, Barbara Nimri Aziz observed a growing dissociation from others around them. "It was most apparent during a four-day-long pilgrimage in Kashmir, where people seemed to become less sociable, less talkative and less concerned with their fellow pilgrims than earlier in the trek when they helped one another and ventured to talk with strangers."

One woman she spoke to on the route to a Himalayan shrine said of the relatives with whom she was traveling: "What they feel about Siva is their own; I do not care about them."

As pilgrims become more and more focused on the divine, what they as individuals want from their sacred journey may become all that matters to them. This is the natural withdrawal of self into self to prepare for a climax.

CHAPTER 9

Arrival: Excitement and Preparation

Here at last, arrived in the sacred place—the place on which you fixed your heart and where, at this time, you want most in the world to be!

The excitement and anticipation are immense, but before you are overwhelmed by all that you have come to see, there are practical things with which to deal. Hopefully, you have arrived a day or two early. If not, you have much to do.

Spontaneity is admirable, but when you are one of several thousand people, if you leave the practical arrangements to chance, you may miss the main attraction.

As I said earlier (Chapter 4), a pilgrimage is like a ballet—it has its choreography and its timing. The best investment of your time before the "show" opens may be a walk-through of the route, like a ballet dancer walking through the steps of a new ballet or a soccer player on the night before a big game, walking through moves on the pitch. Does this walk-through seem unspiritual? I assure you that it is not. Master the physical context, eliminate petty anxieties and uncertainties, place your body in the right position at the right time, and you free your spirit to do its work.

If you are joining a processional pilgrimage, ask in the church or temple, hotel or hostel, or tourist office (perhaps) for a schedule and (if possible) a route map so that you know what is going to happen and when. Begin at the starting point of the procession, and walk the route. (Remember that we are talking about formal processions here, not climbing Mount Fuji!) Whether the procession is to a shrine, a holy well, the sea, or wherever, and you want to see the climax, remember that those at the tail end of a procession have the worst view (everyone else arrives before them). When you have seen the route on the ground, you may decide to accompany the procession, rather than join it, so that you can go ahead. See where the route narrows and will create turbulence, where the blind spots are, where the vantage points. If there is a best position for viewing or participating in the climax, local people will know—ask restaurateurs, store owners, or police officers. If the pilgrimage is highly complex, in an unfamiliar religious framework, you may do better to hire a guide.

> "Our Lord is greatly cheered by our prayer....So he says, 'Pray inwardly, even if you do not enjoy it...though you feel nothing, see nothing.'"
>
> Mother Julian of Norwich,
> *Revelations of Divine Love* (c.1393)

If you intend to take photographs, get locational shots out of the way. You may not have much time, space, or inclination in the heat of the moment. Pilgrim tourists, in particular, may be surprised by the reluctance they develop to distancing themselves from an event by watching it through a viewfinder.

Thinking ahead

Make sure you know where your next meal is coming from. Will stores and restaurants be open? Religious festivals, like folk festivals, sometimes involve the entire community. Suppose that as your sacred journey you have chosen to attend the fire festival of Up-Helly-Aa in Shetland. You will discover that everyone participates (including restaurant and hotel staff), so for your evening meal you will either have to have brought your own or to have organized in advance to share in local people's eating arrangements.

Keep your plans flexible, however, so that if there is an opportunity for eating with other pilgrims, you can take it. A simple meal may turn out to be not so simple: My most powerful memory of Assisi is of breakfast in a convent, where a visiting choir of German nuns sang grace, transforming frugal fare into a spiritual feast of overflowing abundance.

For vegetarians, this is the last chance to find out what will be involved if sacrifice or commensality or both form part of your pilgrimage. For example, after Muslim pilgrims have completed their devotions in Mecca, their pilgrimage continues with visits to the sacred hills outside the city, where they spend the night and sacrifice sheep and other animals. At the same time, Muslims all over the world also sacrifice sheep, which are then cooked and eaten by friends and family. This simultaneous sacrifice is among the bonds that unite the nations of Islam. If you are not a Muslim, you will not be involved, but among other religious groups, you may well witness a sacrifice or be expected to partake in a special meal. Think ahead of how you will handle these issues without offending your hosts' religious convictions.

Crowds

If your pilgrimage involves movement in dense crowds, make sure everything is attached to you, not forgetting glasses and sunglasses. If they are knocked off, you may not be able to retrieve them. Make foolproof arrangements with companions of when and where to meet if you are separated. No one person should carry vital things, such as all the money or the only street plan.

Where are the toilets? Are there any? If not, what are you going to do? And are you ready to wait around, perhaps for hours, in a hot crowd in great heat? This may sound like your memories of a summer rock concert in, say, the Hollywood Bowl, which is quite possibly the best preparation you could have had for a mass procession in a hot country.

Many people have already assembled here. Tomorrow or the next day, there will be more. Are you ready for the sight of enormous numbers of people in one place—the physical pressure of more and more strange bodies, and (wherever in the world and however clean they are) the smell of mass humanity? People on religious occasions are still people. If you intend to participate in some great procession in, say, India, and are not used to people en masse, go and acclimatize in the most crowded place you can find.

By handling the mechanics of your pilgrimage in this way you may lose some of the wonder and astonishment and the sheer raw power of the completely new, but on the other hand, you will avoid fainting or panicking or being away searching for a toilet and missing a crucial moment. Preparation equals liberation to engage in the here and now.

Looking after your body

Anyone who has made a long physical journey may need medication—this is a time for licking your wounds so that you can get on with the least bodily distraction.

It is also a time for cleansing. Like any other traveler after a long journey, you will probably head for the nearest bathtub or shower to wash your hair and refresh yourself bodily all over. Put your mind into this operation: Take your time and really experience what you are doing. If you are a member of one of the world religions or some other spiritual community, you probably have your own rites of purification.

These rites may include regulations or guidance on whether or not to fast. Muslims, for example, come to Mecca fasting. Fasting is a difficult subject in the context of pilgrimage. Not only is it a widespread penitential practice, but it has long been used to achieve altered mental states; for example by Christian mystics and by Hindu holy men hoping to become at one with the *atman*. It is the transformative technique most favored in the Middle East and was used both by Jesus during his forty days in the wilderness and by Muhammad during his spiritual crisis alone in the mountains, before answering their respective "calls."

But if you do not belong to a religious tradition that requires it or if you have had no previous experience of fasting,

SAINTE ANNE DE BEAUPRÉ

Along the path of devotion

It took me about 18 years to get to the Shrine of Sainte Anne de Beaupré. I wanted to go, not so much for myself, but because it had meant so much to women I had met while researching popular devotion in Newfoundland in the late 1970s. Anne is the mother of Mary and grandmother of Jesus. Although the present Basilica dates from 1923, a shrine to her has existed on this site (22 miles from Quebec City, Canada) since 1658.

According to legend, in 1662 St. Anne saved some men shipwrecked in the Gulf of St. Lawrence. Tales of miraculous healings at Beaupré itself have circulated from then until the present day. In 1876, St. Anne was proclaimed the patroness of the province of Quebec. Devotion to St. Anne de Beaupré in Newfoundland has been fostered by the Redemptorist Order, the guardians of the Shrine since 1878. (The Redemptorist Order literally preaches to the converted, its mission being to reinvigorate the spiritual life of Catholics.)

Through the devotional magazine *The Annals of St. Anne de Beaupré*, Newfoundlanders received news of the Shrine and the miracles occurring there. By writing in with prayers to St. Anne, sending thanksgivings for answered prayers, and praying for other letter writers, they were able to participate in a "virtual" pilgrimage, to experience *communitas* despite their spatial isolation. So close was the connection that in one case a copy of *The Annals* was tied around an injured leg for curative purposes! The Newfoundlanders of Irish descent were devoted to St. Anne, but she was particularly popular among the Micmac native peoples, because of the great status they afforded to grandmothers.

For many women, the only trip they ever make outside Newfoundland is on a pilgrimage to Beaupré, one of the most moving and significant experiences of their lives. One woman told me that it had been "like a visit to heaven." I had also been told of the impressive Basilica, which contains a major relic (St. Anne's arm set in a gold casing) and a magnificent lifelike statue of St. Anne. I had heard, too, of the Scala Santa, a replica of the Holy Stairs Jesus climbed to meet Pontius Pilate, which pilgrims ascend on their knees.

The 1895 Cyclorama, affording a panorama of Jerusalem and the surrounding countryside at the time of the Crucifixion, had "brought the Bible to life." Pilgrims stayed at The Basilica Inn, and all brought back souvenirs from the church store, including supplies of St. Anne's oil—oil blessed and burned before the relic of St. Anne in the Basilica—popularly considered to have great healing powers.

The "official" pilgrimage season at Beaupré lasts from early June until early September and has around a million and a half visitors each year. The climax is at the Feast of St. Anne on July 26, which follows nine days of festivities and devotions. Pilgrims arrive by boat and by road. The road from Quebec City, the traditional pilgrimage route still walked by many (particularly on the Feast Day), is marked by wayside shrines and bread ovens.

Mont St. Anne

Saint Joachim

Beaupré

SAINTE ANNE DE BEAUPRÉ

Château Richer

Ile d'Orleans

L'Ange, Gardien

Boischatel

Beauport

Downtown Quebec

Arriving by bus, I entered the Basilica and, to my surprise, wept. I wept with joy at having made it and with empathy for my Newfoundland friends. I wept, too, from an overwhelming sense of this place as the focus of prayers of anguish as well as of thanksgiving and of the triumph of those whose walking sticks and crutches, displayed at the entrance in their hundreds, bear witness to its long healing history. I returned home with a bottle of St. Anne's Oil and a sense of achievement.

Marion Bowman

The feast of St. Anne
From July 17 pilgrims make a novena—nine days of private prayer and public worship—ending in a candlelit procession on the eve of the festival. On the feast day (July 26), the sick are anointed at a ceremony outside the basilica.

"Then our Lord opened my spiritual eyes, and showed me the soul in the middle of my heart. The soul was as large as if it were an eternal world, and a blessed kingdom...a most glorious city. In the midst of it sat our Lord Jesus, God and Man....For in us he is completely at home, and has his eternal dwelling."

Julian of Norwich,
Revelations of Divine Love (c. 1393)

the best advice is: don't. You may not have time to take food during the event itself, so especially if you have had a hard journey, nourish your body and recharge your batteries. However, some abstinence may be beneficial: Foregoing caffeine (tea, coffee, chocolate) and alcohol will give you a clearer mind (although habitual coffee drinkers, in particular, should give it up well before arrival, or they may have the event ruined by withdrawal symptoms, notably headaches).

Such abstinence extends to mind-altering substances including (if your doctor agrees) tranquillizers and antidepressants. The underlying spiritual purpose behind ritualized cleansing is to bring a whole person, in a state as close as possible to the Creator's intention, into the divine presence. That ideal state is usually conceived of as approaching a physical and mental innocence lost somewhere in the history of humankind—the dweller in the Paradise garden, Adam before the Fall.

"[T]here is a great difference in the ways one may be inside the castle. For there are many souls who are in the outer courtyard...and don't care at all about entering the castle, nor do they know...who is within."
Teresa of Avila (1515–1582),
The Interior Castle

Unifying matter and spirit

Because this book is constructed around the stages of a physical journey, readers engaged on an inner pilgrimage may have thought they were forgotten. Not so. The outer journey is a metaphor for the inner, and there are things for you to ponder every step of the way. All pilgrims need to take time now to think about the common equation of inner with spiritual and outer with material.

"OM. In the centre of the castle of Brahman, our own body, there is a small shrine in the form of a lotus-flower, and within can be found a small space. We should find who dwells there, and we should want to know him."

Chandogya Upanishad

Within Christianity, the distinction between inner and outer pilgrimage, and the view that an outer journey is not necessary, go back at least to the twelfth century. During the Reformation this view was echoed by Martin Luther, one of many Protestants who believed that the only legitimate pilgrimage was the inner journey that comes from reading the Scriptures, and that instead of walking about, the true Christian should through prayer and meditation engage in introspection.

His position was not far removed from that of Nanak, the first Sikh guru, who when asked by a Muslim why he did not turn toward Mecca to pray, replied:

"Capacity for contemplation is one with contemplation itself, so that only he who feels he can contemplate is able to do so....Since you will it...obviously you already have it....Please do not worry if you never know more than this....In a word, let the thing...lead you as it will....Watch it if you like, but let it alone....Be willing to be blind."

Anonymous author of *The Cloud of Unknowing* (fourteenth century)

169

One of the most compelling symbols of holiness

Arresting and picturesque with its fortress, towers and circle of walls, Assisi looks down from a foothill of Mt. Subasio onto the orchards and vineyards of the Umbrian plain. St. Francis, son of the richest cloth merchant in the province, was born, buried, and canonized here in 1228. Such was the immensity of his fame and the intensity of the love he gave and inspired, that the city soon became the fourth center of Christian pilgrimage after Jerusalem, Rome, and Santiago de Compostela. It has changed little since.

Close to its handsome piazza you can pray in the little oratory of San Francesco Piccolino, on the site where Francis was born in 1182; nearby the Chiesa Nuova rises from the foundations of his boyhood home. Just up the hill, in the cathedral, you can see the font in which he was baptized and, lower down, the bishop's palace in which at, age twenty-four, he stripped naked and handed back to his father all his worldly goods, swearing himself to God's service and total poverty for the rest of his life.

Less than a mile below Assisi, in an olive grove frequented by hoopoes and nightingales, stand the little church and convent of San Damiano, which Francis repaired with his own hands before going to Rome in 1209 to obtain the pope's approval of his First Order of Friars. Three years later, he installed the eighteen-year-old Clare di Favarone in San Damiano, so founding his Second Order of Poor Clares; she, too, was canonized and lies in a basilica at the eastern end of Assisi. Before long, Francis also founded a Third Order, for the laity, single or married, who now number more than a million.

Many of his later years were spent traveling the world barefoot with his friars, preaching and working himself to death in the care of the poor and the homeless and beggars, cripples and lepers. He crossed the Alps to France and the Pyrenees to Spain, was shipwrecked off Croatia, and ran the gauntlet of the Saracen lines in Egypt, in an attempt to end the murderous battles of the Fifth Crusade. Yet, he always came back to the home he had created for his Order, at the tiny wayside chapel of Santa Maria degli Angeli (also known as the Porziuncula), near San Damiano. It was here, two years after the stigmata—the wounds of Christ—had appeared on his hands and feet and in his side during a night of prayer, that he died at age forty-four in 1226. Today, this touching little shrine is enclosed in a vast church with a looming dome.

For nearly 800 years, Francis's body has lain under the majestic basilica built in his honor by Pope Gregory IX, which rises tier upon tier, at the western end of Assisi. It comprises papal apartments, a convent for the friars, a lower church for their worship, and a soaring church above for preaching to the people—its walls frescoed with 28 scenes from the saint's life, a number of them painted by Giotto. All this, seriously damaged by the earthquake in 1997, has been restored with speed and brilliance. Superb as it is, the building nevertheless defies Francis's conviction that absolute poverty and humility were quintessential to his ministry of love. Because of this, the pilgrim may find the saint's rough stone coffin, bound with a simple iron band, lying silently in a small crypt beneath the basilica, not only a more appropriate memorial but also one of the most compelling symbols of holiness in Christendom.

Today, Francis is the patron saint of Italy and also of ecology. Moreover, inspired by his attempt to make peace with the Muslims, the leaders of all the world's great religions gathered in Assisi in 1987 to pray together for peace, for the first time in history.

Through his love of animals and birds—in fact of the entire universe—memorably expressed in his *Canticle of the Sun*, Francis has become one of the favorite saints in the calendar. Any visit to Assisi is, therefore, incomplete without exploring briefly the mystery and beauties of Mt. Subasio: The little hermitage of I Carceri perched on its flank, in whose caves Francis experienced his conversion; the way up through its enchanting woods—until fifty years ago roamed by wolves and wild boar; and the snowy peaks of the Apennines viewed from its summit—a sunny grassland carpeted with narcissi and orchids, hunted by falcons, and alive with the sublime singing of larks.

Adrian House

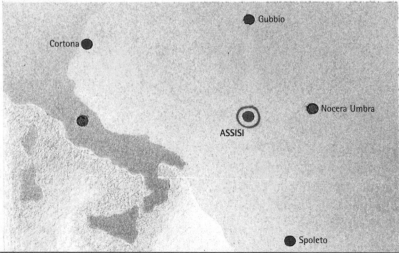

"There is no place where God is not." For Eastern poets, philosophers, and religious teachers, the outer landscape is often less important than the inner. Tibetan guidebooks to holy places teach devotees to recite names and visualize shrines within their own bodies, rather than making physical visits. The Tamil poet Devara Dasimaya says: "To be utterly at one with Siva...[the pilgrim's] front yard is the true Benares."

"We must pray in the height, depth, length, and breadth of our spirits. Not in many words, but in a little word of one syllable. What shall this word be?...let us pray, in word or thought or desire, no other word than 'God.'"

The Cloud of Unknowing

But for many, inner and outer landscapes are not separate. Westerners have perhaps too easily accepted a division of the world by scholars and theologians into two opposing camps: inner versus outer, spirit versus matter. These oppositions have their roots in classical Christian thought about God, which holds that the divine is wholly Other and separated from humanity. But, Christianity also contains doctrines that deny separation: Matter is the creation of spirit (God); Christ's redemption of humankind was spirit acting through matter (the Incarnation); the Holy Sacrament is matter raised to a spiritual dimension. And, as the thirteenth-century theologian Thomas Aquinas said, people forget they are human if they think that bodies play no part in worship: Our bodies are the medium our souls work with. The inner cannot be equated with the spiritual, the outer with the material; Physical acts such as going on pilgrimage may be transcendental.

Oppositional thought draws a sharp distinction between the sacred and the profane. In the influential *Elementary Forms of the Religious Life* (1912), Emile Durkheim wrote that all religions classify things as either sacred, pertaining to the transcendental world, or profane, to the everyday. According to Durkheim, these categories are mutually exclusive: "The religious life and the profane life cannot exist in the same place." But, when we look at what actual Christians *do*, rather than what their interpreters say they *think*, we see something

> "Here at the Fountains sliding foot,
> Or at some Fruit-trees mossy root,
> Casting the Bodies vest aside,
> My soul into the boughs does glide:
> There like a Bird it sits, and sings,
> Then whets, and combs its silver Wings."
> Andrew Marvell (1621–1678), "The Garden"

different. In folk religion, in orthodox religion as it is practiced rather than preached, and in activities such as pilgrimage, there is a continual blurring of categories. Spirit and matter, sacred and profane, are not separate.

Nor is there a distinction between the spiritual and the material in Shinto, the national religion of Japan. This faith, without a founder or dogma, is transmitted not through scriptures but through annual observances and everyday customs. Japanese myths of the Creation say there was an original chaos, which of its own indwelling power produced the *amatsu kami*, or "deities of heaven." From the *kami* descended the islands of Japan, other spiritual beings, and the Japanese people. Thus, human beings, the land,

> "The way we set out on this pilgrimage of 'other-centeredness' is to recite a short phrase, a word that is commonly called today a mantra. The mantra is simply a means of turning our attention beyond ourselves—a way of unhooking us from our own thoughts and concerns."
> John Main OSB, *Moment of Christ* (1984)

and nature are intimately related, and consequently, the whole material world is seen to have a spiritual dimension.

Within this view of existence, there can be no distinction between the realm of God (the sacred) and the realm of humans (the profane). Not perceiving this, we may overlook things in sacred places that offer the possibility of spiritual growth, simply because we read them as "secular"—nothing to do with religion. In the context of Shinto, for example, the traditional Japanese garden is one of the main expressions of faith. Water is an essential element, trickling, falling—the very word for gardener, *kawaracho*, means "he who makes the beds for streams." In a dry garden, such as the great meditation garden in the Tofukuji Temple in Kyoto, thoughts of water are evoked by raked sand or gravel.

The gardens of Islam, too, embody a religious ideal. The name "Paradise" comes from *pairidaeza*, Old Persian for a park or enclosure, and wherever Islam has held sway can be found enclosed, paradisal gardens. These ideal oases of a desert people have trees for shade, and water, revered as an elemental life force, for music and entrancement and its ability to open the mind to inspiration. The gardens of the Alhambra in Spain, the Royal Gardens of Fin in Iran, the Garden of the Maids of Honor at Udaipur, India, are material expressions of Islam and convey more of the nature of matter and spirit than words can express.

Retreat, contemplation, and dedication

It is time for both inner and outer travelers now to retreat a little from the world, perhaps engaging in prayer or meditation.

If these are already habitual to you, follow the methods you have learned. If you have never before done either, you may want to find somewhere to sit quietly—perhaps such a garden as we spoke of above—breathing gently and deeply, contemplating who you are, where you are, and what your purpose is in coming. You may use imagery like that of St. Teresa of Avila, who pictured the inner journey as one into a castle (the soul) with a series of rooms and corridors leading deeper and deeper within to where the king (God) sits enthroned.

Those who have made a long journey will need sleep. Others, whose pilgrimage begins here, may prefer to keep vigil. A vigil is a time when you stay awake (as in *vigilance*). Technically it was the evening service, often continuing through the night, that used to be held before a saint's feast day.

The vigil was a time of heightened expectation. Have you ever wondered why the most magical times in the Western folk calendar are all "eves"—Christmas Eve, Midsummer's Eve, Halloween? Each is the night before a Christian festival: Christmas; the feast of the birth of John the Baptist (June 24); All Hallow's (All Saints, November 1). The festival days themselves coincided with great European pre-Christian celebrations, but the eves received their stamp from Christian practice.

The early Church kept alive the pre-Christian belief in the supernatural significance of dreams. The pagan practice of seeking foreknowledge by ritual incubation (sleeping over) at the shrine of Asklepios, the god of healing, was replaced with nocturnal vigils at the shrines of Christian saints. Vigils were kept in churches on the eve of the feast day of their patron saints and on the eves of great annual festivals. It was important to be

175

wakeful across the temporal divide of midnight, the transition from one day to the next. This was the moment when the epiphany began, the descent of divinity to the sacred place.

"Hail Jerusalem, city of the Great King, glory and crown of the whole earth, joy and delight of the believer's soul. O Jerusalem, Jerusalem, arise, lift up thine eyes round about and see all these pilgrims, thy sons, who have come together from the uttermost parts of the world, who still are coming in hosts that they may see thy brightness, and the glory of the Lord risen upon thee."

Felix Faber,
late fifteenth century

For most of us, our only experience of a vigil is now in a secular context, on New Year's Eve and in a noisy crowd. Yet where we are at the significant moment, on the stroke of midnight, the transition from one year to the next, remains important to us. We have experienced heightened expectation.

You have performed gallant work in coming so far. Now, is the time to remember that in Europe in the Middle Ages the vigil was also the all-night watch sometimes kept by the candidate for knighthood, kneeling before the altar where his sword and armor were laid as a sign that they were to be devoted to Christian service. The lonely night watch is the ritual acting out of dedication: Following in the mythic footsteps of Galahad and Parsifal, the seekers of the Holy Grail, it can be your dedication of yourself to experience the holy in this sacred place.

CHAPTER 10

Climax: Encounter with the Unknown

You are on the brink of something momentous. Your journey through space and time has left behind the habitual and brought you to the threshold of the holy—to the divide between the human and the divine, where power that is usually hidden has pierced the veil and become anchored in human reality. This power is always here, always accessible: In approaching it, you seek to draw it into your life and bring about existential change. This is the place and the moment.

There may be a climax event that will bring about some profound insight, a transformative ritual, a healing of body or mind. No less to be hoped for is the experience of awe, mystery, fulfillment, and the sudden, sharp, astonishing release of joy.

But, you are on your own. For this is the point where words fail—you, me, or anyone else who tries to describe an epiphany, that sacred moment when divinity manifests itself. The experience of the holy takes us to the farthest boundaries of intellect and language.

Knowing broadly what Buddhism is "about," Islam is "about," Hinduism is "about," does not provide you with a blueprint for pilgrimage performance. Go to Sri Lanka, and you will find three major pilgrimage centers, all drawing large crowds: the Sacred City of Anuradhapura, the Temple of the Tooth at Kandy, and Kataragama. Anuradhapura, a Buddhist center that had been capital of the island from the fourth to the ninth century C.E., had fallen into decay but was redeveloped as a regional capital under British colonial rule. After independence, Christian, Muslim, and Tamil Hindu residents were expelled, and their places of worship razed to recreate Anuradhapura as a Buddhist national heartland, fulfilling a role similar to that of Jerusalem for Jews. At the Poson festival, which falls on the full moon in June, the city fills with Buddhist pilgrims who go to worship and make merit. The atmosphere is restrained and calm; there is no procession or spectacle.

By contrast, pilgrims, Buddhist again, come to the Temple of the Tooth in July/August to see the great annual pageant of the former kingdom of Kandy. It lasts a fortnight, with processions every night, getting ever bigger and better toward the end.

"Prayer, the Church's banquet, Angels' age,
God's breath in man returning to his birth,
The soul in paraphrase, heart in pilgrimage,...
A kind of tune, which all things hear and fear;

Softness, and peace, and joy, and love, and bliss,...
The milky way, the bird of Paradise,
Church-bells beyond the stars heard, the soul's blood,
The land of spices; something understood."

George Herbert (1593–1633), "Prayer"

178

Although the pilgrims make offerings in the town temples, they gather here mainly as onlookers, earning merit by simply watching the parade of the illustrious Buddhist past.

At Kataragama, the season of mass pilgrimage in July/ August celebrates the union of the god Skanda with his mistress, Valli Amma. On each of fifteen successive evenings, Skanda's image is taken to her shrine. By contrast with Kandy, pilgrims are active participants; by contrast with Anuradhapura, religious behavior is extrovert, physical, and ecstatic, involving among other things dance and loud rhythmic music, fire walking, and hanging from hooks. Kataragama used to be a place of pilgrimage for Tamil Hindus from Sri Lanka or southern India, but now the majority are Buddhist, as at Kandy and Anuradhapura.

What a pilgrim does and what a pilgrim receives from each of these Sri Lankan pilgrimages is different. (And, what the Hindus, Muslims, and Christians receive who also attend the Kataragama festival is more or less subtly different again.) The substance of pilgrimage lies in the detail. For us to experience it, we need knowledge and observation but most of all a willingness to engage.

Pilgrimage is not about thinking but about doing and feeling. We can learn from descriptions left by early Christian pilgrims to the Holy Land, who stress the experiential nature of the climax of their journey. Its essence often was and is a combination of ritual and physical, sensory experience. Many pilgrimages specify what the pilgrim must see, hear, touch, taste, and smell.

"O world invisible, we view thee,
O world intangible, we touch thee,
O world unknowable, we know thee."
Francis Thompson (1859–1907),
"The Kingdom of God"

This is not an accident but comes by contrivance: Most pilgrimages and processions have been formulated by ritual specialists with long practice in this ancient tradecraft that links Babylonian diviner with Persian mage and Christian priest. If we surrender to their art and give ourselves up to the process, like earlier pilgrims embracing what offers, we may encounter Otherness with their help.

The pilgrim who has arrived at a shrine has arrived at a trifork—a meeting of three ways on the Otherworld journey, where significant place and significant action meet with significant time.

Significant place

"Most of us have a sense of God in places of great natural beauty," writes Martin L. Smith in *Nativities and Passions* (1995). The natural, even raw, landscape acts almost too readily as a conduit for epiphany—the moment of manifestation of divinity—which comes as a sensory experience: I have known it in the desert as a feeling of immanence, a kind of great weight of air bearing down, as if something momentous were descending. After a desert journey, we seem to understand why Moses heard the voice of the Lord on Mount Sinai; why classic Arab music sounds like question and answer—one man's personal dialogue with God; and why many of the early Christian fathers were desert hermits.

Ecologists and conservationists in particular tend to seek God in the natural landscape, "but," Martin Smith continues, "the test of the practice of the presence of God lies in the settings that seem the most barren, anonymous and profane—the malls, the airports, the fast-food restaurants, the subway stations, the crowds." Those crowds—in our case the crowds at great pilgrimage centers—are the milieu in which we must find our own particular epiphanies. How was and is it done?

Because it linked them directly to the figures of sacred history, early Christian pilgrims wanted to see the sites mentioned in the Bible for themselves. Thus in 333 C.E., the anonymous Bordeaux pilgrim visited the place where Jacob wrestled with the angel (Gen 33:24–31), the tree Zaccheus climbed (Luke 19:1–10), even the cornerstone the builders rejected (Ps 118:22). The sites (whether traditional or manufactured to meet the needs of the pilgrim industry) bolstered faith by "proving" the scriptures true and helped pilgrims visualize the events that took place there more vividly. St. Jerome's companion Paula, visiting Bethlehem, declared "that, with the eye of faith, she saw a child wrapped in swaddling clothes, weeping in the Lord's manger, the Magi worshipping, the star shining above, the Virgin Mother, the attentive foster father; and the shepherds coming by night."

> "Ask, and it shall be given you;
> Seek, and ye shall find;
> Knock, and it shall be opened unto you."
> Matthew 7:7

> "God rejoices in his creature;
> and his creature in God,
> eternally marvelling."
> Julian of Norwich,
> *Revelations of Divine Love* (c. 1393)

The proximity of Old and New Testament sites and the practice of reading the latter as fulfillment of the former, seeing allegorical meanings in both, gave a rich, multilayered texture to the Holy Land journey. The Bordeaux Pilgrim saw the place where the prophet Elijah was whirled up into heaven (2 Kgs 2:11) next to the place where Christ was baptized; the birthplace of Christ in Bethlehem near the tomb of King David who had foretold his coming. The dense concentrations of meaning, especially in Jerusalem, made the experience of seeing these sites something more profound than the modern tourist's response to ancient places. What Paula enjoyed in Bethlehem was not the fruits of a powerful imagination but a full-scale mystical experience.

The act of seeing the holy sites was perhaps for these early pilgrims close to the Hindu experience of "taking *darshan.*" *Darshan* means "seeing," and when Hindus go on pilgrimage they go for the *darshan* of a sacred place or famous image. For lay people, on pilgrimage or not, this

> "O Mother Ganga, may your water,
> abundant blessing of this world,
> treasure of Lord Shiva, playful Lord of all the Earth,
> essence of the scriptures and
> embodied goodness of the gods,
> May your water, sublime wine of immortality,
> Soothe our troubled souls."
>
> Hindu invocation

is the central act of worship. Virtually anywhere in India, people can be seen gathering for the *darshan* of the god in courtyards of temples and at doorways of roadside shrines. They will crane their necks over great crowds assembled to watch some deity pass in procession—for they have come both to see and to be seen. This is why images of Hindu deities such as that of Krishna Jagannath at Puri often have enormous saucer eyes, to enable them to "see" large numbers of their devotees at one time. *Darshan* is not a "looking," but an encounter, a mutual touching through the eyes.

Significant action

Seeing and touching were also closely linked for early Christian pilgrims. In the fourth century, Paulinus of Nola wrote: "The principal motive that draws people to Jerusalem is the desire to see and touch the places where Christ was present in the body." And this is the sixth-century theologian Sophronios, speaking of the rock which to this day is believed to mark Jesus' birthplace in Bethlehem: "The shining slab which received the infant God, I will touch with my eyes, my mouth, my forehead, to gain its blessing."

Pilgrims wanted to be physically involved, to kiss the Holy Land's sacred earth, to touch its monuments and relics (genuine or otherwise) in acts of veneration. When the Italian pilgrim Antoninus of Piacenza visited the Holy Sepulchre around 570 C.E., he believed he saw the very board bearing the mocking inscription "This is the King of the Jews" that had been nailed over Christ's head at the Crucifixion: "This I have seen, and had it in my hand and kissed it."

In Antoninus' day, the ritualized reenactment of sacred events also formed a main part of the pilgrim's experience. When he went to Mount Gilboa, where David is said to have killed Goliath with a slingshot (1 Sam 17:41–54), he saw in the middle of the road the place where Goliath was buried and nearby a great heap of stones. He remarks that there was not a pebble left for 20 miles around, as anyone going that way made a gesture of contempt by (in imitation of David) throwing three stones at Goliath's grave. Along with hundreds of others, he journeyed to the River Jordan, so that in imitation of Christ at his baptism he could go down into the water. At Cana, he reclined at the very table where Jesus had reclined at the marriage feast (John 2:1–12), and filled one of two "surviving" water jugs with wine, offering it at the altar. He performed these actions specifically to gain a blessing.

Though less easily beguiled by fake attractions, Holy Land pilgrims of today still place themselves within the ambit of the holy by repeating sacred actions. On Palm Sunday, pilgrims still walk in procession, palm fronds in hand, along the path that Christ is believed to have followed on his triumphant entry into Jerusalem. William Purcell in *Pilgrim's England* (1981) recalls how, when he was leading Holy Land pilgrimages, all sorts of people, including sceptics, would scramble out of the bus to paddle in the River Jordan and collect its water in bottles to take back home. Christ's baptism in the river at one moment in history has rendered the water a continuous, living miracle.

> "I rose early, before sunrise, and rambled off to the holy places on Mount Sion...and on the Mount of Olives...I gathered some of the thorns which grow in the hedges on the side of the Mount of Olives, and of the Mount Sion, and I bound twigs of them together, and wove them into a crown of thorns in the way, and of the thorns wherewith I believe that the Lord Jesus was crowned."
>
> Felix Faber,
> late fifteenth century

To reenact a sacred event is to partake mystically in it. By revisiting sacred scenes, repeating sacred actions, reenacting sacred events, the pilgrim transcends distance in space and time, becoming one with the holy place and the event that made it holy. For Muslims on the *hajj*, this identification is built into the prescribed ritual, that consists not only of circling the Ka'ba, which Muslim tradition says was built by Abraham and Ishmael, the father of the Arabs, but also of kissing or touching the Black Stone. According to some traditions, this ancient meteorite fixed in the lower wall of the Ka'ba is a relic of Adam or Abraham and was kissed by the Prophet Muhammad himself. It is worn down by the lips of pilgrims.

To provide arenas for significant action at home in Europe, the medieval Church evolved architectural and ceremonial strategies. Those who could not go to the church of the Holy Sepulchre in Jerusalem to cut their cross among the myriads cut into its walls by pilgrims, could instead visit an architectural copy. The circular eleventh-century Holy Sepulchre in the cathedral of Aquileia, in northern Italy, is a copy of the Anastasis Rotunda in the Jerusalem Holy Sepulchre, which marks the site of the Resurrection and contains Christ's tomb. The Aquileia copy contains a "tomb" with a removable lid and there on Good Friday a consecrated Host (communion bread), representing the body of Christ, and a crucifix were ceremonially "buried" to be "resurrected" on Easter Morning. Another medieval Italian copy is the church of San Stefano, Bologna, where the distance between the copies of Christ's tomb, in the chapel of San Sepulcro, and Calvary in the central chapel, corresponds to the actual distance in Jerusalem.

Ordinary parish churches throughout Europe had "Easter Sepulchers," either temporary wooden structures or niches, or stone chest-tombs (containing burials) built against the north wall of the chancel. In England, they were banned by the Protestants in 1548 and many were destroyed (although even in

Puritan counties, such as Norfolk, some survive—notably one of the tomb type at East Raynham, where Lady Townshend specifically provided in her will for her tomb to be used as an Easter Sepulcher, thus conferring a blessing on her soul). The ceremonies performed on and around Easter Sepulchers dramatized the events of Easter: the body of Christ being represented, as at Aquileia, by a consecrated Host; and the women discovering the empty tomb on Easter morning played by veiled clergy.

At Chaource in Bourgogne, France, we can make a symbolic descent into an Easter Sepulcher, by going down into the semisubterranean sepulcher chapel of the church of St. John the Baptist. Here the *Mise au Tombeau* (the placing in the tomb) recreates Christ's entombment with life-size, and in some lights, uncannily lifelike figures. The sepulcher, to which daylight is admitted only through two small windows, is guarded by three polychrome stone soldiers in the costume of 1515, when the *Mise au Tombeau* was created. Seven other figures, including the sorrowing Virgin and the Three Marys are gathered round the chest-tomb on which the dead Christ is being laid. The *Mise au Tombeau* is said to have been so designed that the first ray of sunlight on Easter morning strikes the fusion of altar and chest-tomb on which Christ's body lies.

Within the Hagia Sophia in Istanbul, the whole landscape of the Holy Land was reproduced symbolically to provide a total experience. A more modern example is the "Holy Land in America" at the Franciscan monastery in Washington, D.C. (dedicated in 1899), which contains copies of several significant Christian buildings, including a full-scale Tomb of Christ at the correct distance from the Calvary on the other side of the main church. At pilgrimage sites, both biblical scenes and ritual action may be imitated. The shrine of Bom Jesús, near Braga in Portugal, has a Baroque Via Dolorosa (Stations of the Cross) created in the eighteenth century for parishioners who were too poor to go on a pilgrimage abroad. Here they could experience the ritual actions of pilgrims in the Holy City and in their own flesh recreate Christ's journey to Calvary.

Significant time

As well as movement through space on sacred journeys, there is movement through time. Some journeys are repeated within monthly, annual, seasonal, or periodic cycles. There are also particular times when the religious experience is more powerful or divinity more accessible than at others. The interplay of time and space is well illustrated by the Hindu pilgrimage to Pandharpur. Exactly four months and a fortnight after entering Pandharpur, some pilgrims make a second pilgrimage to the tomb of the *sant* Jnanesvar at Alandi. They may go directly from their homes to Alandi or go first to Pandharpur, then make a fourteen-day journey that symbolically retraces the steps of Jnanesvar as he returned from Pandharpur to Alandi after his own pilgrimage.

Pilgrims who make the double pilgrimage refer to their journey as *vari*, signifying the periodic appearance of a person at a particular place at a particular time. They themselves are known as *varkaris* (people who make pilgrimages). Some *varkaris* go once a year, some twice a year, some four times a year, some go every month. These latter are the *mahinemaha varkaris*, the most highly respected. They usually travel singly but often join a group after reaching the holy city and can be relied upon to appear to such an extent that if a man has not joined his group by a certain day, the rest assume he must be dead and perform his obsequies.

Significant time has met with significant place at pilgrim shrines from ancient times. In the Mediterranean world of 2,000 years ago, the Mystery religions were pilgrim-initiation events correlated with the seasons. Crowds of pilgrims sought the Egyptian goddess Isis at her sanctuary at Philae on the Upper Nile, at the full moon of the autumnal equinox. In the second century C.E., the Latin satirist Apuleius joined the cult of Isis and described its rites. The pilgrims dipped themselves seven times in the sea and called on the goddess to appear in the sky, which she duly did, rising as its most brilliant star, the Dog Star, Sirius.

"So hallow'd and so gracious is the time."
William Shakespeare, *Hamlet* (1601)

The secret Mysteries of Eleusis honoring Demeter, three days before the autumnal equinox, drew crowds of pilgrims, who bathed together in the sea outside Athens and then sprinkled their bodies with animal blood. Dressed in saffron robes with crowns of myrtle, they set out for the shrine, a day's walk from the city. There a mimesis or ritual reenactment seems to have been stage managed so that initiates witnessed some kind of metamorphosis, or forms in process of change. At the climax came a baby's cry, then the clash of cymbals and a bright light. Initiates from emperors down confessed themselves profoundly moved by the experience, although not one ever betrayed the exact details.

Christians today participate in a cyclic mystery by entering a cave at Bethlehem. The Grotto of the Nativity, venerated as Christ's birthplace, is a true cave, not the above-ground stable of religious paintings. They make this ritual descent at Christmas, Christ's birthday, packing into the tiny space. By being there at this time, they are mystically present, like St. Jerome's friend Paula, at the Divine Birth.

Pilgrim journeys may also be related to cycles and movements of planetary bodies—especially the sun and moon. This relationship may be a matter of timing—the Pandharpur pilgrimage is organized according to a lunar calendar, so is the *hajj* to Mecca—but may also consciously link human movement through space and time with cosmic motion. The Yucatec Maya word *ximbal* is used to describe both pilgrimage and the passage of the stars through the skies. Maya on local pilgrimages today often avoid modern roads and follow old Maya routes or trails through the bush, as if these were modern equivalents of the ancient *sacbe*, the elevated roadway that led to Maya temples. The Maya still refer to the Milky Way as a celestial *sacbe* over which the deities pass. In medieval England, the Milky Way was known as the Walsingham Way and regarded as a great sign across the sky pointing the way to the Holy House, in which the Holy Family had lived, miraculously transported from Nazareth to Norfolk. In France and Spain, the Milky Way was thought to be a cosmic image of the sacred pilgrim road to Santiago de Compostela. Thus, the cosmic and earthly dimensions are linked—the pilgrims' movements replicating the celestial pilgrimage of the heavenly bodies.

Just as the circling of holy places and shrines is part of the sacred journey, so the same movement is part of pilgrim ritual on arrival at the sacred goal. Circumambulation (walking around) of a shrine is found in Hinduism, Tibetan Buddhism, and some

THE WESTERN WALL

Connecting across time and space

My heart, my eye, my daughter, my mother, great mountain....Jerusalem is known by all these names and at least seventy more by Jewish people around the world. Jerusalem is the pupil of the Jewish eye, it is said; and on that pupil is etched for eternity the image of the holy temple. Solomon built the first temple in Jerusalem, and its successor, erected by Herod, was destroyed by the Romans in 70 C.E.

Muslim quarter

Dome of the Rock

Christian quarter

Moors' quarter

Jewish quarter

Armenian quarter

All that remained was the huge masonry platform on which the temple once stood and to which Jews made pilgrimage for centuries to lament its destruction. In the seventh century, Muslims built the Dome of the Rock on the platform, leaving the Western Wall as the only part of the temple area accessible for Jews. They come as they have always done to pray for the restoration of their temple, which will only rise again, they believe, with the coming of the Messiah and the dawn of world peace and harmony. Until that day, Orthodox Jews everywhere keep an unpainted portion of a wall in their house, to remind them that human existence will be marked by imperfection until the temple stands again.

To pray at the Western Wall is to nurture an image of hope that has held the Jewish people together through millennia of oppression and diaspora. It is to feel connected to Jews everywhere, through all time and across the globe. By extension, it is to feel part of humanity as a whole, for the Wall is a living symbol for the center of the world, where Earth receives the greatest influx of spiritual power from Heaven. "Jerusalem," one rabbi told me as he came away from his prayers at the wall, "is the Gate of Heaven through which prayers ascend and the spirit descends."

One Sabbath morning at the Western Wall, I watched a group of young men dancing around a table piled with the holy books, dipping and bending and singing as they were led by their rabbi in joyous praise. They were American students, sons of modern Orthodox Jews, who had sent them to the homeland for a year of study. Their rabbi, another American, had immigrated to Jerusalem some twenty years earlier. "The Sabbath is always a time of joy and celebration," he explained to me later. "Some sects dance after every prayer. 'All of my bones shall recite, O Lord,' it says in our psalms. Even if most people aren't quite as demonstrative as we are, they still move their bodies in prayer. Look at the people by the Wall."

WESTERN WALL

Moors' Gate

Aqsa Mosque

Women's Mosque

I turned to gaze at the scene behind me. It was true. The people lining the base of the Wall—somber figures, all clad in black with hard black hats; young soldiers, their weapons slung over their arms; boys in jeans, grandfathers in suits and ties—all were vigorously leaning backward and forward, muttering earnest prayers, occasionally sticking petitionary notes in the cracks between the blocks of masonry.

"That rhythmic movement," the rabbi continued, "expresses a need to get closer, to feel physically connected to the temple. We are a soulful people, and the soul for us includes the body and extends to the whole community. We pray here as a community, not from a nostalgia for the past but out of a living vision of the future. That vision, I assure you," he smiled as he turned to rejoin his students, "will be realized. The temple will one day stand here again."

Roger Housden

Practicalities

Pilgrims pray at the Western Wall at any time of year, day or night, but the busiest times are on the Sabbath, beginning on Friday afternoon and continuing through Saturday. Large crowds celebrate the main Jewish festivals, such as Shavuot (May/June) and Yom Kippur (September/October). The dates of Jewish festivals vary each year, following the Hebrew lunar calendar. Following Orthodox Jewish tradition, men and women pray in separate enclosures. Pilgrims of both sexes should cover their legs and upper arms, and women should cover their heads.

The Wailing Wall

The Wall was renamed as the Western Wall in 1967, when the Moors' Quarter was demolished to create the large plaza in front of it.

Christian pilgrimages. By the time of the Madaba Map, a sixth-century mosaic in the church at Madaba, Jordan, that shows Roman Jerusalem, the rock-cut tomb of Christ had been totally separated from the hill out of which it was carved so that processions could walk all round it. Muslims on the *hajj* perform the *tawaf*, circling the Ka'ba seven times; the very name *hajj* derives probably from an old Semitic root meaning "to go around." As we saw in Chapter 4, the direction of circling is most often sunwise (clockwise). The *tawaf* is only performed counterclockwise because Muhammad deliberately changed the direction at the same time as he purged the Ka'ba of its idols, in order to dissociate it from the pagan ceremonial of pre-Islamic times.

> "Thou living Aton, the beginning of life!
> When thou art risen on the eastern horizon,
> Thou has filled every land with thy beauty....
> Thy rays encompass the lands to the limit of all that thou hast made....
>
> When thou settest in the western horizon,
> The land is in darkness, in the manner of death....
> Darkness is a shroud, and the earth is in stillness,
> For he who made them rests....
>
> Thou art in my heart...."
>
> From *The Hymn to the Aton*
> by Pharaoh Ahk-en-Aton
> (fourteenth century B.C.E.)

The sun plays a more direct role in the Japanese Shinto pilgrimage to Mount Fuji, sacred mountain and home of the sun-goddess Amaterasu Omikami. In the nineteenth century, worn-out straw sandals lined the routes to the top, cast off by the thousands of pilgrims who every summer climbed it. Albeit like other natural shrines in Japan it was forbidden to women until 1868, Fuji's summit remained the goal of devout followers of

Shinto up to the end of the Second World War. Today, even for foreign tourists and Japanese vacationers who have joined the pilgrims, the climax of the ascent remains the *goraiko* (watching the sunrise).

The "miracle of the sun"

The *goraiko* on Mount Fuji is a natural epiphany—the rising of the goddess—but the first-ray effect observed in the Easter Sepulcher at Chaource is an ancient piece of ritual stagecraft used in temples and at pilgrim shrines. Modern Druids gather at midsummer at Stonehenge, on Salisbury Plain, to watch the rising sun skim the top of the so-called Heel Stone. This stone cannot originally have been a midsummer sunrise marker because of the change in the inclination of Earth's axis. But, it has been argued that the axis of the trilithons (two upright stones with a third across the top) points to the first gleam of the midsummer sun in 2045 B.C.E. (the best radiocarbon date for their construction).

Perhaps the most dramatic manipulation of light is in the Egyptian temple of Abu Simbel in what was formerly Nubia. This cave, cut into a cliff by order of Ramses II in the thirteenth century B.C.E., was dedicated to the sun gods Amon-Ra and Re-Harmakhis (the rising sun), and the deified Pharaoh Ramses himself. The vast chamber in the heart of the mountain is 59 feet long and 55 feet wide, supported on two rows of columns, each 33 feet tall. About 215 feet from the entrance is the central sacred precinct, where Ramses sits in the role of sun

HOME DANCE OF THE HOPI

Bidding farewell to the spirits

The Great Painted Desert, Arizona—vast, serene, arid, is overhung by an expanse of summer sky so bright that the dark storm dragging its tail over a strangely shaped distant butte only serves to accent the brilliance.

Tomorrow is *Niman*, the Home Dance, when the Kachinas, I am told, go home to the San Francisco Peaks. This is an important dance; a chance to honor and say farewell to all the spirits that have served the people, the Hopi, during the past year. I sit on White Bear's front porch and watch the people arrive. They come from Flagstaff, Gallup, Winslow, even Phoenix—a long haul across the desert to honor the spirits and risk the thong of the Whipping Kachina or the mockery of the clowns. It's a tough journey. The road is dusty and hot. The seat across the width of each pickup truck is jammed full of men, women, and children with long black hair.

So far, the Fords have it. Chevrolets are close behind, then Dodges—great, solid, wind-blasted machines with big tires. At dusk, their lights, one after the other, reach back into the blueness of the sands. A long, straight ribbon of equally spaced twin lights are downshifted as they reach Second Mesa and turn up the gradient by Prophecy Rock—sounding their horns as they pass by the houses of relatives. Occasionally, White Bear says that's so-and-so, and he describes his relationship to them—from way back and to the side, bloodlines reaching through the web of truck lights and square, mesa-top homes.

This is a big pilgrimage. He's eighty-eight, and he says he's never seen so many people come. He says there will be more Kachinas dancing tomorrow than ever. He doesn't talk to me. He just talks into the space across the desert. Now, he talks of from where the people came. He says that the path of the people is a migration through the many worlds. A pickup honks by on the hill. He waves and says it's the family of a niece. All I can see is blackness, the ribbon of lights, and now the stars.

The people, the Hopi, have come through three previous worlds. When the last world was destroyed by flood, they were shown the path into this, the fourth world. "Soon," White Bear says, "it will be time to find the opening to the fifth." The Kachinas emerge from an opening on the top of the *kivas* (subterranean ceremonial chambers) to mark this progression. The path is shown by a line in the petroglyphs, the emergence points are spirals. Together they mark the good road to follow in life. Every year this path is retraced, redrawn in the corn pollen, told of in the stories, in the dances, so the people know from where they have come and to where they are going. "If they did not dance," White Bear says, "the rain would not come, the corn would not grow, the migration trail would not spiral up and on, the land and the people would die."

"Tomorrow," White Bear says, "the Kachinas go home." He indicates vaguely across the road.

I say, "I thought the Kachinas went to the San Francisco Peaks."

"Oh no. That's a story we tell the children. We come from over there."

His finger points upward, over the truck lights on the highway, over the silhouette of the houses on the mesas, into the night sky.

Nicholas R. Mann

god next to the triad of Amon-Ra, Harmakhis and Ptah in his Osirian Underworld aspect.

Nothing here was left to chance: The arrangement of the space was so precise that twice a year, around the vernal and autumnal equinoxes, the sun cast its rays through the entrance. A shaft of light moved down the hallway connecting the entrance to the sanctuary and gradually lit first the left shoulder of Amon-Ra, then a few moments later, after touching Ramses, fell on Harmakhis. After twenty minutes, the light disappears. It never touches Ptah, lord of the shadows.

This illumination of the statues took place in February/March and in October; on February 20 and October 20 the sun is exactly on the central axis of the temple. And, October 20 was the date of Ramses' first jubilee, in the thirtieth year of his reign, and which probably led to the building of the temple. Perhaps just as remarkable as this ancient engineering is the fact that, when the temple at Abu Simbel was dismantled to save it from the rising waters of Lake Nasser in the 1960s, and recreated on higher land, the precise sacred geometry was preserved, and the miracle of the sunlight repeated itself in February 1969.

The power of myth

For outsiders to a pilgrimage tradition, even being in the right place at the right time performing the right actions may not be enough to generate a transformative experience. But, we may "get it" through myth. Understanding the mythological background unlocks hidden meanings that are part of the cultural heritage of the faithful—indeed, they permeate a whole society in often unsuspected ways. In the West, we do not usually think of ourselves as having a mythology, but consider how a Christian myth can transfigure our experience of pilgrimage at Easter, to Jerusalem, and Christ's tomb. This is one of the most important descents I mentioned among patterns of pilgrimage: the reenactment of the descent of Christ into death at the cave tomb.

"Praise be to Thee, my Lord, with all Thy creatures,
Especially to my worshipful brother sun,
The which lights up the day,
and through him dost Thou brightness give;
And beautiful is he and radiant with splendour
    great...

Praised be my Lord for brother fire,
By the which Thou lightest up the dark,
And fair is he and gay and mighty and strong..."
                Francis of Assisi (1181–1226),
                    "The Canticle of the Sun"

"Can there be any day but this,
Though many suns to shine endeavour?
We count three hundred, but we miss:
There is but one, and that one ever."
        George Herbert (1593–1633), "Easter"

In the West, we sometimes underplay the Christ whose greatest festival was not Christmas but Easter, and we increasingly secularize Good Friday. "He descended into hell; The third day he rose again from the dead, He ascended into heaven," says the Creed in the *Book of Common Prayer*, describing the interval between Crucifixion and Resurrection, between Good Friday and Easter Sunday. That lost day has been accounted for by the Church of Latter Day Saints by the belief that in that interval Christ preached in the Western Hemisphere. Medieval Christians filled in that time with the Harrowing of Hell, a story of a power and grandeur to match any in world mythology.

197

According to the apocryphal *Gospel of Nicodemus,* compiled in the fifth century C.E., Christ descended into Hell and harrowed (despoiled) it by releasing its captives. The souls of the dead were in the eternal night of the Underworld, when at midnight there came a light brighter than the sun and a voice like thunder demanded in the words of Psalm 24: "Lift up your heads, O ye gates, and be ye lift up, ye everlasting doors; and the King of glory shall come in." Hell (in the Anglo-Saxon version of the gospel much resembling Hél, queen goddess of the Old Norse Underworld), skulking in the darkness, asks: "Who is this King of glory?" And the answer comes: "The Lord...mighty in battle." Then, the gates of Hell are broken, the dead loosed from their chains, and the victorious Christ, bearing the Vexillum (the banner he holds in Christian art as a symbol of his Resurrection), strides into Hell, his radiance lighting up its farthest and darkest place. Trampling Death underfoot, he binds Satan and leads our forefather Adam out of Hell, together with the righteous who had lived before his Incarnation, and into Paradise.

> "I have come to set fire to the earth."
>
> Luke 12:49

This tremendous myth dramatizes the doctrine that Christ died to redeem all humankind, from the very beginning of time to its end. It is the subtext of the Holy Fire ceremony enacted in the Holy Sepulcher in Jerusalem, part of the Orthodox Easter celebrations. Abbot Daniel, a Russian pilgrim who visited Jerusalem in the twelfth century, tells how "the grace of God comes down unseen from heaven and lights the lamps in the Sepulcher of the Lord." To this day, this mystery is played out at the tomb. One of the clergy goes alone into the empty tomb. Its door is sealed, and all lights in every part of the church are put out. An hour or so later, hundreds of pilgrims waiting silently in the packed church see fire magically passing out from the tomb to kindle torches held by two deacons, who rush off with them to local churches. At the same time, fire leaps from candle to candle in the pilgrims' hands, and suddenly, the whole church is lit into its farthest and darkest corners, just as in the myth.

In Orthodox churches, Easter is generally celebrated with a ceremony of lights, in which the Holy Door (which in the Eastern Church, closes off the sanctuary and altar and represents both the Gate of Heaven and the Jaws of Death), is thrown open at the moment of Resurrection. After a candlelit procession outside the church, the priest censes its main doors, singing: "Christ is risen from the dead, trampling down death by death, and bestowing life upon those in the tomb....We celebrate the death of death, the annihilation of Hades, the beginning of a life new and eternal."

In the Western Church, a similar ceremony of lights began at midnight between Holy Saturday and Easter Sunday. By the time it ended, it would be close to dawn, and the rising sun was greeted by bells ringing as a priest began the first Mass of Easter. These rites celebrating the light of Christ penetrating the tomb (Hell) and subduing Death are entwined with the identification of Christ with the sun, encoded in English in the wordplay between "risen sun" and "risen Son."

It is echoed, too, in the beautiful folk belief that on Easter Day the sun danced as it rose, in honor of the Resurrection. Although Sir Thomas Browne wrote in *Vulgar Errors* (1646): "We shall not, I hope, disparage the resurrection of our

Redeemer, if we say that the sun does not dance on Easter-day," well into the nineteenth century people in England and Wales rose early in the morning on Easter Day in order to see it. Many believed they did see this natural epiphany. The Rector of Ross-on-Wye, the Rev. R. H. Cobbold, wrote in 1879: "In the district called Hockley…a woman whose maiden name was Evans, wife of Rowland Lloyd, a laborer, said she had heard of the thing but did not believe it true, 'till,' she said, 'on Easter morning last, I got up early, and then I saw the sun dance, and dance, and dance, three times, and I called to my husband and said, Rowland, Rowland, get up and see the sun dance!'"

CHAPTER 11

Reflection and Redirection

*T*hat was the journey *to*. There is still the journey *from*.

Whether you undertook your pilgrimage for its own sake or as an act of devotion or for a particular benefit, whether or not you encountered the divine in quite the way you had hoped, you have come far and now must go farther.

You may feel euphoric, or perhaps, mentally and physically drained. Either way, this is a time for reflection. If you have kept a diary, do look it over. Do talk to other pilgrims. Do ask about the expectations they had and how the actuality matched. Do listen if they try to describe their spiritual experience.

Don't go to sleep on your feet. Don't see this as the end of your journey, the aftermath, that frightful time for a child when Christmas is over and the next birthday a long way off.

There are more presents. They include a fuller understanding of where you have been and what you have seen. The most important part of the journey for you may be yet to come.

Sacred geography has great allure on paper and in the imagination, but when you finally arrived at your sacred site, and took part in or witnessed your sacred event, you may have experienced a great range of reactions.

"They set this idol [Juggernaut—Lord Jagannatha at Puri, India] with great reverence in a chariot... and lead it about the city with great solemnity. In front of the chariot there go first in procession the maidens of that land, two by two; and then all the pilgrims that have come from far countries, some of whom out of great devotion to that idol fall down in front of the chariot and let it roll over them. And so some of them are slain, some have their arms and legs broken; and they believe that the more pain they suffer here for the love of that idol, the more joy they will have in the other world..."

The Travels of Sir John Mandeville,
(fourteenth century)

Distaste, disappointment, disillusion

As discussed in Chapter 7, pilgrimages often involve beliefs and observances that would be condemned as heretical if they appeared in your local mosque, synagogue, church, or temple. In particular, they tend to be more tolerant of ecstatic experience. Watching the absorbed and remote faces of the Dervish Dancers of the Order of the Mevlevi, from Konya, Turkey, as they whirl on their axes like celestial bodies is one thing. But, if your sacred journey has taken you somewhere exotic, this may have been the first time you have seen sadomasochistic penances being performed in the streets or witnessed people going into a trance or in the possession of a spirit, rolling their eyes, yapping, howling. You may have felt anything from terrified through appalled to embarassed or—like Margery Kempe's fellow pilgrims every time she created a hysterical scene in the Holy Land—angry at being distracted from your own purposes.

There is often some distance between the idea we hold of a religion and the actuality we encounter. More than one person has gone to India hoping to find a spiritual path in the contemplative disciplines taught in some ashram, only to turn tail on confronting the real-world experience of most Indians. They would agree with Shirley Park Lowry, who in *Familiar Mysteries* (1982), writes: "Most members of 'contemplative' Eastern societies are really too poor, sick and uneducated to know and enjoy the benefits of contemplation. These millions have no choice but to shuffle resignedly from day to day, their greatest hope not a better life but a final release from life."

"Seen on close approach, the mountain of Fuji does not come up to expectations."

Japanese proverb

Again, in Buddhist holy places, we may have seen pilgrims stopping during their circumambulation of the shrine to listen to monks telling stories from Buddhist history and legend. That Buddhists generally visit sacred sites for teaching as well as merit, being concerned more with hearing the sacred word and less with encountering the divine, fulfills Western expectations of the calm detachment of Buddhism. Yet, if we have been to Sri Lanka and joined Buddhist pilgrims to Kataragama, we have seen them behave more like ecstatics, occupied not with knowledge but with direct experience.

There is often also a distance between our idea of a place and what we find on the ground—in some cases literally. That nineteenth-century lover of Japan, Lafcadio Hearn, on close inspection found Mount Fuji to be "a frightful extinct heap of visible ashes and cinders and slaggy lava." The discrepancy

WAR GRAVES OF THE SOMME

"They shall grow not old…"

I was named Colin after Second Lieutenant Colin Graham Sutherland Shields, Royal Air Force. Had he lived he would have been my uncle. But he was posted, "missing, presumed dead" on May, 10 1918, while flying over the Somme. His body was identified after the Great War ended, and he is buried in a British war cemetery at Cerisy-Gailly, halfway between Amiens and Peronne, France. He was nineteen.

Twenty-eight years later, at the end of the Second World War, I was a Captain and company commander in the Lovat Scouts, on active service in Greece. The Lovat Scouts recruit in the farthermost parts of the Highlands and Islands of Scotland, but I was even farther from home than most of the men in my company, as my home was in Argentina. I was nineteen.

Years later, I inherited a few surviving mementos: a cup Colin won for the 100-yard race at school, a framed picture of him as a cadet in London Scottish uniform, a dress version of his pilot's wings, and his last letter home—to his younger sister Barbara. It was not much to show for a human life, even such a short one. He was an only son.

This reminder of my namesake's brief life led to my attending the annual Remembrance Day service at the war memorial in Beaconsfield, Buckinghamshire, where he was born. C. G. S. Shields is one of eighty names, arranged neatly in groups of ten, of those who died in the 1914–18 war. An addition lists another sixty names of Beaconsfield men who died in the Second World War, 1939–45.

It is now more than eighty years since the Great War ended—at the eleventh hour of the eleventh month of 1918—and throughout Britain, simple services of remembrance are still held at war memorials in most villages and towns on the nearest Sunday.

I became interested in war memorials and in what they represent. I began studying them throughout the British Isles, not only those on the village greens and in market squares or those on Scottish hillsides or in country church-yards, but also the memorial plaques inside churches, on the walls of schools and banks, in clubs and factories—anywhere in which people felt there was a need to remember those who had lost their lives serving their country in war.

Until very recently, it was British practice to bury the war dead where they fell and not to repatriate the bodies. The Commonwealth War Graves Commission (CWGC) is responsible for more than 23,000 burial grounds in 140 countries throughout the world. The burial grounds house anything from a few bodies in a foreign churchyard to vast CWGC cemeteries in the places where major battles were fought: Ypres and the Somme and the Dardanelles and Palestine for the Great War; and Normandy and the Low Countries and Libya, Italy, Burma, and the Pacific for the Second World War.

There are also the awe-inspiring monuments to the missing listing all those with "no known grave": more than 73,400 names at Thiepval on the Somme and nearly 55,000 on the Menin Gate at Ypres.

The thought of this kind of oblivion, of nonexistence, must haunt everyone from time to time. Coupled with it is the guilt of the survivor, who is reminded regularly of those who perished—be it on the battlefield, in an airline crash, or in a sports stadium disaster—while he or she did not.

I resolved to make a pilgrimage to my uncle Colin's final resting place at Cerisy, Gailly: Plot 2, Row A, Grave 2. A few years ago, I joined a summer battlefield tour with many others who, like myself, had a relative or fellow townsperson, who had died in that First World War.

Laying a wreath of poppies, emblem of the battlefields of Flanders, on Colin's grave was for me a most meaningful moment. It was strangely cathartic, forgiving. As one of the oldest pilgrims present, I was later invited to stand by the Cross of Sacrifice in another cemetery on the Somme and read the words from Laurence Binyon's poem, in this instance in remembrance of a soldier even younger than Colin:

" They shall grow not old, as we that are left grow old:
Age shall not weary them, nor the years condemn.
At the going down of the sun and in the morning
We will remember them."

Colin McIntyre

Battlefield pilgrimages
Since the end of the First World War, many thousands of pilgrims have joined tours of the battlefields of France and Flanders or made personal pilgrimages to graves of relatives or colleagues. Today, such pilgrimages embrace both world wars and many other conflicts worldwide.

between idea and reality today has taken on a familiar form: Although officially open for only two months of the year because of its snows, Fuji is now climbed by hundreds of thousands of people and the marks of their passing add a false note to the pilgrims' traditional chant of "Be pure....O ye mountain!"

One of the worst shocks of pilgrimage comes from the commercialized, even downright materialistic, nature of some sacred sites. It is a fine line for local populations and institutions to tread between reaping a just reward for providing support systems for pilgrims and going just too far. This can be a particular problem for developing countries with an emerging capitalism; sometimes commercialization kills the goose that laid the golden egg. In the early 1970s, a Catholic shrine in the small village of Devagama, India, suddenly became popular. Its decline after 1975 appears to be because pilgrims were being put off by the degree of commercial exploitation. Sometimes, we seem not to recognize it on our own doorstep—in England, for example, Glastonbury has become a New Age bazaar in my lifetime—but resent it in cultures we perceive as more "spiritual." In the *Rough Guide* TV travel series, several Westerners on the modern Indian "hippy trail" leading to a holy lake at Pushkar, Rajasthan, complained that they were charged to go to the lake. Such public criticisms of how the local people run their *locus sanctus* could lead to the closing of this holy lake to all but Hindus.

Other shocks come from first encounters with relics. You can read differences in attitude toward them in the faces of visitors to the Basilica of St. Claire in Assisi, Italy, as they file past her glass-sided coffin and view her body, turned to leather by time. Some look steadily with reverence, others quickly avert their gaze, evidently judging the display of mortal remains as morbid.

You may have seen some truly vulgar sights within and without the place of the holy: garish colors, crude painting and carving, idiot gods and simpering

"...how canst thou say to thy brother, Brother, let me pull out the mote that is in thine eye, when thou thyself beholdest not the beam that is in thine own eye?"

Luke 6:42

saints. Religious kitsch seems to abound in most cultures, even in ones we judge to be highly aesthetic, such as the Japanese. Westerners are normally most offended by artifacts which do not have the glamor either of exoticism or folk art, such as the mass-produced plastic souvenirs of Christian pilgrimage. You may well see objects even more tasteless than one I saw in France, at Les Saintes-Maries-de-la-Mer—Christ crucified on four clamshells.

Some holy places dumbfound by the inappropriateness of what we see to the sacred history. When I first went to Assisi, I felt physically assaulted by what had been done there in the name of Saint Francis. The touching relics of the man himself—the coarse gray tunic and clumsy heelless shoes preserved in his basilica—were eclipsed by things that seemed to me contrary to his spirit. Chief offender was that church of monstrous vulgarity, Santa Maria degli Angeli (Saint Mary of the Angels), built over the Porziuncola, the tiny chapel given to Francis in 1208 that became the birthplace of the Franciscan Order. How could someone build this florid thing on the spot where Francis himself, returning from the Crusades to find that his friars had replaced their normal shelters of branches with a tiny brick

ARUNACHALA

Bangalore ●
Madras ●

ARUNACHALA
★ Tiruvannamalai

SOUTH INDIA

Into the heart of a sacred mountain

Ramana Maharshi was one of the great Indian saints of the twentieth century. The only words he ever wrote were love poems to Arunachala Mountain. "Arunachala," he said, "was the physical embodiment of Lord Shiva himself." Why go anywhere else? Arunachala, in Tamil Nadu, south India, has been identified with Shiva for centuries. Of all the mountains on the subcontinent, including the Himalayas far to the north, Arunachala is the only one that has a living tradition of the sacred mountain. Tamils revere it as the hill that survives the primordial flood from age to age.

I didn't know of the sacred mountain's reputation when I first arrived in Tiruvannamalai, the town which spreads out at its base. I had come to visit the ashram of Ramana Maharshi. The mountain, though, was the first thing I saw as I drew near to the town. The surrounding area is a large, flat plain, which extends through much of Tamil Nadu. Arunachala looms up from this plain, a solitary pyramid, some two-and-a-half thousand feet high. It was purple and gold in the dusty light, and it drew me like a magnet.

I decided to explore the hill before I did anything else. I climbed up the path from the town, and in twenty minutes, I had arrived at Veerupaksha Cave, where Ramana Maharshi lived for sixteen years in silence and solitude. In the tranquil courtyard outside the cave entrance, a single breadfruit tree shaded a tiny lingam set in a circle of water. Someone had left a red rose on the lingam head and the petals of a yellow chrysanthemum were scattered round it in the water.

Three pairs of shoes were by the tree. I left my own shoes alongside them and passed through into the darkness. Three people were sitting motionless in front of a stone ledge. The air was hot and thick. What a relief to be in darkness after the glare of the sun. I was there for an hour or more when out of nowhere a voice suddenly rang through the quiet of my body. "Just rest," it said. "Just rest." I let the dark cave take me then, hold me; and in that moment it was as if the mountain moved through me. It was then that I felt Arunachala to be truly alive. It was as if the life of the mountain, the cave, and my own innermost being, were one and the same thing.

To climb the hill, to enter the hill through one of its caves, and to circle the hill are some of the ways of honoring the power of this ancient sacred place. The circular walk takes about three hours, and hundreds of people make the walk barefoot every day just before dawn. There have been many reports through the years of visions of Lord Shiva and his consort, Parvati.

The store owner who had served me tea the evening before showed me another way of revering the mountain. I was passing his house when he stepped in front of me and prostrated to a roadside figure of Ganesh, the Remover of Obstacles. Then, he stood up and faced the mountain, his palms together in front of his heart, gazing with devotion. He turned in a circle on the spot, and facing Arunachala, bowed, and made off for his tea shop.

Roger Housden

> When I came to realise who I am,
> What else is this identity of mine?
> But thee,
> Oh thou who standest as the towering Aruna Hill?
> *Sri Ramana Maharshi—Stanzas to Arunachala*

Deepam Festival

Hundreds of thousands of devotees celebrate this festival in November/December. A ten-day reenactment of the story of Arunachala culminates in a climb to the top of the mountain, where a flame is lit to symbolize Shiva's manifestation at the mountain's creation.

convent, tore off its roof tiles with his bare hands? This was not Francis's idea of how to imitate the life of Christ. And, Santa Maria degli Angeli was not my idea of how to honor Francis of Assisi.

You may feel impatient (or guilty because you feel impatient) with the credulity and naivety of other pilgrims. During the great Mexican fiesta of the Three Kings at Tizimin in Yucatan, which lasts 18 days from December 31 to January 17, and when trainloads of pilgrims leave Merida Central Railroad Station at short intervals every day, motorists from as far away as Mexico City drive their cars to be blessed at the shrine. As far as they are concerned, the Three Kings who came from afar, being themselves great travelers, know the hazards of travel, and therefore, afford the best protection.

> "Open thou my eyes, that I may behold wondrous things..."
>
> Psalm 119:18

There is a moral in all of this. Iranian Muslims tell the story of Iskandr (Alexander the Great) and the Kaf. The Kaf is a mountain that encircles the Earth, which is conceived of as a plane or disc. It is a mountain so high that a space equal only to the height of a man remains between its peaks and heaven. Made of emerald, the green of the land and blue of the sky are its reflections. There is another world on the far side of the Kaf: Some say it is the home of the *jinns* and *peris* (demons and fairies), but others that there lives the race of Yájúj and Májúj (Gog and Magog in the Bible), who would have broken through to this side long ago if Iskandr had not built walls against them.

When Iskandr had conquered the world, he went to see the Kaf. He sent a slave up the mountain who, when he got to the top, saw another slave just like himself coming up the other side. So Iskandr sent a second slave, and a third, and a fourth, and every time another slave exactly like him came from the other side. Finally, Iskandr himself ascended the Kaf and looked over, and behold, another Iskandr looked back. Iskandr, who had thought he was master of all, now knew that there were other worlds and other conquerors and died of disappointment.

"'Hey! What's this? I don't understand,' said Pigsy. 'You've just made the other two into Buddhas. Why aren't I a Buddha too?'

'Because,' said Buddha, 'your conversation and appearance still lack refinement, and your appetite is still too large. But...it will be your job to clean up the altar everywhere and whenever there is a Buddhist ceremony and offerings are made. So you'll get plenty of pickings. I don't see what you've got to complain of!'"

Wu Ch'êng-ê n (c. 1505–80), *Monkey*

But the Kaf is no less wonderful and mysterious and miraculous a place because Iskandr has come face to face with himself and lost his illusions.

Looking with better eyes

So our built-in expectations of our sacred journey may have been disappointed. Although unlike medieval pilgrims we have not been expected to sleep many people and both sexes to a bed, we have traveled here perhaps fairly uncomfortably, only to be pestered by hawkers, distressed by beggars, and oppressed by art and architecture that falls short of sublimity.

On top of all of this, we may feel we missed our moment of revelation. Look again. In the Bible, the prophet Isaiah describes the day of the Lord's vengeance: "And thorns shall come up in her palaces, nettles and brambles in the fortress thereof: and it shall be an habitation for dragons, and a court for owls" (Isa 34:13). When I was a child, I could never see why this was supposed to be a curse. Dragons and owls seemed infinitely desirable. It is a matter of perspective. In James Cameron's film *The Abyss* (1989) about alien encounter Lindsay (Mary Elizabeth Mastrantonio) puts it exactly: "You have to look with better eyes than this." We sometimes have to look with better eyes to see what we have seen.

Reconsider your journey. The world is made not only of ideas but also of things, and the world of the sacred is a physical, sensual place, of landscapes, buildings, gardens, graveyards and cemeteries, paintings, sculptures, garments, and objects from bells to begging bowls. All these things have been your windows on the sacred.

In Japan, you have seen arches connecting nothing and in the middle of nowhere, standing in deep forests, beside great trees, on mountain peaks, on riverbanks and seashores. You now recognize them as Shinto *torii*, or shrine gates, indicating that what lies beyond is holy ground. Near the *torii* you have seen the font where before entering the shrine visitors rinse their hands and mouths with water, in a symbolic purification of body and mind. You have learned much about Shinto already.

Not far from Cuzco in Peru, you have met some of the remaining native speakers of Quechua on pilgrimage to a distant shrine. They are going there to venerate not a statue in a cathedral but a traditional image on a rock or crag. Although the rites will be Christian, conducted by a Christian priest, the image tells you that the shrine probably stands on a sacred site dedicated to one of the *apus*. These are the nature spirits who share this landscape, apparently on easy terms, with Christ and Mary and the village patron saints. Whether nature spirit or Mary, the miraculous power these pilgrims seek is vested not in the shrine's relics, as in the European tradition, but in the image itself.

All over the world, continuity of sacred place has built up layers of meaning. The Roman author Varro (116–127 B.C.E.) recounts that before the temple of Jupiter, Juno, and Minerva was constructed on the Roman Capitol, the site had been occupied by the ancient deity Terminus, a boundary stone, who stolidly refused to make room for the new building, and therefore, had to be accommodated inside. At Daphne, near Antioch, the oracle of Apollo ceased to speak when on to its very site Christians introduced the cult of the martyr Babylas. At the conquest of the New World by Spain, Christian shrines were built on sites where pre-Columbian deities were worshiped. Sometimes practices seem to have carried over, too, but now is a good time to abandon any notion of "pagan survivals": The movement is not all one way.

What we see at pilgrimage sites is creative religion: religion with some of the boundaries down answering the demands of human aspiration and human suffering. In India, Hindus are often among pilgrims at the shrines of *pirs* (Islamic Sufi saints), whether these be humble grave sites in small villages or great pilgrimage places, such as Fateh Pur Sikri in Uttar Pradesh. The Muslim saints usually have high reputations for healing. Surinder Bhardwaj, writing in the *National Geographic Journal of India* some years ago, recalled that as a child, he had been taken to a living Muslim holy man for healing and that in his own mainly Hindu village there was a small grave site of a Muslim *pir* at which people used to light earthen lamps on Thursdays to pray for good health and even success in school examinations.

On pilgrimage, the clue to what is happening in people's hearts and minds is often in what we see. That pilgrims offer artificial limbs made from silver or gold to Haji Malang for the relief of bodily pain is the explanation of why the timing of the Haja Malanga fair at Wadi in Kalyan Taluka, India, should be according to the Hindu calendar, although Haji Malang was a Muslim saint. It also explains why prayers at the shrine should be offered five times a day, following Muslim practice, but the priest be Brahmin.

We learn from these offerings of golden arms and feet that the desire to end suffering can temporarily transcend religious difference.

Redirection

Through our pilgrimage we have begun to reach beyond the urgency of our own desires to the wider dimension of the divine seen in the light of human history. We have touched hands across space with pilgrims on other roads, looking, like us, for their glimpse of the divine and cast our gaze backward down the steeps of time to see how those tens of thousands on our road before us went about their search.

Now when we see pilgrims in Asia or the Middle East or Europe sleeping near or touching the shrines of saints, we remember the Old Testament account of the grave of the prophet Elisha (2 Kings 13:21): "And...when the man was let down, and touched the bones of Elisha, he revived, and stood up on his feet." When we see Muslims newly returned from the *hajj* with snippets from the great cloth that covers the *Ka'ba*—necessarily renewed every year, as a gift from Egypt; when we see Christian pilgrims touching pieces of cloth to images and reliquaries; even when we see pieces of rags hung round holy wells in Britain and Ireland, we remember the New Testament story of Paul in Ephesus (Acts 19:11–12): "And God wrought special miracles by the hands of Paul: So that from his body were brought unto the sick handkerchiefs or aprons, and the diseases departed from them, and the evil spirits went out of them."

"We are always in the presence of mysticism when we find a human being...feeling himself, while still externally amid the earthly and temporal, to belong to the super-earthly and eternal."

Albert Schweitzer, *The Mysticism of Paul the Apostle* (1930)

What do I think now of that vast basilica at Assisi? Well, I see it as the result of several centuries of Italian Catholicism, during which the intention of honoring—and accessing the spiritual power of—St. Francis has found different ways of expressing itself. I have learned not to fret about Santa Maria degli Angeli but instead to dwell on memories of Francis's rock-hewn hermitage of the Carceri and Claire's austere convent of San Damiano. I see the town as a whole as the living expression of dynamic faith, not as a time-frozen fossil.

We turn homeward, but the road home is not the road by which we came: It is a different road, for we are different. We have become pilgrims, and we have been changed by our experiences. Never in our lives shall we be the same again. What we do with that new person is something to consider.

But still another step on our journey awaits us, and that is to begin to see what we do on pilgrimage in the light of eternity.

CHAPTER 12

Coming Home

*I*f a man, says Sir John Mandeville, set out from home on a journey and kept right on going, he would come back to his own front door.

Although no one would want this medieval pseudogeographer as a guide, for pilgrimage this is not a bad model. It is when you arrive home, when you come full circle, that you perceive the "truth" of your journey. Although the sacred place is the source of spiritual power, it is at home that the effects of this power on you become visible. Your reentry into everyday life is the test of your pilgrimage.

Will unpacking your mental baggage confirm that there has been transformation? That you are different? That your life has been changed?

How do the people at home see this new person, this pilgrim? Was your experience just for you, or will it enrich lives that touch your life?

And when they ask how this change came about, where will you say that you have been?

What is the "truth" of our journey? The British traveler Freya Stark (1893–1993) once said that when she announced that she was setting out on one of her journeys, everyone asked her why. No one accepted as a reasonable answer that she was going simply to look.

We have been to a sacred place to look, and we do not need to justify our journey or worry too much about how we should benefit from it. By the very fact of going on pilgrimage, we have exposed ourselves to the process of revelation and, if we let it, it will work out largely to its own ends.

> "This is my play's last scene,
> here heavens appoint
> My pilgrimage's last mile."
> John Donne (1572–1631),
> *Holy Sonnets*, No. 1

Our journey toward the sacred has been awakening and humanizing and has perhaps added a heroic dimension to our lives.

Awakening

If we have been abroad, we have experienced culture shock, our removal to another setting bringing about shifts in perspective. We may have discovered how completely unfounded were our beliefs concerning other people and gained a greater understanding of how they see life, the world, and God.

Coming home, like expatriates returning to their home country we experience culture shock in reverse. Because of the intensity of the pilgrimage experience, a shift in perceptions can take place after only quite a short exposure to a different world.

Descriptions of mystical experience, saints' legends, and folk traditions concerning fairies, all speak of the way in which, during encounters with the Other, time runs at a different speed. On the hillside above the ancient abbey of Lleyre in Spain is

Saint Virilar's Spring. Legend says that Virilar, hearing a nightingale, followed it up the slope to the spring and stayed there spellbound until it had finished singing.

When he returned to the abbey, he found that the buildings had changed and that the porter at the gate was a stranger. Three hundred years had passed.

This also describes quite well what happens on a sacred journey. Like Virilar, when we return home we find that familiar scenes and faces look strange. We are seeing them with new eyes, receiving revelations about things we normally take for granted. The awakening may be wonderful or painful—it is always enlarging.

Humanizing

Many of us went to a holy place seeking salvation in one form or another—although not as explicitly, perhaps, as a Hindu journeying to Benares to avoid rebirth. Many will have sought some solution to an earthly problem, especially the three *p*'s: powerlessness, poverty, pain. There we have seen others similarly engaged.

Paradoxically, one of the benefits we bring back from pilgrimage is more pain. We may return raw from the encounter with suffering humanity, our normal defenses against others' unhappiness down. We have seen the search for salvation in individual faces, heard it in voices. We may have become aware that there is little or no direct action that we, as individuals, can take.

We heard earlier of the feelings experienced by a Brahmin pilgrim at the realization that, back home, there could be little

A journey of healing and renewal

Over the past thirty years I have made the pilgrimage to St. Winifred's Well many dozens of times—a benefit of having an ancient sanctuary virtually on one's doorstep. This familiarity has occasioned an ever-deepening awareness, not just of its intrinsic beauty, its extraordinary history, and the nuances of its sacred past, but also of its present potency for renewal and restoration to physical and psychic wholeness. This numinous place, silent except for the murmurings of the water, is alive with power.

A constant current of whispered prayer activates, as it were, the "mandala" of the star-shaped Well, and one senses what this place has meant to the thousands of pilgrims who have scratched or carved names or initials on to its walls and pillars over nearly 500 years. Each name represents a cure or favor obtained or at least devoutly hoped for.

But the Well is most alive, and the presence of its celestial patroness most easily accessible, during the stillness of a solitary pilgrimage, when its powerful present confronts and confirms its powerful past.

One of my pilgrimages requires a special telling. By 1982, I had been suffering from osteoarthritis for several years, unable to walk without a stick. That year, acting on impulse, I went to the Well on November 3, the feast of St. Winifred. Painfully, and very slowly, I walked the last mile. I don't remember praying, or even thinking: Every bit of me was concentrated simply on making it to the Well. It took me about an hour and a half, and it was the longest distance I had walked in years.

There is a time-honored ritual way of bathing at the holy Well. The present shrine, which was erected around 1505 under royal patronage, is two-storied: a large chapel over a crypt. Graceful pillars surround a star-shaped basin at the center of the crypt, and from here, the spring rises. Its stingingly cold water flows into an adjacent bath to a depth of about 4 feet. The pilgrim passes through the bath three times, and three times circles the source, saying a decade of the rosary and finishing the prayers kneeling on a stone in the larger pool outside the chapel. On that day, I simply bathed, said a prayer, lit a candle, and went home. My pilgrimage had been an act of devotion rather than a specific plea for healing. Yet within two months, I found myself cured, and permanently.

The pilgrim's road

St. Winifred's shrine is in the town of Holywell (Treffynnon in Welsh), North Wales. The most evocative approach is on foot, up through the woods from the ruined Basingwerk Abbey one mile to the north at Greenfield: this route follows the last stage of a medieval pilgrims' road.

Practicalities

This Catholic shrine is open all year round and welcomes pilgrims of any faith. Between Pentecost and September 30, a service including veneration of St. Winifred's relic is held at the Well daily at 11:30 A.M. (Sundays 2:30 P.M.). The Pilgrims' Hospice in Holywell is open throughout the year.

The Annual National Pilgrimage is on the Sunday following June 22, when there is a procession through the town to mass at the Well. There is also an annual Pan-Orthodox pilgrimage on the first Saturday in October.

Nor was my cure simply physical: My inner, spiritual life was renewed. If I had not prayed as I bathed, I certainly prayed after my cure and with certainty. St. Winifred's Well appeared, according to legend, at the site of her martyrdom; at the same place she was brought back to life. These events have made the Well a place of continuous devotion and healing for thirteen centuries. In a sense, Winifred and I shared a common experience. My cure gave me a kind of jolt of recognition. From that time, Winifred became for me, not a dead saint—however prayerfully powerful—but a living woman. She and I, I feel, are friends.

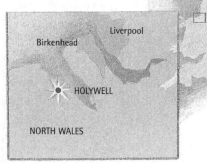

Over the years, I have taken many people to visit the shrine at St. Winifred's Well. One of these, twelve years ago, was my partner; and he came to share my love and respect for the shrine, although he only came to understand it fully at the end. When he died last year, we buried him high on the hillside above the Well and then went to the Well to light candles and to remember him. Home, they say, is where the heart is; and now that I, too, am dying of the same disease, I am very aware that I will follow and rejoin him soon, in like manner. And this, my last pilgrimage, will also be, in a real sense, a coming home.

Tristan Gray Hulse

place in her life for the lower caste women she had traveled with. If, once we are back in the everyday, we want to keep our vision for ourselves, for humanity, or for our planet as clear and bright as it was during our journey, we allow the humanizing memory of pain to work in and through us. Eventually, it will bring about change.

The heroic dimension

Whether we want political or sexual equality, resources enough to feed the world, respect for other life forms, world peace, or planetary healing, the transformation of the world around us will be the result of personal transformation.

One of the terms the Qur'an uses for general sinfulness is *dalal*, aimless wandering, as opposed to the purposeful path of pilgrimage through life. As well as undertaking a pilgrimage that will subconsciously affect the rest of our lives, we can choose consciously to see the whole of our lives as a sacred journey.

Remember King Alfred. His father, King Aethelwulf, had vowed to make a pilgrimage to Rome on behalf of his people. In the event, he sent as his substitute his youngest son, Alfred, then only four years old. The impact of the Eternal City, with its brick and stone buildings and gorgeous processions, on a child from what was by comparison a backwoods, must have been dazzling. There is little doubt that this visit to Rome, and another at age six, were formative experiences, coloring Alfred's entire life and giving him his guiding purpose of creating a Christian civilization in England.

Alfred saw himself as a pilgrim. He speaks of his life as a journey, hoping that God will "enlighten the eyes of my mind

so that I can find out the straight road to the eternal home…"
He also tried to live as a hero, whose achievements would be
remembered long after his
death.

> "It is through the centre…that the
> Holy Spirit enlightens the mind, fires
> the heart, makes firm the will. It is the
> focus of God's action, the sanctuary
> where he dwells."
>
> C. R. Bryant,
> *The Psychology of Prayer*

All pilgrims are heroes: pilgrimage is in itself an heroic
act. The decision to find out
the straight road through life is
a noble decision.

Who are we?

When our families and friends welcome us home again,
what do they see? In one sense, nothing special: just one among
the millions who every year take to the road or the train or the airplane on a sacred journey. Pilgrims need a
proper humility. The Japanese poet
Basho, embarking on a pilgrimage in 1688, recorded in *The
Records of a Travel-Worn
Satchel* that his friends gave
him a good send-off, providing
him with necessities for his
journey—a paper raincoat,
warm winter stockings—and also
threw farewell parties and feasts. He
says, with self-mockery: "I…almost fell a vic-
tim to the illusion that a man of importance was leaving on a
journey."

> "It is a great thing to
> know in our heart that
> God…indwells our soul. Even greater
> is it to know that our soul…dwells in
> the substance of God…we are
> enfolded by him…and he by us."
>
> Julian of Norwich,
> *Revelations of Divine Love*
> (c. 1393)

But in another sense, each pilgrim is very special indeed. We do not just "happen" to go on pilgrimage.

The Persian Sufi poet Rumi (1207–1273) tells the story of a man who always prayed earnestly and most devoutly, late into the night. One night, when he was beginning to tire, Satan put into his mind the question: "For all your calling out 'O God!' have you ever heard God reply 'Here I am'?"

> "Let not your spirit be troubled on account of the times;
> For the Holy and Great One has appointed days for all things...
> He will be gracious to the righteous and give him eternal uprightness...
> And he shall walk in eternal light."
>
> *The Book of Enoch* (first century B.C.E.)
> R. H. Charles, trans.

The man admitted he had never heard even a whisper. Then, God sent a messenger to tell him that all the fear and love he had been pouring into his prayer had been God's gift to him in the first place. "Beneath every 'O Lord' of yours lies many a 'Here I am' from me."

In other words, no one seeks God whom God is not calling. Pilgrims are people who have been evoked by someone or something to seek out the divine.

The journey to the center

Now we are home, we can look again at where we have been. The anthropologist's definition of pilgrimage as a sacred journey that begins in a familiar place and proceeds to a far place, fits many of the popular Christian pilgrimage shrines of today—Lourdes, Fatima, Czestochowa, Guadalupe—located on the edges of cities or at some distance from them. It fits many

Hindu shrines remote from habitation. It fits Mecca, fairly distant from most Islamic states.

Yet, Mecca is regarded by all Muslims as the center of their world. That Jerusalem stood at the center of the earth was said by the Anglo-Saxon historian Bede (*c.* 673–735 C.E.) to be proven scientifically, as on Midsummer's Day a certain column in the city cast no shadow. From the pilgrim's eye view, the sacred place is conceived of as the center of earth and (as mankind once envisioned the earth at the center of universe) the center of the cosmos.

We recognize images of the cosmos in many sacred places: It is often envisioned as the primal mound that at the Creation rose above the waters of chaos and is sometimes surmounted by a pole, pillar, or tree representing the Tree of Life reaching through all planes of existence, or the *Axis Mundi*, the pole around which the cosmos spins. Cosmic imagery is embodied in Babylonian ziggurats, Chinese palaces, Indian cities, Borneo Dyak houses, Buddhist stupas, and in the landscape: For Native Americans of the Rio Grande valley, the center of the world is a mound of loose stones from which rises a tall, barkless spruce, in the exact center of the summit of Mount Tsicomo, New Mexico.

The center is the place of connection. Through the *Axis Mundi* or cosmic tree, it links Heaven and Earth (according to one tradition, Heaven was only 18 miles above Jerusalem). It also connects World and Underworld: The early Romans, like the Pueblos of today, saw the earth's center as a pit covered by a stone, which on special occasions was removed to give the ancestral spirits contact with the living. Similarly, the center of earth for the ancient Greeks was at Delphi, marked by a stone called the Omphalos, the navel. Through the natural image of the navel, in the middle of our bodies, last trace of union with our mother, the center connects us with our human inheritance, with our genetic and cultural coding, who we are.

The center is also the place of orientation. Our world is what we can see all around us, as we stand upright, rotating on our own axis. It is the reference point for the cardinal directions and tells us where we are bound. The Achilpas, one of the Australian Arandi tribes, carry their *Axis Mundi* around with them, represented by a sacred pole. They decide which direction to take according to which way the sacred pole leans: It both centers and orients them, so that they always know where they are and where to go. Their traditions say that the pole was once broken, and the people wandered confusedly for a time and finally sat down and let themselves perish. Loss of centeredness and orientation meant the end of their world.

The inner journey

When Egyptian pilgrims return from the *hajj*, they sometimes have their houses decorated with a stylized pictorial record of their journey. A recurring image is the winged and human-faced creature, Buraq.

Buraq was the steed ridden by Muhammed on his traditional Night Journey to Jerusalem. According to some accounts, Buraq was left tied to the Rock of Jerusalem while the Angel Gabriel led the Prophet up a ladder to the very throne of God. Others say it was Buraq himself who bore Muhammed aloft. Sufi interpreters regarded the Night Journey not as a physical journey, but as an inward experience and a model for the spiritual path. Bayazid al-Bistami suggested that individuals are granted ascension (growth) on the "Buraq of self-forgetfulness," referring to the contemplative goal of loss of self in the absolute of God.

Cosmic imagery, the experience of Sufis and other mystics, and the practice of pilgrimage all say the same thing: that there is a center that can give us meaning (connection) and purpose (direction). This center is the God described by St. Bonaventure (1221–1274) as a "circle whose centre is everywhere and whose circumference is nowhere."

The mystics' perception that God is both within and without is hard to understand. Teresa of Avila asserts: "God visits the soul in a manner which prevents its doubting…that it dwelt in Him, and…He…within it." For centuries, people have hoped to receive this assurance in a sacred place or in the sacred place within: to stand for a moment at once fleeting and eternal before the very throne of God, in contemplation of Shekinah, the divine radiance.

Part II

Guide to Sacred Places

Journeys to Sacred Landscapes

Iona, Scotland

"Iona has cast its spell on the sons of men. In early times, it heard the sweet songs of God sung by Saint Columba and his followers. In later days, greater men than we have found there what they sought. This island set apart, this motherland of many dreams still yields its secret, but it is only as men seek they shall truly find."

This quote from an unknown author now graces the hallway of one of Iona's small hotels and echoes the sense of enchantment that travelers to the island have experienced throughout the ages.

To reach Iona today, travelers must make the lengthy journey to Oban in the West Highlands of Scotland and take the ferry to the Isle of Mull, before crossing the island to Fionnphort and boarding a smaller ferry to Iona. There the imposing abbey stands out facing the waves. Columba's journey was more perilous: Leaving Derry in Northern Ireland, he set sail on a "pilgrimage for Christ" and arrived on Iona in 563, where he founded the island's first monastery.

In more recent times, pilgrims have been drawn to Iona not only to visit the many places linked with the saint and the island's monastic tradition but also to seek something more elusive: inner calm and spiritual renewal. Few tourists and day-trippers venture farther than the abbey and its nearby shops, but the west side of the island, overlooking the Atlantic Ocean, is more rugged and alive with mysterious natural landmarks—the spouting cave, the healing pool, and the bay at the back of the island.

Iona lives at a leisurely pace: It is best to stay overnight to benefit from the island's relaxed rhythm. Accommodations should be booked in advance, as there are few hotels. Cars and camping are not generally permitted on Iona, but there are car parks and a campsite at Fionnphort on Mull. The island is exposed, and you will need rainwear even in summer. Walkers will need good shoes and a large-scale map. The abbey now houses the Iona Community, who hold a Christian service on June 15 in honor of St. Columba.

Lough Derg, Ireland

To Catholic pilgrims the world over, the small island in the midst of Lough Derg (red lake), crowned by an octagonal basilica, is a place where they may spend three long, demanding days in prayer, vigil, and penitential retreat. According to tradition, St. Patrick experienced a vision of purgatory on Lough Derg. His Welsh disciple Davog brought Christianity to the region and founded a monastery on nearby Saints' Island.

The island, known both as Station Island and St. Patrick's Purgatory, has been a place of pilgrimage since the twelfth century, and today receives up to 30,000 pilgrims a year, with the largest numbers coming in June, July, and August. They make their way to the village of Pettigo and then to the shores of the lough, from where they are ferried to the island. Each of them has fasted since midnight and is prepared to eat nothing for the next three days save for one daily meal of black tea or coffee and dry bread.

Following a day's fast, pilgrims must complete three stations, which involves reciting prayers silently while walking barefoot over rocks and stones. Then, they undertake a 24-hour vigil, during which they recite prayers at the last four stations in the basilica. Pilgrims support each other as they symbolically make themselves ready for the coming of Christ. On the morning of the third day, they celebrate the Eucharist in a spirit of rejoicing and community after the rigors of their spiritual exercises.

The pilgrimage is organized by the office of St. Patrick's Purgatory on Lough Derg, which stipulates that pilgrims must be more than 15 years old, without ailment or disability, and able to walk and kneel unaided.

Cameras, radios, and musical instruments are forbidden. Pilgrims are provided with a bed at the hostel and are advised to bring clothes to suit the weather, which can be either cold, windy, and wet or hot and humid. Special one-day retreats are conducted in May, August, and September. These retreats, which must be reserved in advance, do not involve fasting or walking barefoot.

Mont-Saint-Michel, France

Pilgrims have made sacred journeys to Mont-Saint-Michel, a small island off the Normandy coast, since the eighth century. In 708, the Archangel Michael allegedly appeared to Aubert, Bishop of Avranches, and ordered him to build a chapel on the summit. The abbey church was built from granite brought by boat from the nearby Chausey Islands and Brittany and hauled up the steep sides of the hill by ropes.

The original building stood at the top of a cone-shaped hill. To enlarge the abbey over the centuries, a huge substructure of stone and rubble had to be created. The feats of architectural ingenuity required are reflected in the name given to the buildings on the northern side—La Merveille (the Marvel). The abbey rises majestically from a clump of houses at its base and is crowned by a Gothic spire 540 feet above sea level. The French author Maupassant called it "the most wonderful Gothic dwelling ever made for God on this earth." Once, according to Celtic myth, this small island was a sea tomb, where the souls of the dead were taken by boat.

Unusual among pilgrimage places, the cult of Mont-Saint-Michel is centered on the spirituality of the place itself, rather than on a saint or a sacred relic. At low tide, you can walk to the mount, but go with a guide to avoid the treacherous quicksand. Since the building of the causeway in the nineteenth century, siltation has meant that the mount is only completely cut off from the mainland during the high tides of spring and autumn.

Two million visitors journey to Mont-Saint-Michel each year, crossing the causeway to enter the Porte de l'Avancée and walk up the Grande Rue to the abbey. The island is most crowded in summer, when the gates often close temporarily, and admission is by guided tour only. The abbey is open every day except national holidays.

Brocéliande, France

The primordial woodland was an elemental force, both dangerous and miraculous. To early European civilizations it represented the threat of the untamed, wild home of Pan, who could inspire terror and "panic." Forest deities required placatory worship, and early cults adopted the natural temples of groves and glades. But as humans began to dominate their habitat, cutting and burning the trees, perceptions changed. The forest then came to represent freedom from authority or the romance of Arthurian legend.

One such forest is the Forest of Paimpont in Brittany, which entered fable as Brocéliande, the wood where the wizard Merlin was bewitched by the nymph Viviane beside the miraculous Fountain of Barenton. High among the trees, the Fountain is reached from the village of Folle Pensée. A woodland track leads to the ancient spring—walled in moss and stone, set in the roots of a mighty tree, and filled with deliciously pure water. The medieval poet Chrétien de Troyes wrote:

> "its water is colder than marble
> ... shaded by the most beautiful tree
> that nature ever made."

After drinking from the spring, visitors can follow a fifth-century tradition: Those who splash water on to Merlin's stone, the great slab in which the spirit of the wizard is still supposedly imprisoned, can test its power to call up storms and the vision of a black-clad horseman.

The forest lies 18 miles west of Rennes and is easily accessible by road. The village of Paimpont offers a range of accommodations. Although a forest fire in 1990 caused some damage, the countryside remains idyllically unspoiled, rich in associations with an age of chivalry. Here, according to the poets of the Middle Ages, Lancelot du Lac spent his childhood after being stolen by magic from his parents.

Each landmark conjures echoes from a legendary past: from the Rocher des Faux Amants, where Morgan le Fay tempted young men to their doom in the evocatively named Valley of No Return, to the beautiful Château at Comper, the birthplace of the enchantress Viviane. It is said that near the fateful spring where she first encountered Merlin, still farther in the depths of the forest, lies the Fountain of Eternal Youth, hidden from all but the pure of heart.

Lalibela, Ethiopia

Orthodox Christians in Ethiopia follow the Julian calendar, which is currently seven years and eight months behind the Gregorian calendar. During the celebration of Timkat (Epiphany), the time lag seems far greater. In Lalibela, a high mountain town, which boasts eleven ancient churches hewn out of rock, Timkat is observed much as it has been for the past 800 years.

In contrast to the other countries of sub-Saharan Africa where European missionaries introduced Christianity, Ethiopia has its own indigenous variation of the religion. The Ethiopian Orthodox Church was founded in the fourth century and incorporates aspects of Judaism. In the twelfth century, King Lalibela ordered the construction (or, more precisely, excavation) of the town which bears his name. He envisioned a new Jerusalem.

Timkat, which is celebrated throughout the country, is the most important annual event for Ethiopia's Orthodox Christians, and takes place on January 19, twelve days after the Ethiopian Christmas. Pilgrims descend on all of the major religious centers. Those converging on Lalibela from the surrounding countryside travel by mule or on foot (often without shoes) and journey for days. Tourists arrive by airplane, to a rough airstrip.

On the eve of Timkat, the *tabotat* (replicas of the tablets on which the Ten Commandments were inscribed) are removed from the Holy of Holies within each church and paraded, wrapped in damask, to the banks of the river that flows through Lalibela. Pilgrims and priests hold vigil over the *tabotat* throughout the night, when temperatures can fall to close to freezing. At daybreak, the priests bless the pilgrims with holy water, and the processions return to their respective churches.

Timkat processions in Lalibela are dusty, colouful, noisy affairs. People dance, chant, and ululate; drums beat and horns blare. Amid the throng, ceremonial umbrellas embroidered in gold provide shade for a lucky few. Priests are resplendent in their brightest robes and carry processional crosses, while pilgrims wear predominantly traditional white shawls and turbans.

Armanath Cave, Kashmir

A pillar of ice at the heart of a yawning cave is the climax of an annual pilgrimage that draws thousands of Hindus from all walks of life. Perched high in the Himalayas north of Srinagar in Kashmir, the cave is believed to be where Shiva and his consort, Parvati, spent their wedding night. Shiva melted himself and then solidified into the pillar, a giant *linga* that became Parvati's object of adoration. Created from seeping spring water under unusual temperature and pressure conditions, the pillar waxes and wanes with the moon and may grow as tall as 10 feet.

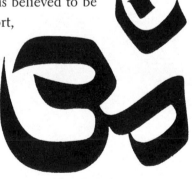

Known as a *yatra*, this ancient pilgrimage is timed to coincide with the full moon in July and August, when weather conditions permit the arduous but rewarding trek through a glacial landscape of sheer escarpments, glorious lakes, and precipitous trails. Despite the disruptions caused by political conflict (would-be pilgrims are advised to check with the authorities before setting out), the *yatra* is very well organized. Pilgrims, or *yatris*, must register at the main starting point at Pahalgam and then move off together for the 4-day, 30-mile journey. Pilgrims are recommended to take a tent, a sleeping bag, waterproof shoes, warm clothing, a flashlight, and a walking stick to use in crossing the snow and ice fields.

Raw, cold, and often wet, the *yatris* arrive at Armanath Cave at dawn on the day of the full moon. Here they wash away their sins in the sacred river Amaravati, where Shiva conferred immortality on the other Hindu gods. After taking off their shoes, they ascend a stone platform and enter the cave. Once inside and past two sadhus—one holding a holy book, one collecting cash offerings—they ring a large bell. Behind an iron grille is the pillar—milky yellow, scattered with rose petals, scarves, and tinsel. Pilgrims have little time to dwell on the experience before they receive the *tilaka*, a red mark on the forehead that symbolizes a devout Hindu, and are ushered out of the cave. The pillar of ice is considered to be the *darshan*, or glimpsing of god. To worship here frees a pilgrim from the fear of death.

Hemkund, India

"And now my own story I tell, how from rigorous austerities I was summoned by God; called from the heights of Hemkund, where seven peaks so grandly pierce the sky ... the place where the Pandava king practiced yogic rites."

Thus, the tenth Sikh Guru, Govind Singh, describes meditating at Hemkund before his incarnation. The Almighty told him, "Preach the way of truth and purge them of every evil way."

Hemkund is regarded as a very holy place by Sikhs, who seek to be immersed in bliss as they submerge in the blue-green waters of the lake, which lies at a height of 15,000 feet surrounded by seven Himalayan peaks. Nearby is the Valley of the Flowers, where more than 200 species of flower (some unique) bloom during the summer.

In the 1930s, Pandit Tara Singh Narottam discovered the site, and a Gurdwara (Sikh temple) was built in 1936. Nearby is a shrine where Lakshmana, brother of the Hindu deity Rama, meditated. Hemkund is 190 miles northeast of Rishikesh in the Garhwal region of Uttarakhand (Northern Uttar Pradesh).

Uttarakhand is a sacred landscape with many *yatras* (traditional Hindu pilgrimages) to a number of sites associated with important Hindu deities, sages, and heroes. The sacred rivers, Ganges and Jamuna, rise here. The landscape is host to ancient Buddhist sites, too. Between May and October many thousands of pilgrims journey to the Char Dhams (four temples) at

Gangotri, Kedarnath, and Badrinath, sources of tributaries of the Ganges, and at Yumnotri, source of the Jamuna. These temples are also the homes of Vishnu and Shiva.

Pilgrims usually travel the first part of the journey by bus but walk the last 13 miles from Govind Ghat or 4 miles from Ghangaria. A visit to these sites must be completed in a day as there is nowhere to stay or camp beyond Ghangaria. Journeys can also be undertaken by hired car, tourist taxi, or trekking. Permission is needed to camp in national parks. You will need warm clothing and rainwear, water, and insect repellent.

Sri Pada, Sri Lanka

Buddhists call the holy mountain in the hill country south of Kandy Sri Pada. *Pada* means "footprint" and *Sri* is a term of respect. Near the peak is a great boulder impressed with a footprint that is venerated as the first place Buddha stood on Earth. On tourist maps, the mountain is called Adam's Peak. According to both Christian and Muslim legend, the giant footprint is the place of Adam's penance, where he was forced to stand on one leg for a thousand years after he had been thrown out of the Garden of Eden.

Few tourists climb the mountain, but thousands of locals make the pilgrimage annually, climbing at night in family groups that include children and grandparents. Steps have been cut into the mountainside for most of the climb. The goal is to reach the summit at dawn when the triangular shadow of the peak is projected on to the mists over the awakening countryside. In some weather conditions, you may see your own shadow floating on skeins of mist looped with a rainbow.

Most pilgrims take a bus or taxi from Ratnapura to one of two starting points, from which it is either a four- or seven-mile climb up stone steps to the peak. As the pilgrimage is not a normal tourist activity, you will need to seek local information. You can make the journey between December and April before the monsoon season, when torrential rains make the paths dangerous. Sneakers are more suitable than boots but take plenty of warm clothing, including rainwear, and a bag in which to carry your clothes for the hot climb down. Stalls sell food and hot drinks; however, many pilgrims prefer not to eat on the way up but to wait for the dawn, symbol of enlightenment, before breaking their fast.

An ancient name for Sri Lanka is *Serendip*, from which comes *serendipity*, meaning "to find something important while searching for something else." This is an appropriate theme for a pilgrimage up a holy mountain to a footprint symbolizing a great spiritual figure.

Fuji-san, Japan

On a very clear day, you can see the symmetrical cone of Fuji-san from Tokyo. Especially in winter, when the peak is capped with snow, it is a sight of awe-inspiring beauty. But, Fuji-san hides a silent volcanic power. The last time the volcano erupted, in 1707, the streets of Tokyo, 60 miles away, were covered in ash.

Traditionally, women were only allowed to climb the mountain on one special day every 60 years because the female mountain *kami* was believed to be jealous of other women. (The Shinto concept of *kami* means something powerful and awe-inspiring.) Today, no such restrictions exist.

The pilgrimage season is in July and August when large crowds of people of all ages, from children to grandparents, follow clearly marked mountain paths to the summit. Pilgrims should not attempt to climb Fuji-san out of season unless they are experienced climbers. At 12,400 feet, it is a serious mountain. Weather conditions can change suddenly, and even in midsummer, the temperature at the top is close to freezing. Climbers should wear boots and take several layers of warm clothing, hat, gloves, rainwear and sun cream, and a flashlight for night climbing. Meals and hot drinks can be bought in the mountain huts en route.

The climb is divided into ten stages, but most pilgrims travel by bus to the fifth station. The idea is to time your climb so that you arrive at the top by dawn. Although freezing cold and windy on the summit, this is the time when the mountain is least likely to be shrouded by cloud, and the sunrise is spectacular. As the first rays of sunlight appear, thousands of pilgrims all over the

243

mountain throw up their arms and shout "Bonsai!," which is like sharing a huge "Hurrah!"

> *"Morning frost,*
> *Mount Fuji*
> *brushed lightly."*

Haiku written by TanTan (1674–1761)

Plaine du Nord, Haiti

The Church of St. James commands the center of Plaine du Nord, a fertile farming area where slave uprisings commenced the Haitian revolution in 1791. Running past the church is a dirt track marked by a series of potholes, which fill during summer rains to become small ponds. Should the rains fail, townspeople will come with pails of water to ensure plenty of mud. For them, these are not potholes but terrestrial emergence points for Ogou, an *lwa* (deity) who is the commander in chief of the voodoo pantheon. These mud pits are his most important shrine in Haiti.

For three days prior to the canonical feast of St. James (July 25), pilgrims descend on the town wearing blue suits and red scarves, or the multistriped garb of a penitent. They have come to fulfill vows or to seek blessings. Pregnant women and tubercular children line up for a bath and a blessing from itinerant herbalists. Bony bulls, with red ribbons around their necks and candles stuck on their horns, become lumbering sacrifices for

Ogou. After the muddy tauracide, the bulls' blood will be used to anoint the pilgrims.

Other pilgrims fall face down in the sludge, not visibly breathing. When they arise they look like primal creatures, flinging their mud-covered torsos in ecstasy. Groups of drummers play sacred rhythms at crosspoints around the mud pits. The music never stops until the morning of July 25, by which time most pilgrims have departed for other festivals nearby.

Throughout the pilgrimage, crowds gather on the steps of the church, which they cannot enter. Iron gratings bar the doors and windows. So they shout prayers and hurl candles, pennies, or rum bottles through the gratings. They aim their missiles at an empty niche that used to contain an image of St. James. Catholic clergy have removed the image, noting that the church is being used to honor a voodoo deity. For indeed, in Haiti everyone knows St. James is Ogou, senior brother of a lineage of divine warriors. Through a long process of appropriation, Haitians have refigured an important Catholic festival in order to honor their own African god.

Señor de Qoyllor Rit'i, Peru

Amid the bleak immensity of the southern Peruvian Andes, three great glacial tongues reach down to the desolate Sinakara Valley. A stone chapel houses a figure of Christ crucified—the miraculous Señor de Qoyllor Rit'i (Lord of the Snow Star)—painted on a rock outcrop. Each year, between the Christian feasts of the Ascension and Corpus Christi, 25,000 pilgrims (predominantly Quechua-speaking highlanders) converge on the chapel in an explosion of color, noise, and ritual movement.

In 1783, it is said, a shepherd boy, Mariano, was befriended in Sinakara by Manuel, a pale-skinned stranger. Church representatives traveled from Cuzco (55 miles away) to see Manuel but instead, on June 23, found Christ's agonized body hanging in a *tayanka* bush. Mysteriously, the body disappeared, leaving only a tree shaped like a crucifix. In the meantime, Mariano died and was buried beneath the adjacent crag.

Later embellished with a painted Christ figure, this crag today forms the focal point of devotion. Pilgrims firmly identify the Señor de Qoyllor Rit'i, or *taytacha* (little father), with the most powerful mountain deity—the 20,000-foot Ausankati in whose shadow the fiesta unravels. They believe that as weather creator he has the power to blight crops or bestow health and fertility.

Pilgrims travel by road to Mawallani village and then trek the five miles to Sinakara. Colorfully robed dancers dominate the scene. Through formalized choreography, village dance groups, or *comparsas*, pay homage to the *taytacha* on behalf of their home communities. Scattered among them, the *ukukus*, or bear men, sport woollen masks and whips to maintain order. Always speaking in falsetto tones, they protect the pilgrims, yet are themselves disorderly.

The central day of the pilgrimage is Trinity Sunday (May or June). The dancing hardly stops all day while an image of the *taytacha* is paraded up and down the valley. Then, in the early hours, maned ranks of *ukukus* ascend the glaciers where they plant candles, retrieve a cross placed there a few days earlier, and return to the valley. Many carry blocks of ice which, when melted, provide a supply of holy water for the following year.

Journeys to Sacred Temples

Westminster Abbey, London

The Abbey's mystique is inseparable from its role as the site of the coronations of the kings and queens of England. The presence within the abbey of two supreme totems, the tomb of Edward the Confessor and the Coronation Chair, make it the heart from which the blood of royalty springs. Here the Celtic, Anglo-Saxon, and Norman roots of Britain meet.

In the eleventh century, when King Edward the Confessor built his new church on the site of a small monastery, the Isle of Thorns (as the Saxons knew Westminster) already had royal associations with both King Offa and King Canute. After the Confessor's death in 1066, the Saxon Bishop Wulfstan, threatened with dispossession, stuck his staff into the king's tomb. Like King Arthur's Excalibur, it could be withdrawn by none but Wulfstan himself. Other miracles followed, and in 1161, Edward was canonized. His shrine has remained one of the most important places of pilgrimage in Britain.

William of Normandy claimed to be Edward's rightful heir. Thus, Edward was the link between the Norman succession and the older Anglo-Saxon tradition in which the vitality of a people depended upon the *mana* (luck) of its monarch. Edward's tomb represents a bridge between Anglo-Saxon and Norman royalty. Beside the tomb stands a far more ancient talisman, the Stone of Scone.

Seized from the Scots in 1296 by Edward I (Longshanks) and housed in the Coronation Chair, the Stone was traditionally thought to be Jacob's stony pillow from the Bible story. Later, it was identified with the Irish *Lia-Fail,* the Stone of Destiny, which revealed the royal line. The founder of the Scottish monarchy, Fergus Mor MacEirc, may have taken it to Argyll in the fifth century. Certainly by 840 C.E., when Kenneth II brought it to Scone in Scotland, it was such a potent symbol of Scottish identity that more than a thousand years later, in 1950, the Stone's "capture" by Scottish nationalists caused a furor throughout Britain. According to legend, wherever the Scots find the Stone they will rule—a prophecy fulfilled when James VI of Scotland was crowned James I of England. Recently, the British government returned the Stone to Scotland, where it is now kept in Edinburgh castle. Only for coronation ceremonies is it brought back to Westminster Abbey.

Stonehenge, England

Stonehenge is probably the best-known prehistoric monument in Britain and ranks as one of the most powerful spiritual sites in Europe. Although crowds and competing interests are a perennial problem for the pilgrim, the great stones of Salisbury Plain, massive and brooding like a council of giants, have not lost their magic.

Stonehenge was not built as a single construction. A series of earth, timber, and stone works were revised and remodeled over a period of more than 2,000 years, from about 3200 to 1100

B.C.E. Many of the original stones are missing or have fallen. The sarsen stones come from the Marlborough Downs 20 miles away, while the bluestones were transported more than 200 miles to the site from the Preseli Mountains in southwest Wales.

This awe-inspiring monument was probably a temple, or a neolithic observatory for predicting solstices and eclipses. However, Earth has tilted farther on its axis since Stonehenge was built, so the alignments of the stones with the sun have changed.

Salisbury Plain is dotted with tumuli (ancient burial mounds) and sites of neolithic encampments. Ley-lines link Stonehenge with places farther afield, such as Salisbury Cathedral, which may have been built on a pre-Christian site, and the Iron Age earthworks of Old Sarum.

In recent years, the site has been fenced to prevent damage to the stones. Even this restriction and the large crowds of visitors cannot destroy the powerful atmosphere of this place. Those who wish to get closer to the stones can arrange with English Heritage (who manage the site) to visit outside the daily opening times.

The monument is near the A303 Road, easily accessible by car or bus. A more evocative approach is on foot from Salisbury, following the route believed to have been used in transporting the bluestones from Wales. The ten-mile walk follows the River Avon northwest to the villages of Middle and Upper Woodford and then through woods to the edge of Salisbury Plain.

The Cathedral, Chartres, France

Chartres Cathedral, the world's most complete and glorious example of Gothic art and architecture, soars above the town it guards from a hilltop that has been sacred for more than 2,000 years. In ancient times, a rough stone dolmen covered a point where invigorating energy was believed to flow from the earth; beside it was a well.

The Druids later had a college here. They carved a statue of a child-bearing virgin seen in a vision and placed it beside the well. In the third century, Christians worshiped her as the "Black Virgin," or the "Virgin about to bring forth," and built a church dedicated to Mary around her. That church, and four after it, burnt down between 743 and 1194.

The most treasured relic, the Virgin's "sacred tunic," escaped the last devastating fire. This was taken as a sign that Our Lady wished an even finer church to be built on the site. The result, today's mighty cathedral, is an extraordinary blend of the supreme in architecture, sculpture, and stained glass.

A legend tells how, during the Crusades to the Holy Land, the Knights Templar brought back the secrets of divine Number, Weight, and Measure from Solomon's Temple and that these were used in building the cathedral. Its interior proportions and symbolism are so powerful that they are said to affect the consciousness.

Traditionally, the pilgrim approaches on foot, and ideally, barefoot. The cathedral's energizing effects can be felt upon entering the western door. The interior is flooded with intensely colored light shining through the great rose window and other windows of vivid jewel-colored stained glass, such as the "Notre-Dame de la Belle Verrière," a masterpiece of early Gothic art. An oddly angled flagstone by the entrance has a "solar nail" which catches the sun's rays at noon on Midsummer Day.

Eleven circles in blue and white stones around a six-petaled rose (see pattern, right) form "The Path to Jerusalem," a labyrinth at the center of the nave. This represents the pilgrim's path to salvation. Esoterically, it is believed, when trodden correctly, to indicate the point where the Druids' thought-converging currents of cosmic power were focused.

Chartres lies beside the river Eure, 25 miles southwest of Paris. To see the stained glass at its best, visit in the bright light of spring or summer. Ideally choose a festival of the Virgin—either March 25 (the Annunciation) or August 15 (the Assumption). A more cosmic moment would be to coincide with Midsummer Day.

The Cathedral, Aachen, Germany

Long before the Emperor Charlemagne built his imperial palace at Aachen, the site was sacred to the Celts because of the hot springs that rise here. The Celts dedicated the waters to their god of healing, Granus. Later, the Romans built bath complexes and shrines, and called the place *Aquis Grani*.

Charlemagne chose the site for his palace because of the springs. He enjoyed bathing in the hot waters, but the spiritual significance of the area was not lost on him either. His aim was to Christianize the pagan holy places, and accordingly, he built his eight-sided royal chapel, spiritual heart of his palace, directly over the Roman baths.

Charlemagne, the first Holy Roman Emperor after the title was revived, was crowned in Rome as protector of the Christian faith. His successors were crowned in Aachen's octagon chapel. In the fourteenth century, a choir was added to the chapel to create Aachen Cathedral, all that now remains of the imperial palace.

The cathedral houses many holy relics collected by Charlemagne throughout his life, such as the swaddling clothes of the infant Jesus and the loincloth Christ wore on the cross. Charlemagne's remains were enshrined here on his death in 814, and 400 years later, were moved to a golden shrine in the east end of the cathedral. His marble throne in the gallery looks down on the altar below. Throughout the Middle Ages, the throne, shrine, and holy relics made Aachen one of the key centers of European pilgrimage. Today, visitors who wish to see the throne must join a guided tour of the cathedral.

Aachen is in western Germany, close to the Dutch and Belgian borders. The city is also known as Aix-la-Chapelle because of the eight-sided chapel, still the spiritual heart of the city.

The Cathedral, Trondheim, Norway

Nidaros Cathedral (Nidarosdomen in Norwegian) stands on the banks of the River Nidelven in Trondheim, the former capital city of Norway and meeting place of the early Norse parliament. For almost 1,000 years, pilgrims have paid homage here to Olav Haraldsson, Norway's legendary Christian king and saint.

Olav was killed in battle in 1030 at Stikelsad by King Canute's armies, and his body was buried near the river. From his grave, springs of water began to flow, reputedly with healing properties, and there were reports of miracles. One year after his death, Olav's body was disinterred and was found to be undecayed, an indication of his sanctity. His body was then removed to the town's only church.

Norway declared Olav a saint and martyr, and in 1070 his nephew Olav Kyrre started building a vast stone church on the site of his first burial place. The oldest parts of this church to survive date from the twelfth century and form part of Nidarosdomen, which was granted cathedral status in 1152. In the Middle Ages, countless pilgrims made the journey on foot to Trondheim—from Sweden in the north and from Oslo in the South. A chain of pilgrim hostels marked the southern route to the shrine.

The Reformation in sixteenth-century Europe destroyed the tradition of public pilgrimage, along with other Roman Catholic forms of worship. However, Nidarosdomen is still the traditional burial place of the Norwegian monarchs and

Trondheim's finest building. Visitors may admire its Gothic architecture, the magnificent rose window, and the Norwegian Crown Jewels. Modern Norway's first king and queen were crowned here in 1906; and the current king and queen, Harald and Sonja, were formally blessed here in 1992.

The best time to visit is in the late afternoon, when the tour groups have departed. On July 29, the official anniversary of St. Olav's death in 1030, carloads of modern pilgrims return to the ancient battlefield of Stikelsad, near Trondheim, to see a reenactment of Olav's last battle in his fight for the evangelization of Norway.

St Peter's Basilica, Rome

The basilica of St. Peter's is the principal shrine of the Catholic Church, and the curving colonnades around St. Peter's Square symbolize the protecting arms of the Church, inviting all who come here into its embrace.

Since the Middle Ages, Rome has been a center of pilgrimages, largely because of the tombs of the many martyrs who were put to death here by the Romans. The obelisk believed to have marked the spot where St. Peter was executed in Nero's Circus was moved to St. Peter's Square in 1586. In the fourth century the Emperor Constantine erected a basilica with the saint's alleged grave, encased in a huge cube of marble, as its focal point. The present basilica, a sixteenth-century building on a far grander scale than the original church, contains works by many prominent artists from the Italian Renaissance.

A thirteenth-century bronze statue of St. Peter has one silver foot—polished by the kisses of pilgrims over generations. At the base of the main altar, which is built over the saint's tomb, oil lamps burn continuously by an open crypt where pilgrims pray.

The Pope holds public audiences every Wednesday in a hall off St. Peter's Square. Admission is by ticket only, available in advance from the Prefettura della Casa Pontificia, also in the Square. On Sundays at noon, the Pope says the Angelus and blesses the crowd from the balcony of the Vatican offices overlooking the square.

The basilica is open daily and attracts large crowds, especially for the major Christian festivals. Rome in midsummer is hot and oppressive, so the best time to visit is in spring or fall. Visitors should dress modestly, with their upper arms covered. Those in unsuitable clothing, such as shorts and miniskirts, are refused entry.

Hagia Sophia, Istanbul

The glory of Christendom rose in Constantinople, the city that Constantine made the center of the Eastern Roman Empire. The Emperor Justinian employed two of the last mathematicians of the Athenian Academy to design a church combining the rectangular basilica of Roman civic centers with the soaring spirituality of the great dome. They succeeded so well that the people thought the dome must be suspended from heaven by a golden chain. And Justinian, on entering his basilica for the first time in 548 C.E., declared: "Oh, Solomon! I have surpassed you!"

Hagia Sophia became a focus of pilgrimage for Christians from Asia and Russia and was famous for its golden mosaics depicting the life of the Holy Family. Many of its treasures and relics were looted during the Crusades. When the Turks took Constantinople in 1453, Hagia Sophia was converted to a mosque and the interior, whitewashed. Thus it remained until 1933, when Kemal Ataturk turned it into a museum and began to restore the mosaics.

Pilgrims can fly to Istanbul, but there is a more interesting route. Those with time on their hands can take a train (perhaps even the historic Orient-Express) from Paris to Venice, and then travel by boat via Piraeus through the Dardanelles to Istanbul. This boat trip gives a first view of the city of domes and minarets over the Sea of Marmora.

It is best to avoid the summer months, which are hot and crowded with tourists. April to mid-June, or September and October are preferable. Clothing needs to be lightweight but modest, as Turkey is a mainly Muslim country.

The Dome of the Rock, Jerusalem

The magnificent golden dome of Jerusalem's most celebrated Muslim shrine dominates the entire old city, announcing both the might and beauty of Islam and the miracle and sanctity of a cave. At the heart of the dome, protected by a fine wooden screen, stands the great Holy Rock, which is also sacred to Jews and Christians. Muslims believe that the dome stands at the center of the world, for it is said that the waters of Paradise flow beneath the cave.

Stairs lead the pilgrim below the rock into a large cave, which according to legend, is where Abraham offered his son Isaac in sacrifice to God. There, too, Muslims believe, the Prophet Muhammad began his miraculous night journey to heaven on his legendary steed, Buraq. Near the entrance to the cave, a shrine contains relics of the Prophet, including a hair from his head.

The Qubbat al-Sakhra, as the dome is known, was built by the fifth Umayyad Caliph, 'Abd-al-Malik, and was completed in 691–692 C.E. Its design, a dome over an octagonal lower storey, is based on intricate mathematical detail. It stands on the masonry platform that was the original foundation for Herod's temple, which in turn was built on the site of the Temple of Solomon. Thus, the Muslim shrine looms over the platform's Western Wall, now the focal point for Jewish pilgrimages.

Islam's third holiest place after the Ka'ba in Mecca and the Prophet's mosque in Medina, the dome is second in importance only to Mecca as a place of pilgrimages. Tourists and pilgrims alike flock here throughout the year, although one of the best times to visit is in April, when the crowds are not at their heaviest, and the temperature is pleasantly warm. Anyone can visit the dome and its cave as long as they are modestly dressed. The building, which is a shrine in honor of the prophet and not a mosque or a place of formal worship, is free of ceremony and ritual. It is a place of pilgrimage and personal prayer.

The Bahá'í Shrines, Haifa and Acre, Israel

Bahá'ís all over the world aim to make the sacred journey at least once in their lifetime to the World Center of their Faith, at the shrines of the Báb and Bahá'u'lláh in the cities of Haifa and Acre in Israel.

Bahá'u'lláh (1817–1892), founder of the Bahá'í Faith, endured forty years of imprisonment and exile for teaching the unity of humankind and the oneness of religions. To several million Bahá'ís worldwide, his resting place in Acre is the holiest place on Earth. The Báb (1817–1850) was a Divine Messenger who was executed for heralding the mission of Bahá'u'lláh in his native Persia. The Shrine of the Báb on the slopes of Mount Carmel in Haifa is popularly known as the Queen of Carmel, and is one of the most distinctive sights in the Holy Land.

The shrines and their surrounding gardens are open to visitors—of which there are currently a quarter of a million annually. These are places of reflection, contemplation, and prayer. The Bahá'í Faith has no fixed devotional rituals, and as long as they do not disturb others, anyone may pray or meditate here as they see fit or simply enjoy the peace and beauty of the gardens. Visitors should dress and behave modestly, in a manner befitting a holy place.

Haifa, a busy port and Israel's third largest city, is accessible from other parts of Israel by road and rail. Regular buses make the short trip from Acre to Haifa, or you can travel inexpensively by *sherut* (taxi). The Shrine of the Báb, which is clearly visible on approaching Haifa, is open each morning. The gardens are open for most of the day, and in the evenings, the shrine is brilliantly illuminated.

The Shrine of Bahá'u'lláh is open in the morning from Friday to Monday; its gardens, too, are open for most of the day. Both shrines and gardens are closed for short periods between July and September, and public access is also limited on nine Bahá'í holy days. Tour-guide agencies in Israel are informed of the exact dates of closure each year.

Mashad, Iran

From Tehran, pilgrims may fly to Mashad or take the train, but the adventurous will go on the "Golden Road to Samarkand"—all 600 dreary miles of it—skirting the edge of the desert. Mashad is Iran's paramount holy city, visited by more than 14 million pilgrims each year. It contains probably the greatest concentration of religious buildings anywhere in the world: a shrine, several sanctuaries, two mosques, five theological schools, libraries, and a museum.

The city grew on the site of the village of Sanabad, where in 817 C.E., the Eighth Imam, Ali Reza, died after eating grapes. Reza's father had prophesied his murder, and most Shi'ites believe that he was poisoned by his father-in-law, Caliph Ma'mun. Nevertheless, Ma'mun built a mausoleum over Reza's grave, which is close to that of his own father, the famous Harun al-Rashid. Sanabad soon grew into a place of pilgrimage, under a new name, *Mashad*, meaning "place of the martyr." A pilgrimage to Imam Reza's tomb was said to equal 70,000 visits to Mecca, and pilgrims now come to Mashad from all parts of the Muslim world.

Mongols sacked the holy city in 1230 C.E., and most of the oldest part dates from the fourteenth century. The jewel in Mashad's crown was the gift of a remarkable woman, Gohar Shad, the wife of Shah Rokh. Between 1405 and 1418, she and her architect Qavam od-din of Shiraz created the mosque which now bears her name and which some art historians call the most beautiful building in Islam.

A golden dome covers Imam Reza's shrine and his sarcophagus is protected by a silver grille. Entry into the shrine is not permitted for non-Muslims. Attached to the sacred precinct, through a garden at the side of the Gowhar Shad Mosque, is the Qods-e Razari Museum, where visitors can see many of the treasures that have been given to the shrine.

Throughout Iran, women must observe the Islamic dress code. This means a scarf to cover the head and neck, long sleeves, long skirts or trousers, and a dark calf-length coat. Feet should also be covered and jewelry and makeup kept to a minimum.

Non-Muslims are granted only limited access to the sacred area at Mashad. It is best to avoid major pilgrimages and festivals—10th and 11th Moharram, 20th and 28th Safar, and Ramadan, in particular. Bear in mind that the climate is changeable and harsh, and in winter, bitterly cold.

All travelers to Iran require visas, and for most nationalities, only a five-day transit visa is available. The easiest way to visit Mashad is on an organized group tour.

Amritsar, India

"I would bathe at the place of pilgrimage, if that would please God, but without his blessing, nothing is obtained," said Guru Nanak (1469–1539), the founder of Sikhism. One of his followers later observed, "if bathing at pilgrimages does any good, frogs are assured salvation!"

The Guru's teaching emphasized the importance of interior religion and was opposed to mindless ritual. The only pilgrimage that matters is inside your own heart. As the "one beyond time" is everywhere, all of space is equally sacred. Sikhs believe that the teaching spirit that passed through the Gurus is now lodged in the Guru Granth Sahib, the Sikh holy book. A copy of it is kept in every Sikh Gurdwara (temple).

The most famous Sikh Gurdwara is the Harmandir Sahib, or God's Temple, (known in the west as the Golden Temple) at Amritsar. This city in the Punjab, northern India, was founded in 1577. The main feature of the original site was the pool constructed by the fourth Guru, where Sikhs still bathe. Many stories recount how pilgrims have been healed here. The original Gurdwara was constructed by the fifth Guru, but several temples were demolished and rebuilt on the site. The present building, which dates from the eighteenth and nineteenth centuries, was mainly built under the direction of Maharaja Ranjit Singh, who ruled Punjab from 1799 to 1839. A long bridge leads across the sacred pool to the temple, with its inlaid marble walls and golden dome.

Festivals associated with Amritsar are Baisakhi in mid-April, and Diwali, which is in October and November. Baisakhi was originally a spring fair, a traditional meeting time, but it is also the anniversary of a massacre which occurred in 1919, when soldiers fired on civilians in a garden called Jallianwala Bagh. During Diwali, the festival of light that Sikhs associate with the release from prison of the sixth Guru, the Golden Temple is illuminated.

The best time to go to Amritsar is between October and March when the weather is coolest. The nights can be cold, so warm clothes are advisable. Wear a scarf or other suitable head covering, and remove shoes and socks before entering a Gurdwara.

Wangdi Phodrang, Bhutan

Bhutan is a secretive kingdom in the eastern Himalayas, without television and largely roadless. Nonetheless, the indigenous form of Tantric Buddhism permeates every remote valley, every isolated homestead. Monasteries and roaming monks relay the message throughout this mountainous country and, once a year, rural people converge on their district *dzong* (an imposing cross between a fortress and a monastery) to attend the Tshechu festival. One such *dzong* stands on a cacti-covered spur above the Puna Tsang River in the town of Wangdi Phodrang, a two-hour drive east from the capital, Thimpu.

Tshechus are dedicated to Guru Rinpoche, who converted Bhutan to Buddhism in the eighth century and take place on the tenth day of the month. The precise definition of the tenth day is determined by the abbot of the *dzong*, and sometimes the festival begins a day or two later than originally scheduled. It lasts between three and five days.

By law, the Bhutanese must always wear traditional dress in public. On the October day of the Wangdi Phodrang Tshechu, the men add to their *gho* (a garment resembling a rugged dressing gown) a decorative sash denoting in color their social status. Sashes range from white for a commoner to saffron for the king. Women wear a *kira* (dress) and their best brooches.

Approaching the *dzong*, a journey that can take several days on foot for those from the farthest-flung reaches of the district, pilgrims pass numerous prayer flags and water-driven prayer wheels. After the hardship of the trek, the Tshechu is a joyous and often raucous occasion, a mixture of the social and the spiritual. The focal points of the festivities in the courtyard of the *dzong* are dances performed by monks and laymen in elaborate masks and costumes. These dances often last more than an hour each and involve athletic leaping and spinning. Between the dances, clowns provide entertainment. On the final day, with the unveiling of a *thangka,* a giant embroidered banner depicting Guru Rinpoche, solemnity returns to the proceedings as the pilgrims are reconfirmed in their religion.

Bhutan restricts tourism to a few thousand visitors each year. The government publishes a list of festival dates each year, and some organized tours are timed to coincide with the Tshechus in the major *dzongs,* such as Paro, Thimpu, and Wangdi Phodrang. For the Bhutanese, the Tshechu is an annual event. For an outsider, it is the experience of a lifetime.

Shwe Dagon, Rangoon, Myanmar

From an aircraft descending out of dark monsoon rain clouds toward the brown parched paddy fields surrounding Rangoon, the Shwe Dagon glistens golden in the sunlight. This most venerated pagoda is one of the wonders of Asia, and one of the largest of its type.

Revered as a pilgrimage center by Burmese Buddhists, it resonates with their joyous devotion. It was built 2,500 years ago to enshrine the eight sacred hair relics given personally by the Buddha to two Burmese devotees. The relics' enshrinement is celebrated at the full-moon harvest festival of Htaname in February. The Shwe Dagon has been enlarged over the centuries to a height of 330 feet, its apex adorned with 5,000 diamonds and semiprecious stones.

Easily reached by taxi from the center of Rangoon, the Shwe Dagon is best accessed from the southern entrance, where you climb up steps past traders' stalls. Their wares are not tourist trinkets; fragrant lotus blossoms, incense, candles, bells, and multicolored flower garlands are essential ritual offerings for pilgrims.

Intricate carvings, mosaics, and symbolic statues adorn more than 82 shrines around the many levels encompassing the immense central *stupa*, the shrine built to house the relics of the Buddha. Some shrines shelter vast reclining Buddhas, while others contain small "spirit" or "Nat" houses, where you can offer incense, food, flowers, and prayers as personal tributes. You might enter the Prayer Pavilion with the 28 incarnations of Buddha, sit still on the floor, and hear a Buddhist monk talk in English of health through meditation, of clearing the mind, and of finding paths to peace and happiness.

Pilgrims should show respect with their manner, and dress modestly, removing shoes and socks before entering the pavilion. The Burmese visit in hundreds in everyday clothes—both men and women wear colorfully woven sarongs. Children play as their elders sit in prayer and meditation; young couples kneel close to each other, press their foreheads to the marble floor, then rise to give thanks and offer praise to Buddha.

Those who wish to ignore the current political realities of Myanmar and the requests of the elected leader to boycott the country, should first contact their respective embassies. Tourists are advised not to stray beyond the limits of the areas officially designated for visitors.

Angkor Wat, Cambodia

"Suddenly, and as if by enchantment, [the traveler] seems to be transported from barbarism to civilization, from profound darkness to light."

So wrote Henri Mouhot (1860), a French naturalist who stumbled across the magnificent ruins of Angkor Wat—the largest and one of the most spectacular religious monuments in the world. Angkor itself was once the capital of a powerful Khmer kingdom, whose twelfth-century ruler, the god-king Suryavarman, personified the Hindu god Vishnu to whom the temple was dedicated.

Created as Suryavarman's tomb, Angkor forms an architectural allegory that depicts in stone the epic tales of Hindu mythology. As a result, Angkor Wat is a colossal, terraced structure covering almost one square mile and crowned by five towers, each in the shape of a huge lotus bud.

Early pilgrims paid homage to the god-king. In later centuries, with Buddhism the predominant form of worship, pilgrims revered the 1,000 statues of Buddha.

The progression from darkness to light that Mouhot expressed is an image of particular resonance to Angkor Wat. Created in the midst of jungle, it became the spiritual and cultural heart of the kingdom until the Thai invasion of 1431. Eventually abandoned, it then became overgrown and lay undisturbed for 400 years.

This period of darkness, more recently compounded by war and devastation, appears to be ending, and Angkor's designation as a World Heritage Site should ensure that it once more becomes a place of inspiration. Since the 1991 cease-fire, visitors—up to 1,000 a day—have returned to Angkor.

Travelers approach the western gate of Angkor Wat along a causeway lined with carvings of sacred snakes, representing the bridge between Heaven and Earth. They then cross the broad moat. Inside, behind a platform guarded by stone lions, the outer gallery contains the 1,000 statues of Buddha.

The best time to travel to the temple complex is between November and January when the monsoon is over and before the hottest weather arrives. However hot and humid it is, visitors to the temple should dress modestly.

The security situation in Cambodia is difficult, and travel is carefully controlled.

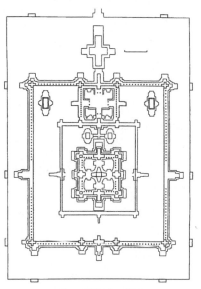

Plan of Angkor Wat

268

Public transport is not recommended. Some travel agents can book internal flights in Cambodia. You will also need to purchase a visa on arrival in the country, for which you will need several passport photographs. Pilgrims are advised to hire a car and driver in Phnom Penh or to fly into Siem Reap, the nearest town, and take a minibus or car tour. You should allow three days to explore Angkor fully.

Wong Tai Sin Temple, Hong Kong

He lived among the mists on a mountain in China, seeking eternal life. Now, immortal, he floats above this magnificent Taoist temple built for him 1,500 years later in Hong Kong, listening to the endless petitions of worshipers. He is Great Immortal Wong: "Wong Tai Sin." During the twentieth century, his temples in China were destroyed. He found refuge in Hong Kong: His image was brought to the city by two believers in 1915. Now, his believers are innumerable and have spread from Hong Kong around the world. Many Hong Kong people living overseas return to his temple to worship and seek his help.

Wong Tai Sin's original speciality in China was healing. A clinic next to the Hong Kong temple offers free Chinese herbal medicines. (Prescriptions from the god can be obtained by divination.) But most worshipers now consult him for advice about career, marriage, business, or emigration. Once, he spoke to worshipers through spirit-writing: A Taoist in a trance wrote his words on a table. Now, most devotees receive his messages by shaking a bamboo cup containing 100 numbered sticks. When one falls out, the number on the stick tells the worshipper which of 100 fortune-poems contains the god's answer. Fortunetellers in booths next to the temple interpret these poems for those who do not understand the god's message. His advice and predictions are so much sought that this temple contains the largest concentration of fortunetellers in Asia.

Once a tranquil religious retreat set among empty fields, this shrine is now surrounded by the metropolis. But, the city fades as visitors walk among offerings of food, clouds of incense, and throngs of worshipers seeking help, advice, or peace of mind. Donations, at the gate and inside the complex, go to hospitals, schools, and homes for the elderly.

To visit the temple, take the MTR (subway) to the Wong Tai Sin Station. The temple is open daily from 7:00 A.M. to 5:00 P.M. but is most busy on Sundays. Large crowds attend at the Chinese New Year (January or February), for Wong Tai Sin's birthday on the twenty-third day of the eighth lunar month, and throughout the seventh lunar month.

Borobudur, Java

The largest Buddhist monument in the world, Borobudur in Java was constructed around 800 C.E., during the reigns of the kings of the Cailendra dynasty. It is believed to have taken 10,000 men

100 years to build, depleting the population of central Java and exhausting five generations.

For about 150 years, this Mahayana-Buddhist monument was the spiritual center of Buddhism in Java. But with the fall of the kingdom of Mataram in about 919 C.E., it was neglected and suffered widespread decay. Interest in it was revived at the beginning of the eighteenth century, and the slow process of restoration has been taking place ever since.

Borobudur sits on top of a hill and is built in the form of a step pyramid, comprising six rectangular stories, three circular terraces, and a central *stupa* (dome) that forms the summit. Together, these different elements resemble a single *stupa*, representing the highest symbol of Buddhism and also replicating the universe.

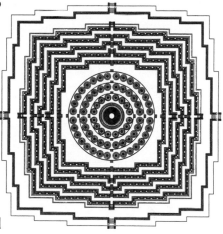

Plan of Borobudur

To visit Borobudur, and to climb it, is truly to experience something magical, but it is important to plan carefully to benefit from this. Go very early in the morning to avoid the heat of the day and the large crowds, and avoid public holidays. Carry drinking water, and protect yourself from the sun. Allow at least two hours to climb the stepped monument. Ten terraces rise from the base to the main *stupa* at the top, each signifying a stage toward perfection in life.

The walk takes you round the temple nine times, past the many pictorial and ornamental relief panels that tell stories from the Buddha's life and take in the entire Buddhist cosmos. In this way, the lower terraces are richly adorned for the senses, while the top terraces are adorned for the soul. The higher you climb, the more heavenly the themes become. The terraces near the top represent the stage in the striving for enlightenment in which desire is eliminated, though the devotee is still tied to the realm of the senses. Perfection is finally reached at the top, where all suffering ends.

Journeys to Sacred Shrines

Walsingham, England

England's "Nazareth" is an Anglican, Catholic, and Christian Orthodox pilgrimage site around the village of Walsingham, inland from Wells on the north Norfolk coast. According to legend, Lady Richeldis, widow of the lord of the manor, had three visions in 1061. The Holy Mother took her in spirit to the house in Nazareth in which the Angel Gabriel had appeared to the Virgin Mary at the Annunciation. Richeldis was told to note the dimensions of the Holy House and to build a replica in Walsingham. As she engaged builders, a heavy fall of dew one night left dry two similarly sized spaces in a meadow. From this "sign," she chose for the house the dry site closest to twin wells.

An Augustinian Priory was built in 1169 to guard the shrine, with a separate Lady Chapel enclosing the Holy House. England's Reformation destroyed the shrine and the priory in 1538, although the wells were still used as wishing wells, at which people drank, then wished.

Walsingham's status as a place of pilgrimage was revived by Catholics in 1897. Today, there are separate shrines for Catholics, Anglicans, and Orthodox Christians.

Of these, the Anglican shrine now exists as a small windowless room lit by candles inside a larger church. Known as a center for the Holy Family, the site holds the Church of England's largest collection of relics, including several fragments of the True Cross. Twin staircases lead from the shrine to the well below. The surrounding gardens hold fourteen Stations of the Cross, which serve as a symbolic journey of contemplation for pilgrims. In an unbroken tradition, each evening at 6:00 P.M. pilgrims may join a gathering for Shrine Prayers. The Rosary is said, and those in need can request the Virgin's intercession. Every afternoon a Sprinkling ceremony offers a blessing and gives pilgrims an opportunity to touch and drink the holy water of Walsingham.

Throughout the year the shrine hosts a number of important events. One of the most widely known of these is the Anglican National Pilgrimage, held on the last weekend in May. This celebration ends with a procession encircling the village. Other special days in the shrine's calendar are devoted to youth and the sick, and a day in May sees MPs asking blessings on their responsibilities in government.

Knock, Ireland

In 1878, the little church in the remote and windswept village of Knock in the west of Ireland was battered by gales in a great storm. The slate roof and windows were damaged, and some statues were smashed. The following year, on the wet evening of August 21, a group of women saw figures standing outside the church and assumed they were new statues. Returning later, they noticed that the figures were moving and ran to fetch family and friends to witness this miracle. These fourteen people claimed to have seen the Virgin Mary, dressed in white and wearing a golden crown, accompanied by St. Joseph and St. John.

Word of the apparition spread, and soon pilgrims began to arrive on foot from all over Ireland. Of the sick and disabled who came or were brought to the shrine, many claimed miraculous healings. At first, the Church discouraged such stories and stood aloof, leaving the pilgrims to create their own rituals. The pilgrims reverted to traditional Gaelic forms of worship, making circuits of the church grounds while chanting the Rosary and the Liturgy out loud.

Knock draws thousands of pilgrims annually, many making their journey in organized church groups. The majority fly to the airport ten miles away, then arrive at the shrine by bus. Knock boasts a basilica that can accommodate 12,000 people and a folk museum that houses craft tools and costumes from the time of the apparition as well as details of the miraculous apparition and cures attributed to attendance at the shrine.

One recent visitor observed that what impressed her most was the prayerful attitude of the people. Young families were circling the grounds together, praying aloud as they followed the rituals developed by the early pilgrims. She remarked that even the youngest children seemed totally engrossed in what they were doing. "The place," she said, "is stark rather than beautiful but has the authentic feeling of spiritual power."

Noyal-Pontivy, France

A traditional Breton prayer runs: "Ste. Noyale preserve us, especially from sin; so that not one person from Noyal will be missing, O our Patroness, from Paradise." Legend tells how that in the sixth century, an Irishwoman sailed to Brittany on a leaf and settled as a hermit at Ste-Noyale—a scattering of farms and a church just north of Noyal-Pontivy. Pestered by a local tyrant, she fled south for some 18 miles to Bezo, where her pursuer found her and beheaded her. Undismayed, the saint picked up her head and walked home to Ste-Noyale, where she was buried.

Noyal-Pontivy, which lies east of Pontivy in the Morbihan, enshrines the memory of its patron saint, Noyale. The ancient parish observes two Pardons (processions to a sacred location associated with the saint and a conventional patronal festival) in her honor. On the Sunday nearest June 24, the only day when the church is open (it is otherwise closed to protect its frescoes of the saint's life), cars and tractors file slowly past the church in a procession after High Mass.

The major Pardon takes place two Sundays later. After morning Masses in the large medieval parish church in Noyal-Pontivy, where Noyale's legend is told in the choir windows, the villagers bear an image of the saint carrying her head and trace one section of her last strange journey. They proceed from the church through the fields to Les Trois Fontaines, a mysterious site in a wooded valley in which three springs rise in a large sunken courtyard. A small Calvary stands in the trees above the fountains. Close by are two other stones, the saint's "bed" and "prie-dieu," which bears Noyale's knee prints. Water from the three wells flows into a large, shallow pool near the shrine and is so pure that local women still come here to rinse their linen. By a stream some 150 feet away is a large stone, Ste. Noyale's "Chair." According to legend, this was the saint's last stop before she reached the village of Ste-Noyale. Here, while the saint rested on her chair, three drops of blood fell from her severed head, causing the three springs to well up. It is said that the three drops are still to be seen in the depths of the well basins—but only by the pure in heart.

On the afternoon of the Pardon, parishioners become pilgrims, bathe their faces and hands in the wells, drink the sacred water, and bottle it to carry home. After Vespers at 3:00 P.M., the procession returns to the town to light the "feu-de-joie" (or ceremonial bonfire), stuffed with fireworks and dance around it.

Rocamadour, France

The mountains curve spectacularly; a medieval French castle and churches cling perilously to a cliff above the Alzou River. Nearby, a cave harbors 20,000-year-old paintings. A Black Virgin, just over 2 feet high and nearly 9 centuries old, is carried through the village in a procession. Pilgrims on their knees mount the stone stairs cut into the cliff. A blind beggar asks, "Has *she* passed yet?" Intense human and divine energy merge in religious climax at Rocamadour.

Rocamadour is located near Souillac, east of Bordeaux, in the Dordogne. The name comes from the Langue d'Oc expression *roc amator*, "He who likes the rock," and from St. Amadour, who in folk tradition was the servant of the Mother of God. According to legend, his body was found buried, perfectly preserved beneath the threshold of the Chapel of the Virgin and was later burned and hacked to pieces. Cathars, a medieval sect that denounced the church's material wealth, were brought here from Provence to renounce their "heresy" in front of the statue.

Only 800 people now live in Rocamadour, but every year on September 8, Our Lady's birthday, thousands surge into the narrow street, barely leaving space for the Black Virgin to pass. A wash of candles glows, each person lighting the next person's as Notre Dame comes closer. Prayers and murmurs hush. She passes. An ever-lengthening column of pilgrims follows the statue. The 223 stairs are unbelievably rugged and steep. Pilgrims mount skyward, some on their knees, some old, crippled, and hurting. They crowd into the basilica and the Virgin's Chapel, having completed the Pilgrim's Way, the passage to forgiveness.

Taizé, France

"Ah, Taizé, that little springtime!" These affectionate words spoken by Pope John XXIII in 1960 express the hope and the lightness of being emanating from the simplicity of the Taizé experience, which since 1957 has attracted increasing numbers of young people from around the world. They come to discover, or be nourished by, the sources of the Christian faith.

Situated on a hill amid the colorful fields and slopes of the Burgundy countryside, the Taizé community is the home of 90 monks. Living rooted in prayer, contemplation, and an alertness to news arriving from every continent, their daily aspiration is to enable the young to become creators of trust and reconciliation.

All year, the pilgrimage of young people continues, increasing to 8,000 visitors at Easter and in summer—the community's busiest times. Visitors share in a daily routine of prayers and multinational meetings with the community's monks. Accommodations are allocated each Sunday afternoon. Families stay at Olinda, a 15-minute walk away, and the over 30s are set slightly apart from the central site. It is advisable to bring a tent, a sleeping bag, and warm clothing and to register in advance, particularly for family accommodations.

On arrival, you are confronted with what appears to be a sprawling campsite. The slightly disconcerting impression is of buses arriving or departing, fields full of tents, and a few inauspicious buildings. There are few visible signs that this is a place of religious significance. Ubiquitous backpacks and a calm sense of youthful anticipation dominate the scene.

To visit Taizé is to experience communion, sharing space, time, thoughts, and routine tasks with others in small groups. Three times a day, everyone files quietly into the Church of Reconciliation. The silence is astonishing as the crowd sits, enveloped by the soft amber glow of candlelight, waiting. Then, the singing begins—the hallmark of Taizé. Simple chanted psalms, sung over and over again, immerse all in a powerful tide of worship. The songs of Taizé are known throughout the world. They are a special gift from Taizé—an aid to prayer, which continues to reconcile, to heal, and to nourish the inner journey.

Lourdes, France

Lourdes, Mary, and pilgrimage—the connection is axiomatic, even for those for whom Mary is no more than a name or a distant memory. Lourdes 150 years ago was little more than a backward village—not even worth connecting with the French national railway—in the foothills of the Pyrénées. Then in February 1858, Lourdes was wrenched from obscurity to ceaseless celebrity by the startling appearance of Mary, Mother of God, to an illiterate asthmatic child called Bernadette Soubirous.

True to her uniquely individual "style," the Virgin Mary chose to make her appearance to Bernadette in the Massabielle grotto on the banks of the River Gave, which was then little more than the municipal garbage dump. With breathtaking audacity in bourgeois France, and thus proclaiming that nothing was beneath her compassion, the Queen of Heaven stood in the dump and proclaimed herself as the Immaculate Conception.

Radiant among the rubbish and already performing miracles of healing as she went, Mary indicated a hitherto unsuspected perennial spring of water to the bewildered but trusting child. This spring has ever since flowed to the "healing of the nations." Mary also requested processions and pilgrims to seek her in that unlikely spot.

At Lourdes, Mary's victory—and thus the victory of compassion and the human spirit—is confirmed. Bernadette became a nun, and her enclosed life made of her a great saint, although she never returned to the grotto. But in her place, millions from all over the world have gone, and still more go, to bathe in the waters and visit the sacred places on the banks of the Gave.

The nightly candlelit procession around the shrine's domain is an unforgettable experience. But, even more impressive is the midnight flicker of candles in the darkness at the grotto, which has been open for prayer continuously since 1858.

More than 6 million pilgrims visit Lourdes each year, mainly between Easter and mid-October. Most pilgrimages are organized by local groups, churches, or societies for the sick, but individual pilgrims are always welcome.

Guadalupe, Spain

The small town of Guadalupe, on the slopes of the Guadalupe Mountains in western Spain, has long been the heart of Christian worship in Estremadura and the goal of countless pilgrims from all over the Spanish-speaking world. Both the Caribbean island of Guadeloupe and the Mexican shrine Guadalupe owe their names to this Estremadura town, whose fame far exceeds its size.

Guadalupe's reputation rests on a relic—the Virgin of Guadalupe—the patron saint of the region. This small black statue, which now stands in the town's cathedral, was reputedly carved by St. Luke. Pope Gregory the Great presented it to Bishop Leander of Sevilla in 580. When the Moors conquered southern Spain in 711, the Christians fled north, taking the statue with them. They buried it in a cave near the Guadalupe River, where in the ensuing centuries of strife, it lay forgotten until the fourteenth century when the Virgin Mary appeared to a cowherd, ordering him to assemble the townsfolk and clergy and dig until they found her statue.

The statue was unearthed, and the King of Spain ordered a chapel to be built on the spot, which soon became a shrine. Reports of cures and healings followed, and wealthy aristocrats donated clothing and a jewelled headdress to the statue. Ferdinand and Isabella, the first monarchs of modern Spain, met Christopher Columbus here in 1490, prior to his first voyage. Columbus's arrival in the Americas is still celebrated here with all the Spanish-American flags flying from the monastery on October 12.

For more than 500 years, the medieval monastery was home to Hieronomite monks, who founded a celebrated faculty of medicine and performed surgery within its walls. The monastery is now occupied by Franciscans who require modern pilgrims to join a guided tour of the monastery. Although not included in the official tour, it is worth requesting to see the Gothic cloisters. As well as the rich Mudejar architecture, the monastery houses eight paintings by the artist Zurbarán, who lends his name to the Parador-Hotel opposite—once a pilgrim's hospital.

Accommodation is easy to find, except during Easter Week, on the Virgin's feast day on September 8, and on October 20. At other times Guadalupe remains an ordinary white-walled town, save for the clamoring bells of the monastery.

Fatima, Portugal

The sun spun and danced in the sky, flashing every color of the spectrum and then plummeted toward Earth and the terrified crowd before whirling back into the heavens. On October 13, 1917, about 70,000 people witnessed this Miracle of the Sun at Fatima, a small village in the wooded hills of central Portugal. The Virgin Mary had promised the miracle to Lucia, Francisco, and Jacinta, three peasant children to whom she had appeared each month since May 13 that year.

In the six visitations, the Virgin revealed three secrets. The first was a vision of hell; the second a prophecy that unless Russia was converted, that country's errors would spread throughout the world, provoking war. This prophecy has been interpreted as a prediction of the spread of communism and also of World War II. The third prophecy, which is believed to foretell the end of the world, was later written down by Lucia and given to the Pope. He judged it too terrible to be revealed.

Two main festivals are held each year at Fatima on May 12 and 13 and October 12 and 13. About 100,000 pilgrims camp around the village. A candlelight procession leads to the vast square in front of the basilica, in which Mass is celebrated at 5:00 P.M. on the 12th. Singing continues throughout the night until a second Mass is held later in the morning of the 13th. The celebration ends at noon, when all the women in the crowd wave white handkerchiefs.

Pilgrims dress respectfully, with covered legs and shoulders. They walk on their knees along the path to the Chapel of the Apparition at the Cova da Iria and follow the Stations of the Cross along the white marble *via sacra*, which leads to the Loca do Cabeço. It was here that the three children claimed to have seen an Angel of Peace in the year before the Miracle. The basilica contains the tombs of Francisco and Jacinta, who died in 1919 and 1920, respectively, fulfilling the Virgin's promise that they would soon go to heaven. The Portuguese say that "Fatima has nothing to satisfy mere curiosity. What matters here is the heart."

Hostyn, Czech Republic

From Tesák the path winds through a forest, past the Machova Studánka Well, with its carved Madonna, to emerge on Mount Hostyn, the most popular pilgrimage place in Moravia. A vast baroque cathedral, a healing spring, and a host of pilgrim hostels now stand on the hill where the Virgin Mary is said to have sent a terrible storm to save the near-defeated Moravians from the siege of the Tatars in 1241.

Her portrait depicts her as Protectress of Moravia, shielding the Christians with her cloak, while from the safety of her arms the infant Jesus hurls lightning at the tents of the Mongols. Whatever the reasons for the sudden retreat of the Tatars from Moravia in the thirteenth century, Hostyn has long since attracted pilgrims to worship the Virgin on its wooded slopes.

In earlier times, around 2000 B.C.E., Mount Hostyn was the fortress of the Lusatian people, and later it lay close to the ancient amber route from the Mediterranean to the Baltic Sea. The Slavic saints, Cyril and Methodius, brought Christianity to Moravia and according to legend, persuaded the people to part with their dedication to their pagan god Radost in return for a painting of the Blessed Mother Mary.

Over the centuries, Moravians have kept faith in Mary as both their mother and protector, despite disapproval from the authorities, the Nazi occupation, and the expulsion of the Jesuits from their monastery on Mount Hostyn. The settlement on the hill has grown and now, as well as the cathedral, encompasses the monastery, a healing spring, and a "water chapel," the Stations of the Cross created by the famous Slovak architect Jurkovic, a small cemetery, and a lookout tower offering panoramic views of the surrounding countryside.

Pilgrims to Hostyn in the spring and summer can walk on the trails through the woods and along the Hostyn ridgeway from Tesák and Rusava. In winter, it is wiser to approach by road, leaving the car at the town of Bystrice pod Hostynem. Pilgrims' hostels on the hill provide accommodations. On the Saturday nearest August 15, the feast of Mary's Assumption draws pilgrims from all over Moravia.

Czestochowa, Poland

The industrial town of Czestochowa in southwest Poland attracts more than 100,000 pilgrims a year. They come to worship at the shrine of the icon of the Black Madonna (Matka Bozka Czestochowska), Our Lady of Czestochowa. The most famous of the Madonnas in Poland, the icon's exact origin is unknown, but it probably dates from the fifth century and originates from the Middle East. In 1655, the icon hung outside the town hall, and the citizens believed it helped them withstand a prolonged siege by invading Swedes. The icon became the focus of a successful campaign to drive out the invaders.

Pilgrimages to Czestochowa began shortly afterward. The biggest and oldest pilgrimage starts in Warsaw at dawn on August 6, arriving at Czestochowa 180 miles and 9 days later, on the eve of the Assumption, the most important feast of Mary in the liturgical year. This pilgrimage has taken place without fail for more than 200 years, surviving partition, Nazi atrocities, and decades of official disapproval.

Pilgrims register in the crypt of Pauline Church in Warsaw, where they are divided into 15 groups of about 1,000 people, who walk as one straggly column. Academics walk side by side with coal miners, teachers with peasant farmers, infants are carried by mothers, and elderly women hobble along in torn sneakers. Most are Polish and active Catholics. They sing and recite the rosary; the rhythm of their prayers keeping pace with their walking. At night, pilgrims sleep in groups of up to 100 on straw in barns. Local people wait along the route, offering gifts of cake, bread, water, fruit, and flowers. Each town and village on the route is adorned with flowers and decorations.

The journey ends in anticlimax at the fortified medieval monastery on a "shining mountain" at the center of Czestochowa. Pilgrims enter the chapel of the Black Madonna and once inside, walk briskly past the icon before dispersing. Although their devotion to the icon would lead most of them to deny it, their behavior on this pilgrimage is in the spirit of the Japanese saying "the path is the goal in itself."

Medjugorje, Bosnia

The actor Michael York said that he had been "spiritually moved" by the peacefulness of Medjugorje when he visited the Bosnian shrine in 1994. He had "felt totally energized" by the experience during the filming of *Gospa*, a film based on the events at Medjugorje.

The actor is just one of millions of pilgrims who have been to this small village in Bosnia, where six young people claim to have seen apparitions of the Gospa (Virgin Mary) daily since June 24, 1981. The Gospa has given them messages for all humankind, and has inspired a more peaceful way of life in the village. Tired from the hustle and bustle of their daily lives and hungry for a deeper relationship with God, many pilgrims respond whole-heartedly to the Gospa's call to repentance, conversion, prayer, penance, and fasting.

In recent years, Medjugorje has been an oasis of peace for people of all nationalities and religions throughout the civil war which engulfed most of the former Yugoslavia. (Rockets and bombs aimed at the church at Medjugorje mysteriously failed to explode.) Many begin their spiritual journey by climbing Podbrdo, known today as the Hill of Apparitions, where the Gospa is said to have appeared to the teenagers for the first time. Most pilgrims also make the steep ascent of Mount Krizevac, which boasts a large cement cross, built by local people in 1933 and where many have reported seeing the sun "dance" and other mysterious light effects. Some make the journey barefoot in the heat of the day as an act of penance and to meditate on the crucifixion.

The overall experience of Medjugorje, however, is centered on the parish Church of St. James in which the priests and visionaries encourage people to attend Mass and join in a collective offering of the Rosary. Pilgrims also speak of miracles at the shrine and of the "Medjugorje effect," a state of euphoria, that follows an initial hostility to believing in the events at the shrine.

Kataragama, Sri Lanka

Hindus, Buddhists, Muslims, and Christians all make their sacred journey to Kataragama, the holiest place in Sri Lanka.

Kataragama is associated with the Hindu war deity Skanda (called Murugan in South India). Buddhists come to visit a *dagoba* (mound) on a site where Buddha meditated. Muslims come to pray at a local mosque. Yet all gravitate to the Kataragama Devala, the principal shrine. In times gone by, the pilgrimage was a dangerous trek through the jungle; now, many travel by public transport.

The biggest crowds gather in July and August for a festival celebrating the union of Skanda with his mistress, Valli Amma. This festival comes shortly after the *Perahera*, the enormous procession at the Temple of the Tooth in Kandy, where Buddha's tooth is kept. Visitors approach through the Menik Ganga (Jewel River). They bathe in the river and buy offerings—lotuses and other flowers—from the nearby stalls. The principal shrine is a white stone building. It is said to contain Skanda's lance, but only priests may see this.

Whatever their religion, people who face difficulties, who have lost something or someone, often make vows. These vows are honored during the festival, which lasts a fortnight. Some pilgrims skewer their tongues, cheeks, and other parts of their bodies. A few are hung up on hooks, which pierce their bodies. A demonstration of faith at Kataragama is shown in fire walking in which devotees—old and young, male and female—walk across hot embers with no visible ill effect. The crowds provide noisy accompaniment by blowing conch shells and beating drums.

At other times of the year, most people simply worship, give alms, and circle the great *dagoba*. The festival finishes with a procession, ending in a water-cutting ceremony. A sacred sword is used to part the water with a circular sweep, and clay pots are filled with water from this circle, to ensure a supply of water for the coming year.

Chimayó, United States

The name Chimayó comes from the Tewa Pueblo Indian *tsi mayoh*, meaning "obsidian chief." Chimayó valley, 30 miles north of Santa Fe, New Mexico, is watered by small rivers and springs. Prehistoric Indians chose to live in such valleys for the alluvial soil, trees, and water supply. Legend says that in the Tewa village in Chimayó there was a pool with mud that had healing properties. This pool dried to dampness when an obsidian chief (a giant volcano) was destroyed while spewing smoke and fire. The nearby sacred hill was believed to be an entrance to the underworld.

The Native Americans left the valley around 1400, and Spanish settlers arrived in 1692. They constructed several chapels in the valley, one on the site of the healing mud. This adobe church with its old painted wooden saints and altar carvings, is called El Santuario de Chimayó and is the site of a major pilgrimage by Hispanics and Native Americans during Easter Holy Week.

Pilgrims walk from a hundred or more miles away across mountain and desert, although it is possible to drive. Some carry tall crosses, some photos of sick relatives, some nothing but water. On Good Friday, about 2,000 pilgrims gather here. The rarely seen Penitentes, or Brotherhood of Jesus Christ, similar to fraternities in Sevilla, Spain, meet in private to suffer for Christ. A century ago, Penitente novices had to kiss the *santa tierra*, the "blessed earth" of Chimayó, as part of their initiation.

From underworld entrance to volcano to mud, Chimayó's history tells of power in the earth and of rebirth. Today, that power is accessed through the earth at the sacred spot in the church. From the sacristy, a narrow, low door leads to a tiny room, with a dry earth "well" in the middle of the floor. Pilgrims take away bags of soil from this hole, or rub the soil directly on their bodies. A priest is on hand to replenish the soil, whose healing powers are attested to by the crutches hanging nearby, the votive offerings, photographs, flowers, candles, and touching stories written in Spanish.

Small images of body parts hang at the shrine, too (see above). Called *milagros* (miracles), each represents a prayer for healing of that part. The Holy Week penitents leave at Easter, the busiest time in the sanctuary's calendar, but other pilgrims visit Chimayó every day of the year to experience the healing, holy earth.

Bibliography

Alfred the Great: Asser's Life of King Alfred and Other Contemporary Sources. Keynes, Simon and Michael, Lapidge, trans. Harmondsworth: Penguin, 1983.

The Apocrypha from The Bible. New Revised Standard Version. Oxford: Oxford University Press, 1995.

The Atlas of Mysterious Places. Westwood, Jennifer., ed. London: Marshall Editions, 1987.

Attar, Farid ud-din. *The Conference of the Birds*. Trans. Darbandi and Davis. London: Penguin Books, 1984.

Aziz, Barbara Nimri. "Personal Dimensions of the Sacred Journey: What Pilgrims Say," *Religious Studies*. 1987: 23.

Basho, Matsuo. *The Narrow Road to the Deep North*. Trans. Nobuyuki Yuasa. London: Penguin, 1966.

Bharduraj, S. M. *Hindu Places of Pilgrimage in India*. Berkeley, Los Angeles, and London: University of California Press, 1973.

Bhardwaj, S., and G. Rinschede, eds. *Pilgrimage in World Religions*. Berlin: Dietrich Reimer Verlag, 1988.

The Book of Margery Kempe. Tony D. Triggs, trans. Tunbridge Wells: Burns & Oates, 1995.

Brooke, R. and P. *Popular Religion in the Middle Ages*. London: Thames & Hudson, 1984.

Bunyan, John. *The Pilgrim's Progress*. London: Penguin, 1965.

Cable, Mildred and Francesca French. *The Gobi Desert* London: Hodder & Stoughton, 1942.

Chaucer, Geoffrey. *The Canterbury Tales*. N. Coghill, trans. London: Penguin, 1977 (revised).

The Cloud of Unknowing. Wolters, Clifton., trans. London: Penguin, 1961.

Coleman, S. and J. Elsner. *Pilgrimage Past and Present*. London: British Museum, 1995.

Collinson, C. and C. Miller. *Pilgrimages: Journeys from a Multi-Faith Community*. London: Hodder & Stoughton, 1990.

Crumrine, N. R. and A. Morinis. *Pilgrimage in Latin America*. Westport, Conn. and London: Greenwood Press, 1991.

Donaldson, B. A. *The Wild Rue*. London: Luzac & Co, 1938.

Duffy, Eamon. *The Stripping of the Altars*. New Haven and London: Yale University Press, 1992.

Eade, J. and M. Sallnow. (eds.) *Contesting the Sacred*. London: Routledge, 1991.

Farmer, D. *The Oxford Dictionary of Saints*. Oxford: Oxford University Press, 1978.

Fiennes, J. *On Pilgrimage*. London: Sinclair-Stevenson, 1991.

Finucane, Ronald C. *Miracles and Pilgrims*. London: J. M. Dent, 1977.

Gallwey, W. Timothy. *The Inner Game of Tennis*. London: Jonathan Cape, 1975.

Hakluyt, Richard. *The Principal Navigations, Voyages, Traffiques and Discoveries of the English Nation.* 2nd enlarged edn. London: 1598–1600.

The HarperCollins Encyclopedia of Catholicism. Richard P. McBrien, gen. ed. New York: HarperCollins, 1995.

Harpur, James. *The Atlas of Sacred Places.* London: Marshall Editions, 1994.

Hearn, Lafcadio. "Glimpses of Unfamiliar Japan," *Writings from Japan.* Francis King, ed. London: Penguin, 1984.

Hilton, Walter. *The Ladder of Perfection.* Sherley-Price, Leo, trans. London: Penguin, 1957.

Karve, Irawati "On the Road: A Maharashtrian Pilgrimage," *Asian Studies* 1962, 30:1.

Kumar, Satish. *No Destination.* Bideford: Green Books, 1992.

MacCormack, Sabine. "Loca Sancta: The Organization of Sacred Topography in Late Antiquity," *The Blessings of Pilgrimage.* Robert Ousterhout, ed. Illinois Byzantine Studies 1. Urbana and Chicago: University of Illinois Press, 1990.

Marsden, John. *Sea-Road of the Saints: Celtic Holy Men in the Hebrides.* Edinburgh: Floris Books, 1995.

Morinis, Alan. "Introduction: The Territory of the Anthropology of Pilgrimage," *The Anthropology of Pilgrimage.* A. Morinis, ed. Westport, Connecticut, and London: Greenwood Press, 1993.

Mother Julian of Norwich. *Revelations of Divine Love.* C. Wolters, trans. London: Penguin, 1966.

Mullikin, Mary Augusta and Anna M. Hotchkis. *The Nine Sacred Mountains of China.* Hong Kong: Vetch & Lee Ltd., 1973.

Nothing Ventured: Disabled People Travel the World. Walsh, A., ed. London: Harrap Columbus, 1991.

Palmer, Martin. *Travels through Sacred China.* London: Thorsons, 1996.

Purcell, William. *Pilgrim's England.* Harlow: Longman, 1981.

Ramanujan, A. K. *Speaking of Siva.* Harmondsworth: Penguin, 1973.

St. Vincent, David. *Iran: a Travel Survival Kit.* London & Sydney: Lonely Planet, 1992.

Smart, Ninian. *The World's Religions.* Cambridge: Cambridge University Press, 1989.

Sumption, Jonathan. *Pilgrimage: an Image of Mediaeval Religion.* London: Faber & Faber, 1975.

Teresa of Avila. *The Interior Castle.* London: Fount Paperbacks, 1995.

Toibin, C. *The Sign of the Cross.* London: Jonathan Cape, 1994.

The Travels of Sir John Mandeville. Moseley, C. W. R. D., trans., London: Penguin, 1983.

Turnbull, Colin. "A Pilgrimage to India," *Natural History.* N. S. 90:7.

Turner, Victor. "The Center Out There: Pilgrim's Goal," *History of Religions.* Vol. 12, No. 3. February 1973.

Warner, Marina. *Alone of All Her Sex.* London: Weidenfeld and Nicolson, 1976.

Watts, A. *Myth and Ritual in Christianity.* London: Thames & Hudson, 1983.

Index

Aachen Cathedral
(Germany), 252–53
Abbot Daniel, 198
abstinence, 43, 168
Abu Simbel (Egypt), 193, 196
Achilpas, 226
Ahmad, 109; *The Pilgrimage
of Ahmad, Son of the Little
Bird of Paradise*, 109
Ajmer (India), 17
Aldersey, Laurence, 100; *Trip
to Jerusalem* (1581), 100
Alfred, 113–15, 222–23
Amritsar (India), 30, 262–63
Angkor Wat (Cambodia),
267–69; plan of, 268
Antoninus of Piacenza, 183
Anuradhapura (Sri Lanka),
178
Aquileia Cathedral (Italy),
185
Aquinas, Thomas, 70, 172
Armanath Cave (Kashmir),
238–39
Arunachala (India), 208–9

Assisi (Italy), 170–71, 207,
210, 215
austerities, 97–99, 152
Axis Mundi, 225–26

Báb, the, 259
Baba, Lotan, 98
Badaun (India), 17
Bahá'í, 259–60; shrines in
Haifa and Acre, Israel,
259–60
Bahá'ulláh, 259
Ballyvourney (Ireland), 127
Basho, Matsuo, 29, 60–61,
146; *The Narrow Road of
the Deep North*, 55–58, 82;
*The Records of a Travel-
Worn Satchel*, 223
Batista, Cicero Romao,
132–33
battlefield pilgrimages, 205
Bayazid-al-Bastami shrine
(Iran), 84–85
Beauraing (Belgium), 131
Bede, 225

Benares (India), 24–26; the five crossings, 25
Binyon, Laurence, 205
al-Bistami, 227
Blake, William, 34
Bom Jesús (Portugal), 187
Book of Enoch, The, 224
Book of Lismore, The, 61
Borobudur (Java), 270–72; plan of, 271
bridge building, 104–5, 108
Brocéliande (France), 235–36
Brown, K. Bradford, 33
Bryant, C. R., 223
Buddhism, 11, 136–37; Buddha's footprint, 137; pilgrimage sites in India, 6
Bunyan, John, 99, 110; "To Be a Pilgrim," 59; *The Pilgrim's Progress,* 7, 45, 112, 113, 137, 138, 151; tomb of, 53

Cable, Mildred, 101; *The Gobi Desert* (1942), 101
Calvin, John, 130
Camargue (France), 40–41
Candomblé, 139
Canterbury, 13, 14; Pilgrim's Way, 15, 67; Thomas à Becket's tomb, 15, 22
Carmina Gadelica, 53, 96
caves, 74–75

Chaco Canyon (New Mexico), 134–35
Charlemagne, 253
Chartres Cathedral (France), 251–52; the Path to Jerusalem, 252
Chaucer, Geoffrey, 13, 32; *Canterbury Tales,* 82
Chimáyo (New Mexico), 290–91
Christianity, 97, 169, 172
Chumpón (Mexico), 139, 142
circumambulation, 189, 192
clothing, 37–39, 42
Cloud of Unknowing, The, 44, 169, 172
Cohen, Israel, 127–28; *A Jewish Pilgrimage* (1956), 127
communitas, 21, 146, 147
Cooper, W. Oliver, 46
Copacabana (Peru), 77
Coryat, Tom, 76–77
Count Eberhard of Württemberg, 102
credit cards, 36
crime, 99–101
Croagh Patrick (Ireland), 94–95
crowds, 164–65
Crusades, the, 92, 152; and the looting of Hagia Sophia, 257

Cuiliacán (Mexico), 13, 16
cultural assumptions, 93,
　96–97
Czestochowa (Poland), 224,
　286–87

dangers, 92–93
Dasimaya, Devara, 172
Davies, J. G., 70
Davog, 232
Desert House of Prayer
　(Arizona), 106–7
Dey, Mukul, 128; *My
　Pilgrimages to Ajanta and
　Bagh* (1925), 128
Dhu 'l-Nun, xv
diaries, 42, 117–18, 201
Diego, Juan, 154, 155
Dome of the Rock
　(Jerusalem), x, 190, 258–59
Donne, John, 218
Doughty, C. M., 54
Druids, 35, 193, 251
Dubslane, 5
Durkheim, Emile, 172–73;
　*Elementary Forms of the
　Religious Life* (1912),
　172–73

Easter, 199–200
"Easter Sepulchers," 185–86;
　Mise au Tombeau
　(Bourgogne, France), 186

Edward the Confessor, 248
Eleusinian Mysteries (ancient
　Greece), 67, 73–74, 188
epiphany, 180
Ethiopian Orthodox Church,
　237

Faber, Felix, 176, 184
Farid-ud-din Attar, 88–89,
　121, 125; *Conference of the
　Birds*, 88
fasting, 43, 165
Fátima (Portugal), 5, 131,
　146–47, 224, 283–84
foot care/footwear, 43
foreign currency, 36
French, Francesca, 101; *The
　Gobi Desert* (1942), 101
Frontinus, 78

Gallwey, Tim, 121, 125–26
Ganges pilgrimage (India),
　18, 25, 98–99
Glastonbury (England), xvi,
　34–35, 206; George and
　Pilgrims Hotel, 77
Guadalupe (Mexico), 5, 50,
　154–55
Guadalupe (Spain), 5,
　281–83
guides/guidebooks, 32–33
Gurdjieff, G. I., 25
Guru Rinpoche, 264

Hagia Sophia (Istanbul), 186, 256–57
hajj, the, 8–10, 36, 46, 184–85, 192; rituals of, 9, 10, 38, 43; as sacred privilege, 9
Hargreaves, Alison, 119–21
head coverings, 39
Hearn, Lafcadio, 56, 75, 79, 203, 206
hearth rites (ancient Rome), 53–55
Hemkund (India), 240–41
Herbert, George, 19, 178, 197
Hilton, Walter, 23, 156
Hinduism, 4, 11, 13, 97; and the *atman*, xvi; and *avataras*, 6; and *darshan*, 182, 239; the four *dhamas*, 25; and life-cycle pilgrimages, 19–20; and *tirtha*, 111
Holy Land, 3, 6, 23, 26, 76, 179, 181–82, 183–84; "Holy Land in America" (Washington, D.C.), 186–87; Via Dolorosa, 26, 27. *See also* Jerusalem
Holy Sepulcher (Jerusalem), 198–99
Hopi, 72, 194–95
hostels, 77
Hostyn (Czech Republic), 284–85

Hotchkis, Anna, 153
Hsüan Tsang, 136

I Ching, 117
incubation, 7, 175
Information for Pilgrims unto the Holy Land (c. 1498), 32–33
Inge, W. R., ix
Ingulph, 99–100
Instruction of Amen-em-Opet, The, 119
Iona (Scotland), 231–32
Islam: Buraq imagery, 226–27; dress code for women, 262; gardens of, 174; and miracles, 12–13; and saints, 6; and *salik*, xv. *See also hajj*, the
Issa, xii
Itinerary (333 C.E.), 6, 32

Jerusalem, 23, 190, 225
Jesus Christ, xvi, 75; and the Harrowing of Hell, 197–99
Jnanesvar, 67, 187
Judaism, and visitation of tombs of prophets and saints, 6
Julian of Norwich, xv, 20, 144, 162, 168, 181, 223; shrine of (Norwich, England), 52–53

Karve, Irawati, 98, 105, 111, 147, 150
Kataragama (Sri Lanka), 179, 288–90
Kateri Tekakwitha shrines (North America), 50–52
Kempe, Margery, 22, 36, 37, 202; *The Book of Margery Kempe*, 22, 100
Khayyam, Omar, 88; *The Rubáiyát of Omar Khayyám* (1859), 88
Khwaja Murad, 89
Khwaja Murad shrine (Iran), 89
Knock (Ireland), 274–75
Kobo Daishi, 87
Kumar, Satish, 59
Kumbha Mela (India), 3

La Salette, 5
Labyrinth of Knossos (Crete), 72
Lake Manasarovar (Tibet), 81
Lalibela (Ethiopia), 237–38
Lives of the Prophets (50 C.E.), 6
Loreto (Italy), xiii–xiv, 138
Lough Derg (Ireland), 152, 232–33
Lourdes (France), xiii, 5, 16, 131, 138, 224, 280–81; Imochigaura Lourdes

(Goto Island, Japan), 138; International Military Pilgrimage to, 105
Luang Phau, 137
Luther, Martin, 131, 169

Macha, 139
Machethu, 5
Maelinmun, 5
Main, John, 173
Malcolm X, 105, 108, 150–51
Malverde, Jesús, 13, 16
Marvell, Andrew, 173
Mashad (Iran), 261–62
Maya, 139, 142, 189
maze running, 64
meals, 163–64
Mecca, 3, 8–10, 12, 18, 20, 38, 152, 163, 225
medical insurance, 36
meditation, 43–44
Medjugorje (Bosnia), 287–88
miracles, 132; healing miracles, 16, 132
Mont-Saint-Michel (France), 234–35
Mosque of Samarra (Iraq), 73
Motupe (Peru), 77–78
Mount Athos (Greece), 62–63
Mount Fuji-san (Japan), 192–93, 203, 206, 243–44

Mount Hiei (Japan), 152–53
Mount Kailash (Tibet), 11, 71, 79, 80–81
Muhammad, 9, 12
Mullikan, Mary Augusta, 153
Mystery religions, 188. *See also* Eleusinian mysteries
mythology, 11, 126, 196–97; and the language of parenthood, 12

Nanak, 169, 172, 262
Newby, Eric, 115–16
Nidaros Cathedral (Trondheim, Norway), 254–55
Nikulás, 42
Nott, Peter, 108
Noyal-Pontivy (France), 276–77
numen, 11, 53

Olav Haraldsson, 254
Old Uppsala temple (Sweden), 78–79
Our Lady of Health (Tamil Nadu, India), 17

Pandharpur (India), 30, 67, 70, 187–88; lunar calendar and, 189; myth associated with, 126
Passover, 3

passport, 36
Path to Jerusalem maze, 4, 64
Paula, 45, 181, 182
Paulinus of Nola, 183
Pharaoh Ahk-en-Aton, 192
photography, 42–43, 162
pilgrim, 4
pilgrim tourist, 23, 82
pilgrimage: anthropological definition of, 224–25; and ascent, 73; circular pilgrimage, 70–72, commercialization of, 206; and descent, 73–75; Greek word for, 66; Latin word for, 66; linear pilgrimage, 66–67; massing pilgrimage, 67, 70; as metaphor for life's journey, 5, 45; opening ritual and, 49; processional pilgrimage, 67, 162; as "rite of passage," 46; spiral pilgrimage, 72–73; tourism marketed as, 27
pilgrimage souvenirs, xii, xiii, 207
Plaine du Nord (Haiti), 244–45
Polo, Marco, 47
Pope Gregory, 114
prescription medications, 36

Purcell, William, 184; *Pilgrim's England* (1981), 184
Purchas, Samuel, 76–77

Qadamagah shrine (Iran), 89
Quarles, Francis, 130

Raleigh, Sir Walter, 38
Ramana Maharshi, 208
Rastafarianism, 142–43
relics, 7, 133, 136, 206–7, 215, 253; Church of England's, 273
Rig Veda, 48
Robinson, George, 100
Rocamadour (France), 277–78
Roger of Wansford, 19
Rumi, xvii, 224

St. Amadour, 278
St. Bonaventure, 227
St. Brendan, 4–5
St. Catherine of Alexandria, 141
St. Catherine's monastery (Sinai), 140–41
St. Claire, 136, 170, 206–7
St. Columba, 231
St. Cyril, 285
St. Francis of Assisi, 170–71, 197

St. Gobnat, 127
St. Helena, 76
St. James, 69; as Ogou, 245
St. Joseph's Oratory (Montreal), 50
St. Melangell shrine (Wales), 133
St. Meriasek, 4
St. Methodius, 285
St. Noyale, 276–77
St. Patrick, 94, 232
St. Peter's Basilica (Rome), 133, 136, 255–56
St. Silvia of Aquitania, 85
St. Teresa of Avila, 118, 168, 175, 227
Saint Virilar's Spring (Spain), 218–19
Saint Walstan's Well (Bawburgh, England), 49, 52
Saint Winifred's Well (North Wales), 220–21
Saint-Gilles abbey (Provence, France), 60
Sainte Anne de Beaupré shrine (Quebec), 16, 50, 166–67
Sainte-Baume (Provence, France), x, 122–24
San Stefano church (Bologna, Italy), 185
Sanford, John, 57

Santiago de Compostela (Spain), 22, 28, 68–69; Camino de Santiago, 28
Schweitzer, Albert, 215
self-care, 165, 168
Señor de Qoyllor Rit'i (Peru), 245–47
Shah, Idries, 152
Shakespeare, William, 115, 117, 188
Shikoku (Japan), 71–72, 86–87, 138, 151
Shinto, 173–74, 212, 243
shrines: and belief systems, xiii–xiv; pilgrimages to as private community events, xi; Reformation destruction of, 77; and the tri-fork, 180
Shwe Dagon (Rangoon, Myanmar), 265–67
Sikhism, 262–63; and the Guru Granth Sahib, 263
Sodo (Haiti), 13, 148–49
Somme battlefield, 204–5
Sophronios, 183
Soubirous, Bernadette, xiii, 16, 280–81
spiritual preparation, 43
Sri Pada (Sri Lanka), 6, 241–42
Stacions of Rome, The, 17–18
Stark, Freya, 218

Stonehenge (England), 193, 249–50
Sufism, 4
syncretism, 139, 142, 245

T'ai Shan (Great Mountain) (China), 61; and "mountain societies," 61, 64
Taizé (France), 21, 278–80
TanTan, 244
Tarik Khana mosque (Iran), 84
Tarot cards, 117
Temple of Tooth (Kandy, Sri Lanka), 7, 178–79
Terence, 139
Theoderich, 23, 26
Thompson, Francis, 179
threshold, the, 47–49
Tizimin (Yucatan, Mexico), 210
Tobias and the angel, 103–4
Torkington, Sir Richard, 31
"trade goods," 42
travelers' checks, 36
Travels of Sir John Mandeville, The, 202
Turnbull, Colin, 156–59

al-Udhma, 18
Underworld cults, 73–74
Universal Sympathy, xvi

Upanishads, The, 17, 169

vaccinations, 36
Varro, 213
Vaughan, Henry, 159
vigils, 175–76
visas, 36
Vodou ("Voodoo"), 139, 149
Voyage of St. Bréanainn, 4–5

Walsingham (England), 13, 30, 31, 273–74
Wangdi Phodrang (Bhutan), 264–65
Way of the Pilgrim, The, 109–10
Western Wall (Jerusalem), 190–91
Westminster Abbey (London), 248–49; the Stone of Scone, 248–49
Wong Tai Sin, 269
Wong Tai Sin Temple (Hong Kong), 269–70
Wu Ch'eng-e, 211

Acknowledgments

Our feature writers have been a great inspiration: I thank them for agreeing to contribute. Particular thanks are due to Marion Bowman and Tristan Gray Hulse, both of whom have been generous with their time. Others to whom I am indebted are David Benham, the Rev. Phillip MacFadyen, Roger Shaljean, and Mrs. Jean Tsushima. On the home front, Barbara Littlewood gallantly came on pilgrimage as friend and interpreter; Jonathan Westwood Chandler, Stephen Brearley, Sharon Fulcher, and Sophia Kingshill kept my life running, and my husband Brian Chandler contributed both material support and constructive criticism. They know what this book owes them.

This book is dedicated to my fellow countywomen Margery Kempe (b. 1364) and Mother Julian (1342–c. 1416), one who went and one who stayed.

Contributors

The following people have contributed to the various chapters of the book:

GŸLNAR BALTANOVA lectures in philosophy at Kazan University in Russia. In 1991 she was among the first pilgrims from the former USSR permitted to go to Mecca.

Mecca pages 8–10

MARION BOWMAN is senior lecturer in religious studies at the Open University, England.

Glastonbury pages 34–35

Sainte Anne de Beaupré pages 166–167

DR. DONALD COSENTINO is Professor of African and Caribbean Folklore at the University of California, Los Angeles, and editor of *African Arts* magazine.

Sodo pages 148–149

Plaine du Nord pages 244–245

CHARLES FLETCHER is a community health educator. He co-ordinates Wilderness Spirit Adventures, which leads treks to remote and sacred regions of the United States.

Chaco Canyon pages 134–135

TRISTAN GRAY HULSE teaches postgraduate studies in the department of Welsh at the University of Wales, Lampeter.

Saint Winifred's Well pages 220–221

Noyal-Pontivy pages 276–277

Lourdes pages 280–281

JAMES HARPUR is a writer and poet. He is the author of *The Atlas of Sacred Places*, *A Vision of Comets*, and *The Monk's Dream*.

Croagh Patrick pages 94–95

ROGER HOUSDEN is the author of *Sacred India* and *Retreat*. He is a director of Open Gate Journeys, which leads groups on sacred journeys to spiritual sites.

Benares pages 24–26

Mount Athos pages 62–63

Saint Catherine's Monastery pages 140–141

The Western Wall pages 190–191

Arunachala pages 208–209

ADRIAN HOUSE, a former publisher with William Collins in London, is the author of *Francis of Assisi: A Revolutionary Life*.

Assisi pages 170–171

SATISH KUMAR is the program director at Schumacher College, England, and the editor of *Resurgence*, an international magazine that promotes ecological and spiritual thinking. He is the author of *Path Without Destination*.

Canterbury pages 14–15

WALTER LOMBAERT lives and works at the Oikoten community in Belgium, which aims to provide alternatives for young people in special care.

Santiago de Compostela pages 68–69

NICHOLAS MANN is the author of *The Isle of Avalon* and co-author of *Giants of Gaia*. He lives in New Mexico.

Home dance of the Hopi pages 194–195

COLIN MCINTYRE is a journalist, former company commander of the Lovat Scouts, and author of *Monuments of War*.

War graves of the Somme pages 204–205

DR JAMES PRESTON is professor of anthropology and chair of the religious studies program at the State University of New York, Oneonta, specializing in Catholic devotions and shrines. He has also conducted extensive research into pilgrimages in India.

Kateri Tekakwitha pages 50–52

DR IAN READER is a researcher at the Nordic Institue for Asian Studies in Denmark. He is an authority on Japanese pilgrimage.

Shikoku pages 86–87

DR MAYA SUTTON lives in New Mexico. She coordinates Sacred and Megalithic Sacred Journeys, helping people to plan their own pilgrimages.

Our Lady of Guadalupe pages 154–155

Rocamadour pages 277–278

Chimayó pages 290–291

PATRICIA STOAT works as an information consultant and has studied Japanese and Oriental history.

Mount Kailash pages 80–81

RITA WINTERS is a former advertising executive and the author of *The Green Desert: A Retreat Diary.*

An American Desert Retreat pages 106–107

Picture Credits

Permission to use copyright material is gratefully acknowledged to the following. While every effort has been made to trace all copyright holders, the publisher apologizes to any holders possibly not acknowledged.

Four-color insert:

Catholic News Service: page 3, top right

Corbis Stock Market: page 1, bottom

Fortean Picture Library: page 2, top right and bottom; page 3, top left and bottom; page 4, top and bottom

Christine Guerth: page 1, top left

The Secretariat of the Basilica, Sainte Anne de Beaupré: page 1, top right

Jennifer Westwood: page 2, top left